Also by Christopher Hobhouse

1851 AND THE CRYSTAL PALACE

FOX

BY CHRISTOPHER HOBHOUSE

WITH A

BIOGRAPHICAL

INTRODUCTION

BY

HAROLD NICOLSON

JOHN MURRAY

ALBEMARLE STREET LONDON

First published 1934
Second edition 1947
Reprinted 1948
Reprinted 1964

Made and printed by offset in Great Britain by
William Clowes and Sons Limited
London and Beccles

Author's Note

I am indebted to the Managers of Brooks's for permission to quote from the Bets Book; to John Murray for leave to quote from Creevey; and to Mr. John Sparrow for his invaluable criticism and encouragement.

Contents

a*

Introduction

BY HAROLD NICOLSON

Christopher Hobhouse, the author of this book, was killed at Portsmouth on August 26th, 1940, a few days only after his thirtieth birthday. On June 11th of that year he had married Miss Gavrelle Thomas, a beautiful girl with whom he was much in love. His daughter, Christina, was born posthumously in April, 1941.

At the time of his death Hobhouse was serving as a second lieutenant in the Royal Marines. His wife had come down to Portsmouth with him and they had rented a cottage on Hayling Island. On the afternoon of August 26th he left her to go on duty, expecting to return that night. Shortly afterwards the sirens wailed and an air attack developed. Fort Cumberland, in which Hobhouse was stationed, received two direct hits; his death was instantaneous.

The impulsiveness, which was part of his charm, and which in his early manhood had rushed him into many strange experiments, had by then been tamed. He had begun to assume a responsible attitude towards himself. He had settled down to a profitable career at the Bar, and he looked forward, with a confidence which was in no way misplaced, to an active political future. In literature he had already made his mark. The war came to destroy our hopes.

Christopher Hobhouse was born at 19 Carpenter Road, Edgbaston, Birmingham, on August 9th, 1910. His father, the Rev. Walter Hobhouse, editor of the *Guardian*, and subsequently Archdeacon of Gloucester Cathedral, was a scholar of distinction, who at Eton had won the Newcastle. After the death of his first wife, the Archdeacon had entered into correspondence with her closest friend, Miss Gwendolen Owen, who was serving as a teacher in a missionary school in Africa and whom he had not seen for many years. In the course of time this correspondence led to a proposal of marriage. Miss Owen accepted this proposal and returned to England. On seeing her again, after so long a lapse of time, the Archdeacon regretted his offer; it was too late to retreat.

Two daughters were born of this marriage and then the boy Christopher.

His was not a happy childhood. He was first sent to a school at Bruton, where he suffered much. When he was ten years old his mother died, and in the same year his father was afflicted with a mental illness from which he never recovered. Christopher and his two sisters were made wards in Chancery and the capital which they inherited was so well administered that on coming of age they each received a sum of £10,000. The children were entrusted to the care of their uncle, the Rev. Jack Penrose, with whom they lived. Mr. Penrose was not an intellectual; he believed in the more muscular brands of Christianity and would seek to persuade Christopher that manliness was the first of human virtues. This incompatibility of temper between himself and his uncle had some effect upon his character. It led him to conceal his sensitiveness, and his abiding desire for affection, behind an outer covering of disdain. It led him to discover in the privacy of his own mind certain pleasurable movements of thought and feeling, which were more bland, more intimate and infinitely more amusing than the physical certainties of his uncle's tenets. And it led him to rebel, not only against what was valueless or inapplicable in Mr. Penrose's philosophy of life, but also against those sound precepts of industry, economy and prudence with which that philosophy was associated. Above all perhaps the spiritual loneliness of his early years, the absence of a consoling domestic background, rendered him self-centred and as such increased his idiosyncrasies. Had it not been for his two sisters, and for his aunt, Anne Penrose (who although an invalid managed to gain and to hold the affections of the three children), he would in his early years never have known the meaning of gentleness.

There was one benefit, however, which Mr. Penrose did confer upon his nephew. He took him away from Bruton and sent him to Amesbury School near Hindhead. This establishment was conducted upon imaginative lines; there was little said about muscular Christianity and a great deal about the proper balance between music and gymnastics. At Amesbury, Christopher learnt that the out-of-door life, and even games, could be a pleasure in place of a compulsion. While there, he developed both in mind and body; eventually he won a scholarship at Eton.

It does not appear that while in college at Eton he left any deep impress of his personality upon his contemporaries. He was retiring and aloof. The good looks, the distinction of carriage, the eccentricity of wit, which rendered him so vivid a figure at Oxford did not develop during his schoolboy days. He left Eton before his full time was accomplished and spent some months at Hanover before going up to Oxford. Yet even while at Eton he had begun to write. He published a careful review in the *Architects' Journal* of Walter H. Kilham's book on Mexican architecture. And he contributed several articles to other periodicals.

At Oxford he found an atmosphere congenial to his temperament. He discovered that he possessed original social gifts; he discovered that his comments on life and art were regarded as amusing; he found that interesting people thought him interesting. It may well have been that this startling discovery swept him off his feet. His hospitality became extravagant; his delight in conversation inordinate; his eccentricity marked. Disdaining the grey flannel trousers and the sports coat of the ordinary undergraduate, Hobhouse was always dressed in a neat London suit of tweed. In his first two years his tweeds were of the subfusc variety; but in his third year he came to favour sporting checks of a more violent pattern. This phase did not survive his Balliol period; on coming to London he adopted the black coat and hat, the pin-stripe trousers of the City magnate, the rising lawyer, the obviously successful and conservative politician. The Oxford of 1928–1931 was passing through a period transitional between the hedonism of the earlier twenties and the puritan revival of 1933. Hobhouse was temperamentally more attuned to the former of these two periods. He made lasting friendships with such varied contemporaries as Jock Murray, John Betjeman, Osbert Lancaster, Randolph Churchill, and Harry D'Avigdor Goldsmid. He widened and elaborated his early taste for architecture and deepened his interest in political history. He came under the influence, at once stimulating and gentle, of such older counsellors as Sligger Urquhart and Father Darcy. Nor did he allow the excitement of this sudden expansion wholly to distract him from more serious studies. He obtained a creditable second in Modern Greats. And on leaving Oxford he plunged immediately and impulsively into politics.

It will be remembered that the Labour Government which assumed office in 1929 under the leadership of Ramsay Mac-Donald proved unable to cope unaided with the financial crisis

which thereafter arose. On August 23rd, 1931, MacDonald re-
signed and on the following day formed a Coalition or National
Government. Parliament was dissolved on October 7th, and a
General Election took place on October 27th resulting in a
National Government majority of 493.

The part which Christopher Hobhouse played in these events
was inconspicuous, but humiliating. Sir Oswald Mosley, who
was rightly regarded as one of the most forceful of the younger
members of the Labour Party, had early in 1930 found himself at
variance with his own leaders. He had been attached to Mr. J. H.
Thomas who had been entrusted by the Cabinet with the special
function of solving the unemployment problem. Mosley became
convinced that this problem was not being tackled with adequate
energy, determination or foresight; his justifiable indignation with
the conservatism of the older members of the Labour Party ex-
tended to impatience with the dilatory methods of Parliament
itself. He decided to form a Committee of Action from among
those members of the Labour and other parties who shared his
conviction that only the most drastic measures could prevent a
social and economic catastrophe. Had he possessed the patience
to restrict himself to influencing his own party from within, there
can be little doubt that his great abilities would have placed him
before long in a position of authority. Unfortunately, he decided
to break with the Labour Party and to form a "New Party" on his
own. Many of the experienced parliamentarians who at heart were
in sympathy with Mosley's programme and energy, were disconcerted by this rebellion; they withdrew their support. Mosley
found himself in the wilderness, surrounded only by eager amateurs. He realised that the party machine was determined to break
him, and being a man of fierce endeavour, he believed that he
could break the party machine. His complete failure to achieve this
object induced in him, as the years passed, a mood of rancour; he
began to look with envy upon those foreign dictators who could
impose reforms without being hampered by the selfishness, the
timidity, and the slow mental movements of other men. That was
a tragic development.

The "New Party" was regarded by its original members solely
as an action committee within the House of Commons; there was
little fear at the time that its leader might develop totalitarian
tendencies; and when the leadership principle began undisguisedly

to establish itself in Sir Oswald's mind, the "New Party" dissolved as snow upon the desert's dusty face. In September, 1931, however, the "New Party" was young, vigorous, reformative and alert. It is not surprising that a man of Hobhouse's impatient energies should have been attracted by its spell. In September, 1931, he became a member of the Party; in October he stood as New Party Candidate in the election at Ashton-under-Lyne. His electioneering card bore the strange slogan "Vote for Hobhouse, The Children's Champion." The electors were startled to observe this very young, and most Etonian, candidate presenting himself as the apostle of radical socialism. His speeches, which in substance were more than progressive, were delivered in the style of Gibbon; they were greeted with yells of distaste. Hobhouse, as indeed most of the other candidates for the "New Party," forfeited his deposit.

Such was his only electoral experience. In after years he would pretend, with his usual amused defiance of his own humiliations, that he had enjoyed it all enormously. It is more probable that his political impulsiveness then received a salutary shock. His future approach to politics was more sedate.

The election of October, 1931, was not, however, the end of his association with Sir Oswald Mosley. It had already been observed by some of those who had been connected with the "New Party" that the disaster which had overwhelmed them at the General Election had increased in Sir Oswald those symptoms of totalitarian illness which had already occasioned some disquiet. It was suggested that it might be a good thing if the leader of the party were accorded a course of homeopathic treatment. He was taken to Rome. Christopher Hobhouse, who was to join him there, first travelled to Munich. At a *conditorei* in that city he was introduced to Adolf Hitler. The Führer assured him that it was always a pleasure to him to meet young Englishmen. Hobhouse replied that for him it was indeed an honour to meet the Führer. Hitler thereupon embarked upon a voluble monologue on the subject of Oliver Cromwell: "a subject," as Hobhouse thereafter remarked "upon which I knew far more than he did." Hobhouse continued his way to Rome quite unimpressed by the personality of Adolf Hitler.

The Rome visit, from the homeopathic point of view, was not successful. Hobhouse—as indeed all those who knew Mosley intimately at that period—never ceased to regret that such high gifts of mind and character should have been diverted, almost by mischance, into unfortunate channels. Hobhouse returned to England via Berlin and Hamburg. He decided, for the present at least, to avoid politics and to devote himself to literature.

His early interest in architecture has already been noted. "His taste," writes Mr. John Betjeman, "was essentially sober, but never conventional. In the early thirties and late twenties, when most young men were keen on flat roofs, vita glass and a cactus in the window, that hygienic simplicity (which one would have thought exactly suited to Hobhouse's requirements) proved unattractive to him. He admired Lutyens above all modern architects. Time has proved his judgment sound."

He might well have become a professional architect, had it not been that he was totally unable to draw. He thought of writing a life of *Wren* but was deterred by lack of material. But throughout his life he remained an alert architectural critic and contributed several articles and notices to the *Architectural Review*.

For some time he had been toying with the idea of writing a biography of one of the most distinguished members of his own family, namely John Cam Hobhouse, the friend of Byron, and the begetter of the interesting phrase "His Majesty's Opposition." He was deterred from this purpose, partly because most of his friends were at that time writing books about the Byron period, and partly because he came to the conclusion that John Cam Hobhouse, in spite of his early escapades, was essentially an unadventurous man. He then conceived the idea of writing a study of George III and thereafter a biography of Lord Chatham. But the quality which most appealed to him was that of genial recklessness, combined with deep internal integrity. He found that quality in Charles James Fox. He became immersed in the life and character of that remarkable man; the pleasure which, with his taste for sombre elegance, he would in any case have derived from his membership of Brooks's Club, was much enhanced thereafter by the presence beside him of so magnificent a ghost. He was happier during the two years in which he was preparing his book on Fox than he had ever been in his life. The book was written partly in the Temple, where he was sharing chambers with me at No. 4 King's Bench Walk, partly at Portmerion in North Wales, and partly at Chagford in Devonshire. It was published by Constable and Co. in 1934 and was well received. At the conclusion of this introduction some suggestions will be given as to the angle from which Hobhouse approached the theme of his most important book.

Meanwhile, on coming of age, he obtained possession of his own capital, which he sought to increase by operations on the Stock Exchange. The City phase in his career inspired much anxiety among his friends. Hobhouse possessed a sense of the dramatic as well as a sense of the grandiose; he flung himself with such relish into the role of a City magnate, he would scan with such expert concentration the columns of the *Financial Times*, that it was feared that his natural impulsiveness, his brilliant impatience, might outrun his experience. As a matter of fact he did succeed in a speculation upon the gold market and invested his profits in an old mill in Suffolk which he furnished, somewhat sparsely, and at which he delighted to entertain his friends. In the end, however, his financial speculations were not remunerative and after two years the mill was sold. He thereafter wrote a short and amusing book about the Crystal Palace and another more serious book about the architecture of Oxford University. For some months he edited and contributed to *Cameo*, which ceased publication on the outbreak of war.

From 1935 Christopher Hobhouse, who although an individualist was always strangely ready to listen to advice, came to agree with those of his friends who urged him to adopt a regular profession. He began studying Law and was called to the Bar in 1937. He worked in chambers in Crown Office Row, first under Sir Charles Hodson and thereafter under Mr. Seymour Karminski. He was a most careful and conscientious lawyer and rapidly made a name for himself at the Probate and Divorce Bar. He was assiduous, precise, obstinate, unperturbed, incisive and convincing. After only two years' practice, he earned as much as £1,500 in a single year. With Mr. Karminski, his wife and children, he established relations of affectionate friendship and spent many happy weekends at their house.

By 1939, therefore, he had discarded his early experiments; he had written three books, two of which had increased his reputation for brilliance, and one of which, the present volume, had earned him a reputation for solid historical interpretation. He had at last discovered the profession to which he was best attuned and had, almost within a few months, begun to derive a handsome income from that profession with a lively expectation of more to come. The noble gift of self-confidence, which had in him been retarded by his boyhood experience, was at last vouchsafed to him. He had no doubt, and his closest friends had no doubt, that in front of him there stretched a firm pathway of legal, political and literary success. In spite of the intense and defiant amusement which he derived from being the spectator, and even the dramatist, of his own fortunes, he began to assume (and wholly without arrogance) the self-assurance of a successful man.

Already in 1938, foreseeing the inevitable catastrophe, he had sought to obtain a commission in the Territorial Army. During the previous year, however, he had been afflicted by a mysterious form of spinal illness which would at moments cripple him entirely. Only to his most intimate friends would he disclose the anxiety, even the despair, which this sinister malady imposed. He was rejected on medical grounds, first by the Army, and then by the Navy. With the outbreak of war he redoubled his efforts to enter the fighting services. For a short period in 1939 he served in the London Fire Brigade, but his illness returned to him and he was invalided out. By devious paths in 1940 he managed to elude the vigilance of the doctors and to obtain a commission in the Royal Marines. He was obliged for this purpose to pass an examination in mathematics, a science to which he was ill-attuned. The strength of his determination was shown by the zest with which he applied himself to the uncongenial task of again learning sums.

It is never convincing to describe in biographical terms an inheritor of unfulfilled renown. There were many other men of equal promise who were killed between 1940 and 1945. Yet in Christopher Hobhouse there was some special blend of imagination and persistence, of impulse and reason, of enjoyment and application, of eccentricity and common sense, of ambition and self-derision, which only found its formula, and synthesis, a few short months before his marriage and death. His friends had always been aware that he possessed the ingredients of a striking personality; they feared that these ingredients were too disintegrated ever to coalesce; this fusion was accomplished between 1938 and 1939 and his friends then foresaw that something remarkable must result. They did not foresee that tragic afternoon at Fort Cumberland.

Nor did they foresee how difficult it would be to describe the charm which is imprinted for ever on their memories. Christopher Hobhouse was not, in the conventional sense, a charming man. In spite of his carriage and presence, he was often tactless. Although he longed for the affection of others, and was deeply grateful when he received it, he could only on rare, and startling, occasions express affection himself. The repressions of his childhood had induced him to adopt many self-protective devices, and among these the illusion of existentialism, or the fallacy that each man, by egoism, creates his own life. His selfishness was always apparent; his unselfishness (and it was constant and touching) operated by stealth. He possessed a deep affection for his friends, but that affection expressed itself, in their presence by amused disdain, in their absence by almost ferocious loyalty. He was capable of being very rude indeed. If he met an American he would dwell with incisive acumen upon the defects of the American Constitution; if he met a Frenchman he would analyse, with considerable brilliance, the corruption of French politics, whether municipal or national. He would ask one of his contemporaries to luncheon, buy a newspaper on his way to the restaurant and read the newspaper very slowly during the early stages of the meal. When confronted with elderly or distinguished people he would not (or not always) flagrantly expose their ineptitude; he would listen quite patiently to their opinions; he would then lean back in his chair, close his eyes slowly, and utter the one word "Gosh!" All that was most disconcerting.

On one occasion he was taken by a friend to visit Mr. George Moore, in Ebury Street. He had been warned in advance that there were certain topics, such as modern painting and Thomas Hardy, which it would be wise to avoid. Casting a glance of rapid disdain at the Berthe Morisot portrait above the mantelpiece, Hobhouse embarked upon the thesis that the greatest of our modern stylists, in truth the greatest of all our men of letters, was Thomas Hardy. George Moore waved his white hands in frantic expostulation. The interview was quickly terminated. "What was it," Hobhouse asked his friend, "that the old man hissed at you when we were leaving?" "Well," his friend replied, "if you really want to know what George Moore said to me, it was 'Never in any circumstances bring that young man to see me again'." With what relish, with how deep an inner chuckle, did Hobhouse recount this story thereafter!

Yet although few people took to Hobhouse at their first meeting, very few people failed, when they got to know him, to be affected by his charm. What was the nature of that charm? In the first place audacity of opinion, audaciously expressed. That was stimulating. In the second place the awareness on the part of any sensitive person that his apparent arrogance was in fact humility pathetically disguised. That gave the pleasurable sensation of a personal discovery. In the third place the consciousness that a man who regarded himself as so extremely ridiculous could not in fact be really conceited. That increased one's desire for further investigation. In the fourth place zest and curiosity, the most clubbable of human qualities. And behind it all, an active intelligence, perplexing and mysterious in that, so obviously, it had not yet quite discovered itself. As a companion he was original, uncertain, always surprising; as a friend he was constant beyond compare; and as a character he was fascinating in that, even when he was nearly thirty, he was forming himself gradually, painfully, before one's eyes.

Something of this entrancing combination of sense and fantasy is reflected in the book to which this is a preface. It may have been that Hobhouse was not by temperament suited for the age of the common man, but with the uncommon man he felt an almost uproarious affinity. It is the zest with which he wrote of Charles James Fox which renders this biography so living.

Since the first edition of Christopher Hobhouse's *Fox* in 1934 certain material has come to light which would have induced him to modify some of the opinions expressed. There has in the first place been Mr. Romney Sedgwick's edition of the letters of George III to Lord Bute. Mr. Edward Lascelles has been so good as to draw my attention to the fact that had Hobhouse read these letters he would have formed a different conception of the relations between George III and his favourite, and of the character of the monarch himself. These letters show that many of the current conceptions of George III are incorrect. It was not his mother only who bullied him; it was also Lord Bute. It was not so much that he was a Hanoverian intent on rendering the British monarchy a paternal despotism on the Continental pattern; it was rather that he was a shy, diffident and neurotic young man, anxious in everything to do what his "dearest friend," Lord Bute, dictated and desired. Had he read the Bute correspondence, Hobhouse would certainly have redrafted the second paragraph on page 41 in which he attributes to the Princess Dowager the young King's panic escape from Lady Sarah Lennox. The marriage, as the correspondence renders abundantly clear, was vetoed, not by the Princess so much as by Lord Bute; and it was the King himself who hurried on the German marriage and sent an emissary to the continent to find a suitable bride.

In the second place there has appeared, since the first edition of *Fox*, Sir Philip Magnus's admirable biography of Edmund Burke. Sir Philip had been given access to the Fitzwilliam papers which until then had been concealed from the historian's eye. While writing his book he had frequent discussions with Hobhouse, with whom he was on terms of close friendship, and it is certain that had the latter himself been able to prepare a second edition of *Fox* he would, in the light of this new evidence, have revised in many important respects the estimate of Burke's character which he had included in Chapter VI. He had assumed (as most people had assumed until Sir Philip Magnus published the results of his researches) that Burke was wholly immune to the political corruption of the age. It is in any case difficult to explain how Burke who, in 1758 was completely penniless, could have been able ten years later to purchase the estate of Gregories in Buckinghamshire and to adorn the walls of his saloons and galleries with a superb collection of Poussins. It is now proven that Edmund Burke speculated considerably in East India stock; it is also clear that his brother Richard was an unsavoury character and that the extent to which his friend, William Burke, juggled in Indian finance exceeded even the then accepted boundaries of chicanery. "An odour of financial adventureship," writes Sir Philip Magnus, "surrounded Burke's most intimate domestic ties." It may be true that Burke never indulged in corruption for his personal benefit; but it is also true that he condoned corruption as practised by his brother and his friend.

More specifically, Hobhouse would have been obliged, after the publication of Sir Philip Magnus's book, to revise the section on pages 41–52 in which he deals with Fox's resignation. Horace Walpole recounts the story that Fox resigned because Lord North refused to give the Burke family a concession in the West Indies. Hobhouse ignored this story, regarding it doubtless as typical

Walpole gossip. Sir Philip Magnus's revelations make it clear that it was something more than gossip. Had Hobhouse been given the opportunity to prepare this second edition he would have been bound to examine these allegations, if only to refute them. He would have found them difficult to refute.

It is not suggested that the new material which has become available since 1934 has in any way rendered this book obsolete. Such emendations as he would have made are incidental only. The book remains one of the most precise and vivid portraits of Charles James Fox that has ever been penned. It remains, moreover, a model of incisive style.

All biographies are to some extent a collaboration between the author and his subject. If a biography is to come alive, as this biography has come alive, there must exist between the artist and his sitter something more than ordinary interest, something more even than respect; there must exist ardent sympathy. How came it that Christopher Hobhouse was so ardently sympathetic to Charles James Fox?

He was by nature resentful of all forms of cant; he possessed particular disdain for those historians who seek to extract from history generalisations upon righteousness; he loathed what he called "Whig uplift." Being a confirmed individualist he believed that history is shaped, not so much by social or economic changes, as by the energies and ambitions of uncommon men. Being himself adventurous he felt attracted to an age in which adventurers could enjoy themselves lavishly. He did not approach the eighteenth century in a mood of disapproval; he approached it in a mood of half-envious and half-amused nostalgia. It is with sympathy, and not in irony, that he states that the first Lord Holland's "sensitive nature felt acutely the storm of indignation that his unscrupulous avarice had aroused." It is with realism, rather than cynicism that he can refer to the Whig leaders as people "of vast wealth, as befitted men who had ruled for fifty years." It came naturally to a man of his patrician instincts to refer to Cromwell and his Puritans as "that reptile rule." He was not deterred by contemporary fashion from using the brave words "the common herd."

Fascinated as he was by the eighteenth century, he saw in Fox the embodiment of all the courage of that age. He recognised in Fox many of the eccentricities and sincerities of his own temperament together with a convincing power of self-assertion which he would himself have longed to possess. His admiration for his hero is based upon the forcefulness with which Fox triumphed over incessant mistakes; his affection for his hero, which is very personal, arises from the realisation that those mistakes were, in the eighteenth century terms, exactly the same sort of mistakes as he had made himself. He loved Fox for his eccentricity: "He was never normal; whenever he did not rise above the accepted standards of conduct, he fell below them." He loved him for being incalculable: "He had inherited the fatalism, the lack of judgment, the recklessness, the intemperance, the consistent bad luck, the unreliability, the un-teachableness of a Stuart." He loved him for his frankness towards himself: "He had barely enough introspection to be ashamed, and far too little ever to be conceited." He loved him for the manner in which he muddled his personal relationships. "I am a bad hater," Fox once remarked. "And so he was," comments Hob-house affectionately, "for he hated the wrong people." "It is an attractive thing about Fox," he writes in another passage, "that his best friendships were his worst mistakes." Hobhouse found in Fox a powerful affirmation of his own hostility to conventional opinion and the dominance of majorities. Fox to him was "the last man in the world to be impressed by a unanimous opinion." He admired his hero's "absolute refusal to conciliate public opinion." He loved him for his generosity; for his profound integrity; for his capacity to inspire lasting devotion; for his union of "all that makes a statesman with all that can undo a politician." For Hobhouse, who until he was almost thirty had failed to integrate his curiously divided temperament, Fox became a model of vehement self-integration. His book, therefore, is something more than a clever analysis made by a most gifted young man; it is written in a passion of sympathy. And it is this, as I have said, which renders it so alive.

Hobhouse derived much benefit from the writing of this book. It gave him confidence. His ambition, which was strong within him, became thereafter more co-ordinated and less dispersed. He gave up toying with experiments and short cuts and settled down to a stubborn tramp along the high road of success. Assuredly, had he lived, and had his health not failed him, he would have achieved power. But he did not live.

The text book for all those who practise at the Probate and

Divorce Bar is *Rayden on Divorce*. When the fourth edition of that classic work was issued in 1942 it bore a dedication to Christopher Hobhouse. The words of that dedication were well conceived:

TO

C. B. H.

Qui ante diem periit
Sed miles
Sed pro patria.

1. His Origin

Charles James Fox was born on January the 24th, 1749, at a house in Conduit Street, to which his parents had removed while Holland House, which they had lately taken, was in the hands of the builders. The plebeian and the aristocratic were fairly balanced in his blood. His father, Henry Fox, was the son of Sir Stephen Fox, and Sir Stephen Fox, though he died surrounded by riches and honours, had been born in total obscurity, and is said to have been a choir boy at Salisbury. Even his public career is little recorded. Of his ability, we know that he was a valued servant of four kings; of his courage, that he stood beside King Charles on the scaffold; of his generosity, that he gave a princely endowment to Chelsea Hospital; and of his physique, that he was a father at eighty. Though an eminently successful man, he was still by the standards of that time a *parvenu*, and it was left to Henry Fox to consolidate the family's position; an end which he achieved in the first place by a successful elopement, and in the second place by his usefulness as a politician.

In 1744 he ran away with Caroline Lennox, the daughter of the Duke of Richmond and the great-grand-daughter of Charles the Second by Louise de Kéroualle. That a commoner, the second son of a self-made man, should aspire to marry into a ducal, a semi-royal family, was not at all to the liking of a close society, and Henry Fox's marriage was the outstanding scandal of the day. But it brought unblemished happiness to them both, and it produced in Charles a clearly recognisable mixture of the vices and virtues of Charles the Second, balanced by the public virtues of one of his most faithful servants.

In politics Henry Fox was as successful as in love. He proved himself an able and serviceable debater, and his blunt, colloquial style is a curious foretaste of his son's. His attention was concentrated not on fame but on money, and in this pursuit his success was phenomenal. The Pay Office was lucrative at any time, as the Paymaster was entitled to use the large sums passing through his hands as if he were a private banker. In time of war it was an Eldorado, and in the hands of Henry Fox the Paymaster's share constituted a high, steady, and yet a perfectly legitimate percentage of the total military expenditure. Not only was he entitled to the interest on the balance in his hands, but to any capital profit he might make by its investment. He has explained the procedure himself in a most disarming way. "The Government borrows money at twenty per cent discount. I am not consulted or concerned in making the bargain. I have, as Paymaster, great sums in my hands, which, not applicable to any present use, must either lie dead in the bank, or be employed by me. I lend this to the Government in 1761. A peace is thought certain. I am not in the least consulted, but my very bad opinion of Mr. Pitt makes me think it will not be concluded. I sell out, and gain greatly. In 1762, I lend again: a peace comes, in which again I am not consulted, and I again gain greatly." Nothing could be more candid, if only he had alluded to the scale of these innocent operations. The facts were that he was Paymaster General almost throughout the Seven Years' War; that £49,500,000, the equivalent of a third of the national debt, passed through his hands; and that some of it was still in the hands of his executors nine years after his death and eighteen years after his resignation.

Henry Fox, or Lord Holland as he became, was fabulously rich. He was at the same time the best hated man in England, and his sensitive nature felt acutely the storm of indignation that his unscrupulous avarice had aroused. His declining years are full of pathos. Mistrusted by the untrustworthy, despised by the despicable, cheated (as he thought) out of his office, baulked of the earldom on which he had set his heart, he turned his back on politics, branded, in the words of a City of London petition, as "the public defaulter of unaccounted millions." He had built himself a country house in a curious situation on the North Foreland, devoid of either beauty or shelter, always notorious as a paradise for smugglers, and now to become "another name for paradise" to Lord Holland, who had a propensity for bathing in the sea.

> "Old, and abandoned by each venal friend,
> Here Holland formed the pious resolution
> To smuggle a few years, and strive to mend
> A broken character and constitution."

So wrote Thomas Gray when he viewed this Formian villa from the sea. At Kingsgate Lord Holland was happy so long as he could forget about public life. In his wife, his children and his friends—all of whom adored him—he could find a substitute for an easy conscience and a refuge from the public fury. Of money and of love he had all that any man could want: but they were not everything. He was always a little querulous, always cynical about the gratitude of politicians, always teaching his sons the philosophy of a man who has been very wicked, but not quite wicked enough. "Aspire, Charles, to the first employments," he would say; "but don't ever *trust* as I did."

But at Holland House he was a different man. It was there that he lived while he was still amassing money and unpopularity. Charles was fourteen years old when his father became Lord Holland and twenty-five years old when he died. The son therefore saw both how success is achieved in a corrupt age, and how failure is requited. During those twenty-five years the whole influence of the father was directed to making the son, who was already an abler, a harder man than himself.

2. *His Upbringing, 1749-1768*

As a child, Charles Fox, his second son, was the greatest consolation of Henry Fox's uneasy life. Perhaps nobody except a royal infant has had a better documented childhood. There is no need to rely on the retrospection of aged contemporaries to find out what a wonderful child he was. Stacks of letters exist to tell us how beautiful he was at two, what good company at three, how sensible at four, how argumentative at five, how stage-struck at six, what a good scholar he was at seven. What is interesting is less the child's intelligence than the peculiar form in which the father showed his fondness.

Henry Fox had strong views on education. Unlimited indulgence was his system. Nothing was ever to stand between a child and its happiness; a child was never to receive a command; and what a child had been promised, it was to have. "Young people," he said, "are always in the right, and old people in the wrong." To someone who wished to deprive his child of some satisfaction, he said: "Let nothing be done to break his spirit.

3

The world will do that business fast enough." And to his children he used to say: "Never do to-day what you can put off till to-morrow, or ever do yourself what you can get anyone else to do for you."

These were not speculations or witticisms: they were his rules of conduct. If Charles wished to stamp on a gold watch, to wash his hands in a bowl of cream at dinner, or to throw an office despatch in the fire, "Very well," his father would say, "if you must, I suppose you must." To show Charles that a promise to a child was as important as any other, when he had dynamited a brick wall at Holland House in Charles' absence, forgetting that he had promised that Charles should see the explosion, he rebuilt the wall and dynamited it again. And Charles was half a Stuart; so that heredity and environment conspired to produce the spoiled child of history.

Never having been pushed, Charles became a passionate seeker of knowledge. At the age of seven he caught his mother in an inaccuracy on a minor point of Roman history and declared that her tuition was a menace to his scholarship. "Charles," wrote his father, "determines to go to Wandsworth." To Wandsworth he went, to the academy of a Monsieur Pampelonne, until two years later, at the age of nine, he "determined" to proceed to Eton.

Eton in the eighteenth century is a very hazy picture. Savage discipline and complete anarchy, extreme youth and extreme sophistication, exclusiveness and latitude—all these contradictions defeat us when we try to recapture that most elusive of atmospheres. But it is not necessary. Fox always altered his surroundings. more than his surroundings altered Fox, even when he was a boy. We have no less an authority for this than Chatham, who, in recording his intensely unfavourable opinion of Lord Holland, declared that "he educated his children without the least regard to morality, and with such extravagant vulgar indulgence, that the great change which has taken place among our youth has been dated from the time of his sons' going to Eton."

There are only scanty records of his career at Eton. Some testimonies to his pre-eminence in oratory: some Latin verses in praise of his cousin, Susan Fox-Strangways, which were sent up for good: some French verses in dispraise of Chatham. But his precocity attracted attention beyond the limits of the school. On one of his frequent visits to London, he was noticed—a small but

4

attentive figure—listening to a debate in the Lords from the steps of the throne. "That," said Lord Mansfield to his neighbour, "is Fox's son Charles, with twice his parts and half his sagacity." It would serve for Charles' epitaph.

Before Charles had been five years at Eton, his father, thinking no doubt that he was getting too fond of his books and leading too regular a life, decided to take him away for a few months of more advanced studies. The place selected was Spa, the education was in games of chance, and for four months Charles (now fourteen years old) was provided with five guineas a night to lose among a smart crowd of cosmopolitan gamblers. At the end of that time he went back of his own accord to Eton, where he spread the gaming habit like an epidemic. It was not long before Eton was under a cloud of fashionable disapproval, and Charles' name a byword for dissipation. At fifteen he had outgrown a public school: he was homesick, having already begun to lose his heart in all directions: it was just as well that he left before his reputation as a gambler had overshadowed his reputation as the most eloquent speaker and the most sought-after friend in the place. It was the custom at that time for a boy on leaving to present the Provost with a portrait in lieu of a tip, and Fox's, which still hangs in the Provost's Lodge, is the work of Reynolds. Among a crowd of contemporaries he stands out, the most mature, the least self-conscious. He is already ugly, swarthy, strongly Semitic: already in his portrait the sardonic voluptuousness of Charles Stuart is lit up by brilliant intelligence into the fine, human, fascinating features of Charles Fox.

It was in 1764 that he went up to Oxford, to Hertford College, where he remained for two years. These were years of almost uninterrupted hard work: in spite of all his father's efforts, scholarship had become a passion with him: he even spent his vacations at Oxford, sending home bulletins of his latest intellectual adventures. From trigonometry to pre-Restoration plays (of which he claimed to have read the lot) his curiosity was universal and unchecked. There was the same violence, too, about his physical excursions; he once walked the fifty-six miles from Oxford to Holland House in a single sweltering day, pawning his gold watch at Nettlebed for some bread and cheese and porter. There was no question about Charles' animal spirits.

His labours were crowned at last with a unique reward: he

was implored by the head of his college to do less work. "Application like yours," wrote Dr. Newcome, "requires some intermission." Fox kept the letter, and in later life he would produce it from his pocket-book as a defence against his friends' well-merited accusations of idleness. Idle he was throughout his life. Like Johnson, he acquired his knowledge by fits and starts. His idleness had a very different cause from Johnson's: no man suffered less from hypochondria than Fox, but he suffered instead from being put to tasks too easy for him, and brought up in conditions that taxed his powers too lightly. "I am afraid," he once wrote, "my natural idleness will in the end get the better of what little ambition I have, and that I shall never be anything but a lounging fellow." His career will not be notable for any lack of worldly ambition, but the temptation to lounge was always present to a man so full of private intellectual resources.

He took Dr. Newcome's advice, and went off to Paris, where he pursued Parisian pleasures as ardently as in Oxford he pursued the pleasures of Oxford: so ardently indeed as to arouse the attention of the Secretary of the British Embassy, none other than David Hume. Hume warned Holland "that the dissipation of this kind of Parisian life might check his ardour after useful knowledge, and lose in all appearance a very great acquisition to the public." But Holland was fully hardened to criticism of his method of educating Charles; knowing his son's worth, he continued to let him do as he pleased, with results that entirely refuted the grave anticipations of philosophers.

Leaving Oxford at seventeen, he went abroad for two years. It was an expensive, but a rewarding, trip. Paris, Nice, Naples, Rome, Florence—each of them added as much to his knowledge of life and of letters, as they reduced his patrimony. Some people travel alone, absorbing meticulous culture as though nothing must escape them; others travel in swarms, behaving abroad exactly as they behave at home, and enjoying no novelty but the climate. Fox avoided both extremes. Wherever he went, he saturated himself in the language, the literature, the dissipations of the place; but equally he took his friends with him, and enjoyed with them an unending series of amateur theatricals. Besides his family, who were good enough company for anyone, there were Richard Fitzpatrick, his brother-in-law, and throughout life his most intimate friend; Carlisle, an Eton friend who later drifted apart from Fox, and later still filled a small *rôle* in Byron's life; Fitz-william, who has an unhappy place in Irish history; and one Uvedale Price, who went with him to take a cup of chocolate with Voltaire. Surrounded and sought after by such a circle as this, still he managed to soak himself in the pleasures and culture of each country. He became fluent in French and Italian. Though he is said to have got through £16,000 in ten days at Naples, it was there that he conceived his passion for Italian poetry. Though he is said to have travelled post from Paris to Lyons to buy some silk waistcoats, it was in Paris that he laid the foundations of a fluency that was to be exercised upon Napoleon, and a culture that opened new worlds to his devouring mind. Always against his historic extravagances, we must set the fact that he was laying up intellectuals treasures for himself.

3. His Wild Oats, 1768 Onwards

When Fox returned to London at the age of nineteen, his literary and academic equipment was kept well in the background. For the time being he was determined to outdo all rivals for the part of the insufferably sophisticated travel-snob and man of the world. He would astonish London, not as a scholar or an intellectual, but as a Macaroni. "An egregious coxcomb," exclaimed one gossip, and another echoes: "A prodigious dandy!" If not the best dressed, he was by general consent the most strikingly dressed man in London, with his red heels, his odd little French hat, his smuggled lace and smuggled velvet, and a buttonhole the size of his head. It was surely the ultimate triumph of style over looks, that converted ugly, slovenly, and rather dirty Charles Fox into the unchallenged beau of the day.

He spent little of his time now at Kingsgate or at Holland House. With Fitzpatrick he shared rooms in Piccadilly over Mackie's Italian Warehouse; but the bulk of his time was spent at Almack's, which he had joined in 1765, and which was not until 1778 taken over by the immortal Brooks, a shady wine-merchant:

"Brooks, whose speculative skill
Is hasty credit, and a distant bill.
Who, nursed in clubs, disdains a vulgar trade,
Exults to trust, and blushes to be paid."

Almack's was not at all what we should call a club: it was a glorified casino, where every night and all night a circle of men played for stakes as high as now prevail at any baccarat table in the world. Walpole says that there was usually £10,000 on the table: and fifty guineas a player was the minimum at some tables. Some of the losses sustained almost defy belief. After one wretch had lost £70,000 and his carriages in a night, Fox moved to pay him an annuity from the pool on condition of his leaving cards alone. Fox himself thought nothing of losing or winning a few thousands in a night: and his brother Stephen was almost as wild. Between them they once lost £32,000 in three nights. There is good reason to believe that the play was crooked. A few men lived by cards, and are referred to in Fox's letters as the Hounds. Though he was overjoyed to win anything off the Hounds, and rated his debts to them below his debts of honour and only just above his bond debts, he continued to play with them. For he soon reached the stage when the thrill of even chances palled: he played for the sake of losing, and lose he did.

To make matters worse, the settlement of debts was facilitated by a swarm of moneylenders who battened on this mania for high play, and who soon found two victims after their own hearts in Charles and Stephen Fox, heirs to a millionaire, and apparently determined to see how little of their patrimony they could inherit. Charles' friends had to thrust their way to his bedside of a morning through a crowd of "Fox-hunting" duns; a special room had to be set aside for them, which Fox called with sublime insolence his Jerusalem chamber.

> "But hark, the voice of battle sounds from far;
> The Jews and Macaronis are at war;
> The Jews prevail, and thundering from the stocks,
> They seize, they bind, they circumcise Charles Fox."

So runs a contemporary ballad. In constant trouble with money-lender after money-lender, Fox borrowed immensely from his friends: Carlisle among others was seriously embarrassed by his advances to Fox. He borrowed from the waiters at Almack's. He borrowed from the chair-men in St. James's Street. When Brooks came on the scene, he borrowed from Brooks. He borrowed untold sums from the unfortunate Mackie. And later in life he achieved what must be the palm of insolvency—he actually borrowed money from Sheridan.

There were one or two bright spots on this horizon. He was a capital whist-player, and could have made several thousand a year by it: only it seems that this very facility spoilt his pleasure in the game. Again he was a most successful backer, and used to come back from Newmarket anything from ten to fifteen thousand richer than he went. But that was a drop in the ocean of his losses at faro; and it was the game of chance alone that really gripped him. It seemed as though nothing could ever restore him to solvency. "Ld Clermont," runs a famous entry in Brooks's betting book, "has given Mr. Crawford 10 guineas, upon the condition of receiving 500l. from him whenever Mr. Charles Fox shall be worth l.100,000 clear of debts." Among other remedies that were proposed, several heiresses were hunted up for his inspection in the hope that their fortunes would stop the rot if only Fox would spare the time to marry them. "I earnestly hope so," said Lord Holland, when he heard that one of these alliances had matured, "for then he will be obliged to go to bed on at least one night of his life." His desperate straits were made to serve the purpose of an excellent practical joke. He was sent to see a Miss Phipps, a West Indian heiress of legendary wealth, with the specific instruction that Miss Phipps was only partial to fair men. Poor Fox, with his Levantine complexion, irrepressible beard, and bushy black eyebrows, presented himself for this interview half suffocated with face-powder.

Fox's personal expenditure was forgotten beside his gambling losses, but it must have been immense. He kept a string of at one time as many as thirty horses at Newmarket in conjunction with Lord Foley, and Lord Foley is known to have spent an inheritance of £100,000 in single-minded devotion to the improvement of the national breed of racehorse. If his earliest biographer is to be trusted, Fox entered into the joys of ownership with unexampled zest. "He placed himself where the animal was to make a push, or where the race was to be most strongly contested. From this spot he eyed the horses advancing with the most immovable look: he breathed quicker as they accelerated their pace; and when they came opposite to him, he rode in with them at full speed, whiffing, spewing and blowing as if he would have infused his whole soul into the speed, courage and perseverance of his favourite racer."

Such exertions on the part of a prominent politician, who turned the scale at over thirteen stone, would add interest to the proceedings at Newmarket today.

With all these expensive diversions, Fox extracted the last ounce of pleasure from many occupations that cost nothing at all. One night at Almack's he had lost so much money that his friend Beauclerk was apprehensive that he might take his own life, and followed him to his lodgings, only to find him engrossed in Herodotus:"What would you have a man do," he gaily demanded, "who has lost his last shilling?" At Kingsgate he could be happy for weeks on end with his devoted father and his horsey brother and lovely Susan Fox-Strangways who had eloped with an actor, and still lovelier Sarah Lennox whose King had so nearly eloped with her. There he was indefatigable in cricket and tennis, but perhaps he was happiest of all in the library. Poetry, he would say is the only thing after all. He was an enthusiastic, if not a very lethal shot; and regularly spent several weeks every autumn at various houses in Norfolk. And after the shooting he would repair to Winterslow in Wiltshire, where his brother Stephen had built a private theatre, in which the Fox family gave amateur performances which attracted the whole county.

Fox's life of pleasure was a full life if ever there was one. Reading the gossip of the period, which centres so largely round his single figure, one wonders faintly how he found the time. But admiration turns to astonishment, when one considers that all the countless exploits, with which London and Paris echoed, were merely offshoots of his main activity. Fox was not simply discounting the future. All the while that he was squandering his money and his reputation in sociable follies, he was building up another sort of position for himself that nothing would impair.

In March, 1768, while he was still in Italy, having only recently celebrated his nineteenth birthday, Lord Holland had his son elected, for a consideration, to represent Lord Montagu's interests at Midhurst in Parliament. That autumn he took his seat, still eighteen months short of the minimum age. An indulgent House of Commons, having heard of his prowess in many fields, overlooked his legal disqualification as an infant, and waited the prodigy with generous eagerness. They were not disappointed. Fox's success in Parliament was instant and entire: as his financial position went from precarious to hopeless, as his name became more and more frowned upon in the austere household of the King or among earnest congregations of dissenters, simultaneously it became every day more clear that this versatile scapegrace was not destined to the ordinary fate of beaux and bankrupts, for Parliament had set him on a pedestal of his own, as "the phenomenon of the age".

CHAPTER TWO

1. *The State of Politics, 1768*

The sudden transformation of the political system that took place on the accession of George the Third was due less to the new king's personal qualities (though his ability was considerable, and his determination immense) than to external circumstances. The first two Georges were paragons of constitutional monarchy, but through no fault of their own. Much as they would have preferred to rule England as they ruled Hanover, it was not in their power. For as long as the Stuarts could maintain a presentable candidate to the throne, the Hanoverians were only here on sufferance. They were painfully aware that two of their three kingdoms regarded them as usurpers, and that the vast majority of the clergy of the established church felt more allegiance to a family of Popish reprobates than to the best of German Protestants. Bound hand and foot by the Jacobite menace, and handicapped by ignorance of the language, they made a virtue of necessity, and ruled as the Whigs would have them rule.

Though Jacobite feeling was strong, it was only strong enough to make the Whigs omnipotent. That great party had centred ever since the revolution around a few powerful families, some English (such as the Russells and Cavendishes), some Dutch (the Keppels or the Bentincks). It was they who had put the King on the throne, and it was they who kept him there: and they were not the men to let him forget his obligation. For fifty years their stranglehold was unbroken: the King ruled as a Whig nominee. During this time Toryism was a form of disloyalty: whoever was not a Whig was under the imputation of being a Jacobite, and was debarred from public life: even the parliamentary opposition was carried on by one set of Whigs against the other. Two successive Jacobite invasions only cemented the power of the Whigs, reducing the King and the Tories alike to greater impotence. And so long as there was any probability of another Jacobite attempt, it was clear that arrogance of the Devonshires and the Bedfords and the Portlands would remain unmitigated.

Bullied in this way by their friends the loyalists, the Hanoverians turned longing eyes towards the other party. If once it proved that the Whigs had no monopoly of loyalty, it would be all up with the Whigs. Better for a monarch to come to terms with the Jacobites than to remain a puppet in the hands of his supporters. The first of the Hanoverians who seriously explored this hope of liberation was George the Third's mother, the Princess Augusta. Guided by Bolingbroke, the most eminent of the oligarchy's victims, she collected round her at Leicester House, in the last years of George the Second's reign, a few men who were to help her son to break the Whig party. Their object was simple enough: it was to oust the other party. But it was converted by Bolingbroke into a noble aspiration, a new and purer political philosophy. "Mettre le roi hors de page," was one of their catchwords; "measures not men" was another; "government without faction" was the favourite formula of George the Third himself. All of which meant simply that in escaping from the Whigs the King had no intention of putting himself at the mercy of the Tories. In future the King would take no cognisance of parties or connections: he would distribute offices to whom he pleased: every government would be a coalition of the most suitable men: the Hanoverians, dividing to rule, would be *Kings* at last.

By 1760, these plans were ripe. The essential condition was fulfilled—the Jacobite menace was dead. The old Pretender was dying disreputably in Rome: the Young Pretender had succumbed to drink and Miss Walkinshaw at Basle. The Jacobites were absolved from their impossible allegiance: Toryism was no longer sedition. The hated Scotch—the Butes, the Murrays, the Elliots—showed their faces in London again. A court party was formed. The young king was popular. Prerogative, which had hardly been mentioned for half a century, was the catchword of the day.

The Whigs, up to the very moment of George the Second's death, were at the summit of their power. Pitt ruled, and was conducting the Seven Years' War: the war was so successful and so lucrative that the Whigs for once were popular in the country. George the Third realised that he must put an end to the war if he ever wished to be rid of the minister. Within two years he had put his old tutor, Bute, the arch-enemy of the Whigs, in power, with the immediate object of concluding peace with France. And this was where Henry Fox came in. Fox was employed by Bute to force the treaty through the House of Commons, and never was a disagreeable task better done. Whoever voted against the treaty, he and his dependants were stripped of every honour and emolument of which Government had the power to deprive them. The Whigs, showing their true colours in the moment of defeat, complained that everyone was turned out, whom they had brought in, except the King. From a privy councillorship to a wounded soldier's pension, all that the Whigs had either earned or grabbed in their years of prosperity was snatched from them—that is, unless they voted for the treaty. For by no means all the Whigs were equal to this trial of faith. Fox's prescription of the Whigs was intended to break them, but to do this primarily by splitting their solidarity and in this it was brilliantly successful.

Henceforward there are three Whig Parties, and it is of the first importance that they should be kept distinct. First there were the Bedfords, a compact and powerful family group, political gangsters without pretence, whose sole public object was to lay their hands on public money; they came to terms at once; and much as he hated them, the King always knew where he was with the Bedfords. Secondly, there was the Rockingham party. Rockingham himself, Richmond, Portland and Sir George Savile were Whigs of the old school. Of vast wealth, as befitted men who had ruled for fifty years, they were the most determined enemies of the royal prerogative. They failed to adapt their minds to the change in the King's position which had come about with the disappearance of the Jacobite menace. The rump of the "Venetian oligarchy," they regarded the renaissance of the Tories as the end of the English constitution—that constitution which they had brought into being in the great and glorious year 1688, and under which they had governed the country so lucratively ever since. Open republicanism would have been a less sterile and unattractive doctrine than the disguised republicanism of this faction. With their eyes riveted on the bad old times, the Rockinghams would soon have disappeared from the scene, but for Edmund Burke, who became Rockingham's secretary in 1765. He could transform their ineffectual regrets, their sighs and tears over the corpse of the English constitution, into words that shook the throne. He was at bottom as much a *laudator temporis acti* as any of them, loving the very imperfections of the precious constitution as much as they did, and without their self-interested reasons; but he had an eloquence and

14

a passion that the leaders of the party lacked. The motive power, the moral force of the Rockingham party, came from him. It was in recognition of this important obligation that they always excluded him from their cabinets.

The Bedfords and the Rockinghams were offshoots of the Whig party: the third and real Whig party was the Earl of Chatham. But Chatham was not the man that Pitt had been. Gout and megalomania were beginning to affect his powers: but he had a disciple who was quite worthy of his mantle. Lord Shelburne had attached himself to Chatham, and was more his equal than his subordinate. Young, rich, noble, industrious and immensely able, Shelburne was capable of playing as large a part in the second part of the century as Chatham had played in the first. He looked to the future as steadily as the Rockinghams looked to the past. He saw how unworkable the old constitution of 1688 had become. He saw the danger of reducing the King to the status of a rubber stamp. He saw how grossly the great Whig oligarchy had abused their power. He saw how obsolete was the foreign policy they had inherited from the Prince of Orange. He was the first free trader and almost the first Parliamentary reformer. How this great man failed of the influence he deserved we shall see in due course: but the statesmanship that he inherited from Chatham was bequeathed through him to Chatham's son, and found its fulfilment after an interval of twenty years.

By 1763, therefore, there were four political parties: the Court party, the Bedfords, the Rockinghams, and Chatham's party. In that year Bute and Fox, having forced through the Peace of Paris, fell from power. Having failed to maintain a Court party in spite of the most desperate measures, the King tried each branch of the Whigs in turn before he formed the coalition of his dreams. For two years, the Bedfords ruled, but their close solidarity was no more in accordance with the principles of Leicester House, than their lack of private morality with the new *régime* at Windsor Castle. The King found that his prerogative was as worthless under this arrogant and rapacious clique as even George the Second's had been. Preferring to rule through his worst enemies, provided they were weaker, he snatched at the chance of putting the Rockinghams in the place of the Bedfords, but he only kept them for a year: for though weak, they were inflexible. In 1766 was formed a Government much more to his liking, because more heterogeneous. Under the leadership of Chatham and Shelburne it included some true Whigs such as Lord Chancellor Camden and Barré; a few deserters from Rockingham's party, such as Grafton and Portland; and a number of political hacks. It was in fact not a Chatham Government at all, but a coalition formed by Chatham to rid the King of Rockingham. And with the increase in Chatham's gout, the Cabinet became more anarchical every day, until after two years in 1768, between the time of Charles Fox's election and the time he took his seat, it had to be remodelled entirely. Chatham who had long been absent from London, resigned, and with him of course went Shelburne. The voting strength of the new coalition was to come from the Bedfords: but owing to the King's dislike of their patronising manners, the head of the Government was the Duke of Grafton.

Grafton, who was thus serving the Bedfords as he had served both Rockingham and Chatham, is one of the worst maligned characters in our political history. Junius made him into a legendary figure, raked up scandals about his private life, and served them up hot for the delight of the public. But Junius, though a very good pamphleteer, was nothing more than a pamphleteer, and it is beneath the dignity, though not beneath the practice, of later Whig historians to take his racy libels for gospel truth. This "black duke," who takes his mistress to the opera and gets horsewhipped at Newmarket, turns out on investigation to be a mild and rather pathetic character, whose lack of will power led him to make as great a muddle of his public as of his private life. His facility for getting into compromising situations was only equalled by his inability to get out of them. Anyone who studies his relationship with Nancy Parsons will see exactly why it was that having got into the Government under Rockingham, he remained in it under Chatham, and continued in it as the titular head of a Bedford clique until he had no reputation left. Always a stupid man, he was clay in the King's hands at a time when the King particularly wanted a pliable minister. We shall see what ample amends he made for his public errors: for his private wrong-doings, of which Junius makes such a salacious story, he atoned by spending the evening of his life in the composition of Unitarian tracts.

Grafton's principal lieutenant, the Chancellor of the Exchequer and leader of the House of Commons in the reconstructed ministry of 1768, was a very able and public-spirited Tory, whom the House of Commons loved for his wit and capacity and good nature—Lord North. "A consummate debater" in Fox's view, and the most kind-hearted of politicians, he was from the King's point of view a perfect leader of the House. For the majority of the Commons would do whatever North told them to do, and North would do more or less exactly what the King told him to do. So the King had at last got a government he could sincerely support, in which the Bedfords voted and took their pay without approaching his person, while a man of straw presided over the cabinet, and a completely faithful retainer controlled the House of Commons.

Such was the political scene when Charles Fox came back from Italy and took his seat in the autumn of 1768. With the worldly experience of a boy of nineteen, and unhampered by a single resident constituent, it is not to be wondered at that he represented nothing but his father's prejudices, which were chiefly personal dislikes. First among Lord Holland's many hatreds was Shelburne, who had been too clever for him over the retention of the Pay Office; Chatham was a good second; the Bedfords as a whole were anathema; and he had little love for any of the revolution families. In short, Holland had a separate quarrel with each separate branch of the Whig Party, and none of the victims of the proscription of 1762 had much fondness for Holland. It was this, rather than any Tory predilection, still less any subservience to royalty (for the King loathed Holland), that drew Charles Fox, as his father's representative in Parliament, into the wake of Grafton and North. That those two gentlemen were worthy to be his leaders he never doubted; and years later, after he had served with both of them and fought against both of them, his esteem for neither of them was diminished.

2. The Wilkes Affair, 1769-1770

The ministry on which the King set so much store was not destined to a long life, and for its difficulties he had no one to thank but himself. The struggle which overthrew so strong a government, the struggle in which Charles Fox won his spurs, the struggle which lost the King the last vestiges of his popularity, the struggle which made John Wilkes into an eighteenth century Hampden, deserves a longer study than is appropriate in a life of Fox. Obstinacy is always a fascinating spectacle, taking its victims so far beyond their destination into fairylands of punctilio and face-saving: between the revoltingly obstinate vengefulness of George the Third and the engagingly obstinate resilience of Wilkes, the ministry was crushed as between two millstones; while the law, and still more the lawyers, halted between two opinions.

Wilkes was a scamp, but a formidable scamp. Gay and feckless, by general consent the most amusing talker of the age, "the phoenix of convivial felicity," nobody was more likely to enjoy setting the government by the heels, or to do it better. Having been ruined already by fast living when the new reign began, he had turned his hand to demagogy, for which he discovered a notable gift. It was left to Wilkes to find the Achilles' heel of the renascent Tory party, which lay in the fact that most of its members were Scots. Toryism had been so effectually stamped out in England, that George the Third was obliged to bring almost all his new favourites from across the border. The few English Jacobites who survived were brought back into favour: three hundred pounds a year persuaded Dr. Johnson that it was no longer decent to drink King James' health in King George's wine. But the vast majority were Scots, from Bute himself and Mansfield, who came from a militant Jacobite family, down to the court architects and the court painter, the Adam brothers and Allan Ramsay. Wilkes knew that the Scots were regarded by the Cockneys as an almost aboriginal race. His organ, the *North Briton*, existed, as its name implied, to abuse the Scots. So long as Bute was in power, this was a safe card to play. It was not libellous to call a man a Scotchman. But when Bute was succeeded by the Bedfords, Wilkes was drawn on to more treacherous ground. In his forty-fifth number, he launched a violent if deserved attack on the King's Speech drawn up by the new government. Though it was as generally understood then as it is now that the King's Speech was the unaided composition of the ministry, and although there was little in this particular King's Speech that the King could have wished to claim as his own, yet it was decided that Wilkes had at last put himself in a position where the law could catch him. Possibly he had: but the law was put in motion in the wrong way, as ministers discovered to their cost. Wilkes was arrested on a warrant that did not mention him by name, but covered generally the authors, printers and publishers of the *North Briton*. That warrant was not legal; and having been released from the Tower on the grounds of Parliamentary immunity, Wilkes proceeded to sue the Secretaries of State for wrongful imprisonment. The Lord Chief Justice, Camden, held that general warrants were illegal, and gave him heavy damages. That same Lord Chief Justice was subsequently Lord Chancellor in Grafton's cabinet; and Grafton himself went to visit Wilkes, as an old friend, in the Tower.

Such a rebuff as this from the lawyers would have been enough for most politicians, but the Bedfords were nothing if not thick-skinned. One of their number had been a fellow-member with Wilkes of the notorious Hell Fire Club, and recollected that Wilkes had thought him a sufficiently prurient fellow to be admitted to a private reading of an obscene poem called the *Essay on Woman*. Having failed to get Wilkes punished for his political activity, the government were delighted by the idea of getting him convicted on a charge of indecent publication. Unfortunately, the poem had not been published, and it was necessary for them to ransack his rooms before they could themselves publish it in the most effective possible way—by reading it aloud to the House of Lords and printing a sizeable edition "for official use". This stratagem served its purpose; Wilkes was convicted. But by this time he was safe in Paris: sentence was postponed, and meanwhile he was outlawed for contumacy.

This was merely the prologue to the main drama. Whatever Wilkes was concerned in, was certain to be played to a finish; publicity was his life blood, and litigation was his native element; he would prefer to be in prison and in the public eye, than to enjoy the wealth of Alderman Beckford in obscurity. For four years he lived abroad, a much sought-after outlaw, *civiliter mortuus*, but otherwise very much alive. Once he returned to England on a wild-goose chase, in 1766: but he found that the Rockinghams, who had posed as his champions when they were in opposition, were not prepared to lift a finger in his defence when they had got into power. They offered him a bribe to stay away, but the general election of 1768 made him long for home and the limelight once more. He boldly returned, put up as a candidate for Middlesex—one of the few popular constituencies of the time—and was elected, at the same time as Fox was elected for Midhurst. That was in March; in April he surrendered to his outlawry and, avoiding with difficulty the crowd of his supporters, insinuated himself into the King's Bench prison. In June he came up for sentence: his outlawry was declared void, but he was fined £1,000 and sentenced to two years' imprisonment on the combined charges of indecent publication and seditious libel.

At this point the King took a hand, by pointing out to his ministers the propriety of expelling from the House of Commons a member who was under the sentence on charges of such a serious nature. The House is entitled to expel whom it pleases, on any grounds that seem to it sufficient: but the case of Wilkes was not normal. Popular feeling was rabid in his favour, and in Parliament itself there was considerable sympathy with him. The doubtful legality of one charge and the glaring hypocrisy of the other, the length of time that had elapsed since the original offence, and the pains taken to secure a conviction; all these aspects of the case convinced many members of Parliament that Wilkes had been persecuted enough, and his previous conduct convinced them that it would be dangerous to pursue him any further. With these considerations in mind, the cabinet, including as it did the very man who awarded Wilkes his damages against the Bedford government, refused to carry out the King's wish by vacating Wilkes' seat for Middlesex.

Wilkes, however, was not a sleeping dog; if ministers wanted to let him lie, he would soon see how far their patience could be tested. In December, after he had been in prison for less than eight months, there appeared a letter in the press that could only have come from Wilkes. It was written to call attention to some instructions issued by the Secretary of State to magistrates about the use of troops to supplement the inadequate constabulary. These instructions were described as "a hellish project, brooded over by some infernal spirits, without one moment's remorse." Wilkes, hauled to the bar of the House, acknowledged the letter with pride and waited for the authorities to do their worst.

There was only one more card the government could play: they acceded to the King's original suggestion. When Parliament reassembled in February, 1769, they moved to expel the member for Middlesex. The grounds for this expulsion were of unequal validity. In his most recent offence, the Secretary of State who had been libelled was a noble lord so that it was for the Upper House to deal with that. In the case of Number Forty-Five of the *North Briton*, now six years old, he had already been expelled before he went to Paris. The case of the *Essay on Woman* was without precedent and remains fortunately without parallel. But that the House had a right to expel him on the fourth and comprehensive charge, that he was under sentence of the courts, there can be no doubt.

On February the 3rd, Wilkes was expelled: on the 16th he was re-elected unopposed. On the 17th, he was again expelled: on March the 10th, he was elected the third time, again unopposed, the government having found a candidate, but no proposer or seconder. On the 11th, he was expelled the third time; and on April the 13th he proceeded to a fourth election. This time the government made a serious effort. They found an indomitable man, one Colonel Luttrell, to oppose Wilkes, and backed him with all their influence, including the assistance of Lord Holland. Luttrell was proposed by Charles Fox's elder brother Stephen, and actively canvassed for by Charles himself: but in vain. Wilkes polled 1143 to Luttrell's 296.

On the next day, April the 14th, the Commons were prepared to play their familiar part in this protracted Punch and Judy show. But the ministers had thought of a new move: instead of moving that Wilkes be expelled they moved that Colonel Luttrell had been duly elected. It was at this point that they overstepped the law. The issue was perfectly plain. If the electors of Middlesex chose a man who had been expelled from Parliament, they simply lost their representation. There was no necessity to expel him again or to proceed to further elections: it was only the King's passion for teaching his subjects a lesson that forced on them the necessity for that false move. But on the other hand, if Middlesex preferred to have no representative than to have anyone but Wilkes, there was nothing government could do about it. They could not appoint another member: it made no difference whether Luttrell got no votes or 296 votes—he could not sit for Middlesex. No man can sit in Parliament by virtue of having fought a seat: he must have won it. A defeated candidate is not to be considered as a second best choice: the mere fact of his defeat argues that he is unacceptable to the majority of the voters: the successful candidate may be disqualified in a number of ways, by being a peer or a lunatic or an infant, but the unsuccessful candidate is disqualified absolutely by the verdict of the constituency.

The law was clear: even clearer was the commonsense of the question. If the House, because it objected to Wilkes, could co-opt Luttrell, was any member of the minority safe? The rules of privilege are elastic: bribery at that time was widespread. Who could be sure that he would not be turned out of his seat, and superseded by his opponent, for bribing successfully the very electors his opponent had bribed unsuccessfully? It was a new weapon in the hands of the majority.

The case against Luttrell was overwhelming: just such a case as needed Charles Fox to oppose it. Both he and Stephen spoke to the motion, and fulfilled the lively expectations of the House. Stephen was an unimpressive speaker, a figure of fun, and contented himself with abusing the Middlesex electorate; but Charles, according to Horace Walpole, "with infinite superiority in parts, was not inferior to his brother in insolence." Lord Holland swelled with pride: "I am told that few in Parliament ever spoke better than Charles did on Tuesday. Offhand, with rapidity, with spirit, and such knowledge of what he was talking of, as surprised everybody in so young a man." It was easy to be insolent in a schoolboy way about the "scum" of the electorate: it was less easy to stand up to some of their champions. That was the next step in Fox's galloping rise to prominence. In May, a petition from the electors of Middlesex was before the House, and was supported by a weighty speech from Burke. Burke, as Goldsmith said,

> "Too deep for his hearers, still went on refining,
>   And thought of convincing, while they thought of dining."

But he terrorised the House while he bored it, and could intimidate his opponents even when he was making himself ridiculous. Fox moreover had known Burke intimately since his Oxford days, and could appreciate the full worth of one who was often under-rated. But even at that he was not alarmed; far from it, "Charles Fox, not yet twenty-one, answered Burke with great quickness and parts, with confidence equally premature." Again his father was in ecstasies: "I am told (and I willingly believe it) Charles Fox spoke extremely well. It was all off hand, all argumentative, in reply to Mr. Burke and Mr. Wedderburn, and excessively well indeed."

Of both these speeches Lord Holland notices with special pride that they were *offhand*. That had been Henry Fox's gift, and it was Charles' in a supreme degree. Of any of his most famous efforts it could be said that it was "all off hand, all argumentative, in reply to somebody or other, and excessively well indeed." Charles Fox was a considerable orator, and could open a debate as well as most, but oratory was always his second string. It was in reply, in the answering of debating points, in unprepared arguments, that he transcended any speaker in the history of Parliament. His speeches were things of the moment, never prepared and seldom recorded, mere flashes of genius, but the Commons valued them above all the classic periods and intricate exposition of his rivals. On the first two occasions that he spoke, he made it clear in which sphere he was going to excel.

The action of the House of Commons in selecting Luttrell in preference to Wilkes, if it had no other extenuation, at least secured a respite for the rest of the year from this degrading controversy. Fox, sensitive to the more peaceful atmosphere, went off to Paris for a few months of gambling which left him several thousand louis the poorer. While he was abandoning himself to these delights, Lord Chatham's gout was reaching an agonising climax. By the end of the year it was over: in the first days of 1770 the sufferer was able to return to London. If he had descended in a chariot from the clouds, instead of in a bath chair from the pump room, his first words could not have been awaited with greater apprehension: and in the general panic, none trembled more than the Duke of Grafton, to whose weak will it was due that Chatham's ministry had become the King's. Their worst fears were confirmed when Chatham went to the King himself and told him outright that he had been wrongly advised in the matter of the Middlesex election. Fox dashed over from Paris, forfeiting in the customs a supply of embroidered suits he had bought for his twenty-first birthday, and reached London in time for the debate on the address. The opposition were truculent, and ministers were cowed, but Fox was no more afraid of Chatham than of Burke: he made himself conspicuous once more, speaking "with much applauded fire" in a debate which was notable for the new-found moderation of the majority.

If the Commons were subdued by Chatham's return, the Lords were paralysed. Camden from the Woolsack pleaded forgiveness: "I have often drooped and hung my head in Council, and disapproved by my looks those steps which I knew my avowed opposition could not prevent." That was the end of Camden's ministerial career: on January the 13th he surrendered the great seal. "The seals are to go a-begging," wrote Shelburne, exulting in his leader's return: "but I hope there will not be found in the kingdom a wretch so base and mean-spirited as to accept of them on the conditions on which they must be offered." No more there was. Not for the first time in English history, the legal profession closed its ranks in unanimous refusal to serve the ends of the executive power. One man, to be sure, whose father had been a great Lord Chancellor, succumbed to the temptation to accept that office under the strongest pressure: but he was only Lord Chancellor for three days before he cut his throat.

Charles Yorke's suicide was the deciding point with Grafton: his conscience was at last aroused by the spectacle of such remorse. He threw in his hand, having survived the return of Chatham by less than three weeks.

CHAPTER THREE

1. *Junior Lord of the Admiralty, 1770*

In spite of Grafton's sudden collapse, the panic that had seized the House of Lords, and the refusal of the legal profession to sanction the illegal proceedings against Wilkes, the King was not yet at a loss. He had in North a servant who would confront any adversary, and pursue any policy, to please his master; and he had still the means of financing a majority through thick and thin. It was easy to make North Prime Minister in Grafton's place; the more serious difficulty was to find a successor for Camden. But even this could be circumvented: the Great Seal was put into commission: three amenable lawyers of no importance were set to fill the place of one, leaving Chatham without any opponent of weight in the House of Lords.

In the Commons ministers were little better off. With Wedderburn and Burke against them, North's easy-going wit was an inadequate defence. North, "the Palinurus of the State," could sleep undisturbed through any invective, or when he happened to be awake could parry the enemy's thrusts with a skill that everyone admitted; but he could never return them, he had no gift for taking the offensive. His manners was cynical and deprecating, soothing the consciences of restive followers, and often intimating all too clearly that the policy he was called upon to advance was not his own, but had been forced upon him by his royal master. This was not at all what his party wanted. The mass of those who voted for North were by no means as black as they are painted. A few, no doubt, were in Parliament for money, and it is these few whose names the Whig historians use like a stage army over and over again to make them look like a whole party. But the bulk of them were honest country gentlemen, sitting in Parliament as they sit there now, because they always had sat there. They needed no bribes to induce them to vote about a bumptious, cross-eyed agitator of low extraction and only too evident intelligence. There is little reason to suspect even those who were bribed of voting against their convictions. To read Lord Holland's letters is to understand the sentiments of a highly intelligent man, prejudiced only by his wealth, about the Middlesex mob, and even about so reputable a body as the Corporation of London. Lord Holland was in politics for money, if ever a man was, but it is clear that no imaginable bribe would have induced him to vote in favour of Wilkes, or against sending the Lord Mayor to the Tower.

With these sort of men for his party following, North's affable cynicism was out of place. They were embarrassed by the insinuation that the official policy was a painful necessity, that it was not the wisest policy, but that after all their lord-lieutenancies and colonelcies depended on voting for it. What they wanted was a little intelligent backing for their own unintelligent sincerity: and that was what Charles Fox gave them. His speaking was the antithesis of North's. He was always on the offensive, truculent, aggressive, dangerous; he could turn in a moment from juvenile insolence to what seemed like passionate sincerity; from heaping raucous abuse on Burke (with whom as likely as not he had just dined) he would suddenly drop to a level of deep-throated emotion as he explained by a succession of brazen paradoxes that the liberties for which their ancestors had died in the field (and his own, he might have added, on the scaffold) depended on the arrest of some pettifogging pamphleteer. He spoke so fast that the amazing perversity of his arguments escaped undetected; what remains of them is a monument of ingenuity and insolence, coming from a young man of twenty-one, and addressed to an assembly of retired military men and squires. But there was a fearlessness, a passion, in his manner that let him get away with anything. The staggering sophistries, the inconsistencies, the outrages that Fox committed on both reason and commonsense, in his struggles to talk the House of Commons off its feet, though in cold print they only raise a smile, were meat and drink to his fellow-members, who only wanted a little conviction in the midst of so much sophisticated insincerity.

That was what made Fox indispensable to North. He had stood up to Burke: he could stand up to Wedderburn: he had the ear of the House more than most men of twice his age. It was obvious that Fox would have to be squared by the administration: but there were two objections. First and most obviously, his youth, for he had only come of age four days before the ministry was born. Secondly, there was the King. George the Third considered Lord

Holland one of the most odious of his subjects; but if there was anyone he disliked more it was Lord Holland's son. All Charles' achievements at Almack's, at Newmarket, and in Paris, were faithfully reported to that virtuous monarch, who disliked Wilkes the rake fully as much as Wilkes the demagogue. The King was always solicitous for his ministers' moral welfare: it was a great tie between him and North that they were both faithful to ugly wives: and though he would tolerate moral errors in men of established position such as Sandwich, it seemed to him very reasonably that it was in vain to set an example to his people by purging the court of doubtful ladies-in-waiting if a young man, whose dissipation was of European fame, was to be presented with a government job on attaining his majority. The King hesitated, but not for long. Within the month two things turned the scale. Lord Holland came to court yet again to ask for his earldom, and yet again had to be refused: and Fox scored off one of the opposition's most formidable figures.

The ministry's weakness, and the opposition's strength, was in lawyers: and the most prominent lawyer in the House was Alexander Wedderburn. As clever as he was wicked, mistrusted even by his fellow-lawyers, hated even by his fellow-Scots, at a time when lawyers and Scots competed for the hatred of mankind, Wedderburn was at the present moment working with the Rockingham party, whom he had joined by the first of that endless series of tergiversations and betrayals, by which he ultimately became Lord Chief Justice Loughborough and Lord Chancellor Rosslyn. He later appeared in Fox's history in one dishonourable capacity after another, until he died leaving, in the words of George the Third, "no greater rogue behind him in all my dominions." This was the man whom Fox bearded when he laid down the law about the Middlesex election. "Charles Fox, of age the day before," (the mistake is Walpole's) "started up and entirely confuted Wedderburn even in law, producing a case decided in the courts below but last year, and exactly similar to that of Wilkes. The House roared with applause." This performance made him indispensable to the ministry. Amid the wreckage of so many reputations, Fox's name was made. The King's scruples were overcome: and the next day, at the age of twenty-one years and a month, Fox became a Junior Lord of the Admiralty.

"I hope," wrote Lady Holland from Nice, "I hope Lord North has courage and resolution. Charles being connected with him pleases me mightily. I have formed a very high opinion of his lordship, and my Charles will, I dare say, inspire him with courage." He did: and sorely the new Prime Minister needed it. The Parliament was now two years old, and in that time its only notable achievement had been the addition of Colonel Luttrell, no great adornment, to its ranks. The whole business of government had been side-tracked, at the royal instigation, into a futile and apparently endless struggle to muzzle and suppress the complaints of a single constituency. The Middlesex affair was supremely unimportant by any practical standards. Nobody lost a night's sleep because Wilkes was out of Parliament, or found himself a penny the poorer because Luttrell was in. It was, as Johnson said, a "false alarm." But neither the King nor the people looked at it in that light. The King shared his people's passion for turning trifles into test cases: he was as litigious as the worst of them. Both he and the Middlesex electors were determined to play the game to a finish. Wilkes, the popular hero, impartially regarded both his enemies and his supporters with sovereign contempt: to him the quarrel brought all he wanted—fame, hard cash, and pretty admirers. And there were others who were keen to share his agreeable martyrdom. By imprisoning and expelling Wilkes the government had raised a hundred pseudo-Wilkeses and would-be Wilkeses to transient importance. With each step that the House of Commons took to protect its prestige it became more ridiculous and hateful in the eyes of the country. By the time North succeeded to power, so many false moves had been made already that the public had lost all patience with its rulers. Government had landed itself in a position, in Chatham's words, "where ordinary inability never arrives, and nothing but first-rate geniuses in incapacity can reach." There was nothing for it but either to surrender without terms—to admit Wilkes, to leave the press uncensored, and to swallow the insults of the City of London: or to go on with the losing struggle. North himself was strongly in favour of surrender: it was the King who insisted on the continuation of the campaign, and directed its every move. North at this period was in utter despair: he wept in public: he pleaded in the royal presence to be allowed to drop the lamentable game: he often envied the fate of Charles Yorke: and if he could have foreseen that he would be in office for twelve equally harassing years, there is little doubt that he would have chosen the same way out. But the King was inexorable: he would never accept the resignation of so loyal a servant, and he would never be deflected from his resolve to govern the people of England as the people of Hanover were governed.

Lord North's misgivings were not shared by the youngest member of his ministry. Fox believed with perfect sincerity that the struggle must go on, and there was a basis of arguable sense in his opinion. The first consideration was the nature of the provocation given by the popular electorates and the popular press. The type of propaganda that the King (and Fox) wished to suppress was beyond all conception foul and mendacious. In a century of culture and polish, for the members of a proud and decent aristocracy to be assailed with daily outpourings of humourless filth, which did not even spare their wives and daughters, was an injustice past all bearing. The only remnants of this type of journalism that have survived are Gillray, whose bawdiness sometimes deviates into wit, and Junius, whose veracity has had the good fortune to satisfy the unexacting standards of Whig historians. If Junius, as is now generally supposed was Philip Francis, a clerk in the War Office, then Fox was unusually lucky in this particular antagonist. For Francis owed his job to Fox's father, and Fox owed his early education to Francis' father. But even these obligations did not prevent Junius from provoking the "Black Boy," as he called him, to the point of issuing a challenge, which was of course declined. We have seen too how ridiculously Junius, and those who take their facts from Junius, traduced the Duke of Grafton. Yet Junius was a model of veracity and moderation beside the common run of opposition scribblers. The twentieth century is not noticeably proud of its journalistic standards: we do not point to the purity and probity of our most successful newspapers as among the heralds of a better age: but not even the worst of our modern newspapers would dare to reproduce the obscenity of an eighteenth-century lampoon, and not even during a general election would a modern editor descend to the lies and slanders that our ancestors daily endured.

Today, Junius and his publisher would be in gaol twenty times over for criminal libel and contempt of court. The law, in its ordinary course, would see to that, without the interference of the

House of Commons. The grand mistake made by the King, and by North, and by the exasperated victims, was in attempting to fight this evil with the machinery of parliamentary privilege. "The House of Commons," said Burke, "as it was never intended for the support of peace and subordination, is miserably appointed for that service: having no stronger weapon than its mace, and no better officer than its sergeant-at-arms, which it can command of its own proper authority." It was the incompetence, not the injustice, of their efforts that brought the Commons into contempt; how little the King understood this weakness is seen by his unhelpful suggestion that perhaps it would be safer to bring the miscreants before the House of Lords.

The history of the next few years is the history of a desperate attempt on the part of the legislature to supply the deficiencies of the penal law. The obvious method of protecting themselves against misrepresentation was to forbid the reporting of debates, but it was an impracticable method. Publicity could not be prevented beforehand: it could only be punished afterwards. It was the attempt to punish the press that brought North's Government into disrepute; and it was the disrepute of his colleagues that threw into strong relief the youthful abilities of Charles Fox. Among the doubts and misgivings of experienced men, Fox never faltered in his mission. He was a House of Commons man: as he emphasised in one speech after another, the privileges of the House of Commons had been won with bloodshed from the Crown, and must be preserved, if necessary with bloodshed, from the encroachments of the mob. While no one else pretended to do more than apologise for the royal policy, Fox invested it with an air of robust ancestral virtue. What so many Pyms and Hampdens had defended from the sovereign, he, Fox, would preserve inviolate from the rabble. The Commons stood midway in the constitution, bearing a double responsibility; and as in the last century they had defended the people from the sovereign, so now they must defend the sovereign from the people. Perseverance was the only essential: even though, each time they struck at a single individual, they raised up a hundred fresh enemies, still they must persevere, for if Parliament once wavered in the defence of its hard-won privileges, if one breach were made in those elaborate defences, the whole sea of popular intimidation would rush in, to drown in anarchy and confusion the peaceful landscape, the exquisitely planned cities, of our constitution. That was the tenor of Fox's speeches as a member of North's government; that was the basis of what seemed his paradoxes; and among so much diffidence and pretence, it was that amount of conviction that won him the respect of everyone except the King.

2. *The Fight with the City, 1771*

Fox had many chances in the coming years of elaborating these curious lines of argument, and none better than the quarrel of the House of Commons with the City of London, which arose, by the fatal progression which attended all their high-handed actions, out of the attempt to prevent the publication of debates. Such publication was in fact a breach of privilege, but it was one that the House had wisely ignored until the Wilkes affair made popular journalism profitable, and called forth such a flood of libels as no governing class in any age could be expected to tolerate. In March 1771 the House set about demonstrating that its indulgence should be abused no longer, and ordered the arrest of a batch of printers. Unfortunately, most of London's printers lived east of Temple Bar, within the bounds of the City of London: and the City of London from the Lord Mayor downwards was Wilkite almost to a man. Wilkes himself, having completed his eventful term of imprisonment in April of the previous year, had been elevated direct to the dignity of an alderman, to become in this year a sheriff and four years later Lord Mayor. Filled with this intense jealousy of the authority of Parliament, the City authorities were determined to come to a trial of strength whenever the Speaker's writ should be executed on their territory. The test case was that of a printer called Miller. As soon as the Speaker's officer tried to arrest him, Miller gave him in charge for assault and false imprisonment, on which he was committed for trial by a bench consisting of Lord Mayor Crosby, Alderman Oliver and Alderman Wilkes. Here was a clear cut issue between the authority of House and City: once again the House had to choose between an ignominious retreat, by letting its officer go to prison, and the alternative of embarking on just such a ding-dong battle as it had fought with the electors of Middlesex. It was the King who chose to go on: at his instigation the Mayor and Alderman were ordered to attend the House, Crosby and Oliver in their seats as members, Wilkes at the bar. Oliver admitted freely what he had done and defied the House to do its worst, whereupon the government moved to commit him to the Tower. It was in speaking to this motion that Fox displayed his theory of the constitution in its most startling colours.

"Are the people at large," he demanded, "or this House, the best judges of the public welfare? For my own part, sir, I shall not hesitate to pronounce positively in favour of this House. What acquaintance have the people at large with the arcana of political rectitude, with the connections of kingdoms, the resources of national strength, the abilities of ministers, or even with their own dispositions? If we are to believe the very petitions which they have lately presented to the throne, they are unequal to those powers which the constitution has trusted to their hands. They have the power of electing their representatives: yet you see they constantly abuse that power, and appoint those as the guardians of their dearest rights, whom they accuse of conspiring against the interests of their country. For these reasons, sir, I pay no regard whatever to the voice of the people: it is our duty to do what is proper, without considering what may be agreeable: their business is to choose us: it is ours to act constitutionally, and to maintain the independency of Parliament. Whether that independency be attacked by the people or by the crown is a matter of little consequence: it is the attack, not the quarter it proceeds from, which we are to punish; and if we are to be controlled in our necessary jurisdiction, can it signify much, whether faction intimidate us with a rabble, or the King surround us with his guards? If we are driven from the direct line of justice by the threats of a mob, our existence is useless in the community. The minority within doors need only assault us by their myrmidons without, to gain their ends upon every occasion. Blows will then carry what their arguments cannot effect, and the people will be their own agents, though they elect us to represent them in Parliament. What must the consequence be? Universal anarchy, sir. Therefore, as we are chosen to defend order, I am for sending those magistrates to the Tower who have attempted to destroy it: I stand up for the constitution, not for the people: if the people attempt to invade the constitution, they are enemies to the nation. Being therefore, sir, convinced that we are here to do justice, whether it is agreeable or disagreeable to the people, I am for maintaining the independency of Parliament, and will not be a rebel to my King, my country, or my own heart, for the loudest huzza of an inconsiderate multitude."

This sort of thing was wormwood to the Whigs. Here was all their favourite jargon, slightly better put, appropriated to serve an autocratic defence: here was Burke's speech to the electors of Bristol parodied by anticipation: here was a man who upset their comfortable assurance that they made up in brains for what they lacked in numbers. Though they saw the ingenuity of it, they pretended to regard it all as mere insolence: Horace Walpole airily remarks that Fox "as if impatient to inherit his father's unpopularity, abused the city as his father used to do, but ministers were moderate." Or as the song writers put it:

> "If that black face, and that black heart,
> Be not old Holland's counterpart,
> Holland himself's unlike the devil."

Two days after this performance, it was Crosby's turn to be sentenced. The Houses of Parliament had been beleaguered throughout the proceedings by a city mob, and never was it thicker than on this day. Many members had the utmost difficulty in getting to the House, and when the Prime Minister arrived the disturbance reached its height. His coach was destroyed and his person severely ill-treated before he was rescued by a gallant opponent. As he picked himself up, bruised and in tatters, it was with mixed feelings that Lord North listened to the explanation that he had been mistaken for Charles Fox. Physically there was some resemblance, for it would have been hard to find two uglier men in London; politically, it was a disturbing reflection for a Prime Minister that the government's tail had already begun to wag the dog. But for the present his feelings were soothed by the sight of the Junior Lord entering the House a few minutes later, bruised to a pulp. The business of the House proceeded on a subdued note. Crosby, like Oliver, was sent to the Tower: and it remained to tackle Wilkes. The King, however, had learnt wisdom in dealing with this one of his subjects: he informed North that Wilkes (whose fame at this period had eclipsed even Chatham's) was beneath the notice of the House: and on the day Wilkes had been ordered to attend, the House did not assemble. Miller, meanwhile, went scot-free. Six weeks later the session ended: Crosby and Oliver were automatically released; in their fight with Wilkes *alias* the City of London, as in their fight with Wilkes *alias* the County of Middlesex, the Commons had their way at the expense of their own prestige.

3. The Portland-Lowther Case, 1771

Horace Walpole, to whom every biographer of Fox is deeply in debt, records an episode that throws a flood of light on Fox's innermost views. On one occasion a speaker, he says, "reflected on Lord Holland as the author of the proscriptions at the beginning of the reign. Charles Fox said he did not believe his father had had any hand in them, but if he had, it was right to break the power of the aristocracy that had governed in the name of the late King. Charles Fox asked me afterwards in private if the accusation against his father was just. I replied, I could not but say it was."

As we have seen, Bute was the author of the proscription of the Whigs in 1762, but Holland was unquestionably the instrument, and incurred the greater part of the odium. What is interesting is not Fox's misplaced filial piety, but his extenuation of the deed. "It was right to break the power of the aristocracy that had governed in the name of the late King." That was a battle-cry to make the Rockingham party tremble: that had the authentic ring of the infuriated seventeenth-century Tory calling for Whig blood.

Proscriptions in the previous century had been a matter of course. As each party came alternately to favour, it secured as far as it could the disgrace and impoverishment of its opponents. Titles were attainted, impeachments were instituted, positions of honour vacated, and lands forfeited, with every successive swing of the pendulum. Since the great and glorious revolution of 1688, things had been more stabilised. William of Orange had behaved with singular moderation towards his opponents; and had been content to balance the account by a quite unprecedented lavishness towards his supporters. At a time when fully a quarter of his subjects thought of him as an usurper, and most of the remainder as no more than a trustee for the Stuarts, William proceeded to alienate a great tract of English land, Crown land, Stuart land, as a reward for a Dutchman. Bentinck's services to his prince, and to the land of his adoption, would be hard to exaggerate: but if William had deliberately wished to ruin Bentinck in the opinions of Englishmen, he could not have found a more invidious method of rewarding him. The outcry was loud and long.

The Bentincks had become Earls and then Dukes of Portland; they had attained a consequence and a connection second to none; they had been foremost among the Whig oligarchy; they had held their grants of land for seventy years, well into what seemed a more settled age. Proscriptions, as the events of 1762 showed, were still possible: impeachment, though much talked of, was never practised: confiscation was thought to be out of the question. But there was one family in the north of England to whom seventy years were a moment in time, to whom the Portlands were still a family of Dutch upstarts basking for a few decades in the royal favour. The eighteenth century had run two-thirds of its course unnoticed by the Lowthers, who still ruled Cumberland as the Lords Marchers had ruled Wales, or as Argyll had ruled the Highlands. When the discomfiture of the Whigs began, Sir James Lowther decided that the time was ripe to oust his neighbour from a property which marched with his own, and would form a serviceable addition to his electioneering influence as well as to his interminable rent-roll. In accordance with the time-honoured procedure of the previous century, when to inform against land tenures was a recognised profession, Lowther informed the Treasury that the manor of Carlisle and the Forest of Inglewood were being wrongfully withheld from the Crown: the Treasury was grateful and not wholly unprepared for the information: and Lowther was rewarded by a lease of the entire district for three lives at thirteen shillings and fourpence a year.

The consternation that followed this news was not confined to the Whigs. Thanks to the favour they had so long enjoyed, the Whigs were by far the greatest landowners—at one of their party meetings an observer calculated the magnates present to be worth £800,000 a year in land alone. It was their land that enabled them to counterbalance the whole resources of the Treasury and the whole favour of the King at election times. The land was at the bottom of their power; and however little they cared for prerogative, on the question of prescriptive right, a Rockingham or a Savile or a Burke was sound. The Tories by comparison were mere small-holders. Charles the Second, by his "act of indemnity to his enemies and oblivion to his friends," had failed to redress the balance of the Commonwealth: he had anticipated William the Third's generosity to his opponents but not his generosity to his supporters: the very territories that Charles had withheld from his long-suffering Cavaliers had been heaped by William on his Dutch friends. Since William's time, fifty years of disfavour had effectively deprived the Tories of any hope beyond that of clinging to the few granges or manors that had been too insignificant for even Cromwell to plunder.

Now that Lowther, who was more a feudal baron than a Tory baronet, had set the example of obtaining redress against the proud Whigs, he found himself, not merely not imitated, but reprobated and disowned. His methods were not to the liking of the worthy men who supported the government. The Whig possessions might be larger, but the Tory possessions were older and dearer. Expropriation was a game that two could play: and a good Tory squire would prefer to sleep soundly on the thousand acres of abbey lands he derived from Henry the Eighth, than to covet the county that his Whig neighbour had been given by the Prince of Orange. So it came about that both parties united to make a signal example of this turbulent and hubristic Lowther. A law was passed to render sixty years' tenure of land irrevocable. *Nullum tempus occurrit regi* had been the legal basis of Lowther's claim; and the Nullum Tempus Act was the usual designation of the new law, which was no sooner passed than to emphasise their disapproval, the House unseated Lowther for the County of Cumberland by a majority of 152 votes.

Lowther, however, was not the man to worry about a few votes of the Lower House, to which he sent a whole bevy of members on his own account. He found that the Nullum Tempus Act left him a loophole: he had a year's grace in which to establish his claim: and deciding to try his luck in the courts, he served simultaneous writs of ejectment on four hundred of the unfortunate inhabitants of Inglewood Forest. These were the methods of the middle ages: an eighteenth-century Parliament was not inclined to tolerate a barefaced gerrymander, prosecuted in defiance of its own emphatic verdict. The House of Commons had been angry and all but unanimous before: they were furious now. Burke, that firm friend to property and not least to Whig property, was in full cry: Lowther's hired members hung their heads: the most respected of the Whigs was put forward with a bill to strike out of the Nullum

36

Tempus Act the provision under which Lowther was litigating for his claim.

But between the time when the Nullum Tempus Act was passed and the time when this amendment became necessary, Charles Fox had appeared on the scene, the last man in the world to be impressed by a unanimous opinion, and convinced, as we have seen, of the necessity of breaking the power of the Whig aristocracy. He decided that Lowther's defence, such as it was, should not go entirely by default. Not caring a fig for landed property himself, he stood forward as the champion of a man who was using legal intimidation to secure the only corner of a large county which he did not already possess.

The pose was that of injured innocence, of outraged sensibility hitherto suppressed. "My silence," he began, "has been owing to my astonishment. I was astonished. I was amazed. For though I viewed this bill at first in the same light in which I now behold it; yet, when I looked round me, and saw who the honourable gentlemen are who introduced it; that they are men of character, men of ability, men of knowledge, men of reputed integrity: I hesitated, I strove to persuade myself that I must rather be mistaken myself, than that anything so bad, so violent, so lawless, so monstrous, could be advanced by men such as those who proposed this bill. But I could not long remain undecided; I soon beheld the proposition in all its naked, genuine deformity; then, sir, as I was at first struck dumb with astonishment, I was seized with horror and indignation: for who that has a reverence for justice, a sense of liberty, or a regard for the constitution, can listen to a proposition which at one blow destroys our constitution, our liberty, and our laws . . .? Mr. Speaker, it is under the law that every man holds his property, and enjoys his liberty in security and ease. But I firmly believe that no man can have a better title to his estate than the very title which the crown has vested in Sir James Lowther to the estate in question. If that title is to be taken away by act of Parliament, why not bring in an act to take away any other part of his estate? Why not of another man's? For if bills are thus to pass for transferring the property of one man to another, there can be nothing sacred, nothing secure amongst us."

Few speeches turn votes, and of all speeches the least likely to do so is a pert speech from the baby of the House. But behind his barrage of impudence, Fox had contrived to make the only hit that could be made against the amending bill, and to make it with deadly aim. The Nullum Tempus Act, though provoked by an individual case, set up a general principle; the amending bill on the other hand was openly aimed at an individual. The House of Commons hates particular or retrospective legislation, except when it is relegated to the procedure of a private bill. Particular legislation had been the instrument for some of the worst party excesses of the troubled times before 1688, and even for such regrettable cases as Fenwick's attainder in later years. In that century divorce, as in the last century railway legislation, and in this century municipal legislation, constituted the limits of what the House cared to undertake by way of what is more properly a judicial function. And here they were, caught red-handed by their youngest member, on the point of passing by acclamation a perfect specimen of a particular law—adjudicating in advance on a case between two individuals which was at that very moment *sub judice,* and hurrying to take it out of the province of the courts after the writs had been served. It was the very thing they were most ashamed of having done in the past, and most determined never to do again. All the squires who had been preparing to vote for the security of their property turned round in an instant to vote for what they valued even more, the independence of the judicial bench. The amending bill was actually defeated by ten votes, a performance that wrung from Walpole the reluctant admission that Fox was "the phenomenon of the age." He had made a complete fool of the House: Lowther's litigation proceeded: and it was only when he was non-suited on a technical point that the worst consequences of Fox's sophistry were averted.

CHAPTER FOUR

1. *The Royal Marriage Bill, 1772*

Up to this point we have been concerned with a few examples chosen from many of the extraordinary ingenuity with which Fox applied himself to the defence of the most unwise and high-handed acts of government, and abused the people with the catchwords of the popular party. These performances had struck awe into all beholders, and had filled the crowds, whom Wilkes had turned into amateur politicians, with profound hatred and fear of Fox: but there were some observers who saw beyond the levity and the foolhardiness to a generous heart beneath. It had been mostly against self-appointed democrats that his operations were directed; and though he was never tired of repeating that the people's representatives were the only judges of the people's welfare, he had shown for his own part a sound appreciation of the people's welfare in standing up for a modification of the criminal code. He was now, after two years of office, to show that his resistance to popular measures, on whatever principles it was based, did not proceed from a love of office or any courtly servility towards the King. The perverted sincerity of his first years was suddenly justified and explained by a triumph of candour over self-interest.

George the Third carried his simple theories of government, and of morality, into the affairs of his own family. One of the first duties of a King, as he saw it, was to supervise every detail of the conduct of the royal family. His efforts in this direction were as unsuccessful as in every other: and the successive marriages of the Duke of Gloucester with Lady Waldegrave, herself the daughter of an unmarried sempstress, and of the Duke of Cumberland with Luttrell's sister, Mrs. Horton, exercised him very much; he could not decide which shocked him more, the thought of a royal prince marrying like the former for love, or like the latter to avoid a scandal. If either practice were to be condoned, his prestige would be gravely diminished, and the chances of convenient continental alliances would disappear. His brothers should marry plain German princesses, as he had done, not pretty English widows. He sent for his law-officers to draft a law.

When the Royal Marriage Bill appeared before Parliament, which was asked to enact that no descendant of George the Second to the end of time (unless a foreign subject) might marry without the King's consent, there was the devil to pay. Society was in a frenzy of indignation. It was described as a Bill to Encourage the Royal Princes to Seduce our Wives, and to Forbid them to Marry our Daughters; it teemed, said Walpole, with the seeds of future civil wars. The friends and the enemies of public morality outdid one another in abuse of the bill. The government damned it openly, and cursed the day they had undertaken to serve such a pig-headed King. But the King was inflexible. He watched the bill through the Lords with intense vigilance, and when it arrived in the Commons he inundated North with instructions and warnings. "I shall remember defaulters" was his message; and every member who hoped for promotion in the army, or wanted a living for his poor cousin, knew what the King meant. Large wagers were laid on the result, and the odds were against the bill passing. There were some limits beyond which servility could not go: there were some insults the English aristocracy would never swallow from a Hanoverian prince. A desperate courage took possession of the rank and file, who knew that by disobedience their livelihood and patronage would be forfeited to some creeping Scottish courtier. Parliament was up in arms: the hearts of the ministers sank within them.

If ever Fox had been wanted, he was wanted now. However unreliable he might be when the government was on safe ground, he was always good at a pinch. In all the ministry's tight corners he had stood forward to defend the indefensible and make the worse appear the better cause. Here was a situation made for him: here was a measure no man could defend if Fox could not. If he could repeat his performance on the Lowther case, he was a made man. Gone would be that implacable disfavour with which the King regarded him and all his family. Holland might have his earldom: Charles might regain solvency: he could sell his support on almost any terms. What was more, here was an opportunity that could never recur, of reinstating himself with the King, without increasing his unpopularity out of doors. The King cared more for this measure than for any other of his reign: the mob was absolutely indifferent—the press was silent. Normally it was a choice between pleasing the King and pleasing the people: but here Fox could gratify the King, and not even the gutter-press would care a straw. The King, the ministry, the whole House looked to Fox at this moment to enhance his reputation, to retrieve his broken fortunes, and to put himself in the way of attaining the position his ability so patently deserved.

What Fox did was to resign. The sensation could not have been more profound if Burke had joined the government. Brooks's and White's between them failed to reach a passable explanation; and the light in which they regarded politics, and Fox's politics in particular, is shown by their tortuous conjectures. Possibly he was holding out for better terms? But Lord North had thought of that, and had been snubbed for his pains. No explanation was to be had from Lord Holland, who was as angry as any of his friends: Holland had good reason to know that resignation is *always* a mistake. Charles himself was perfectly definite as to why he had resigned, but his explanation was received with open disbelief. "I should not," he said, "have resigned at this moment merely on account of my complaints against Lord North, if I had not determined to vote against this Royal Family Bill, which in office I should be ashamed of doing. I think myself very safe from going into opposition, which is the only danger." No wonder he was heard with incredulity: not many politicians of that day were thought to be susceptible to shame, and Fox less than most. Odious to the King, odious to the people, financially more to the bad than any man in England, Fox resigned.

Fox had a reason to be disgusted with the Royal Marriage Bill that he could share with only his brother Stephen. In the family at Holland House and at Kingsgate, Sarah Lennox had been an adopted member. Though she was his mother's sister, she was only Charles' senior by four years, and he had loved her with all the passion of which a boy is capable. "Lady Sarah," Walpole has said, "was more beautiful than you can conceive. No Magdalen by Correggio was half so lovely." Everybody loved Sarah Lennox, but her easiest conquest had been over the young King himself, just after his accession. He had proposed to her. She was amused: Lord Holland was elated: the Princess Dowager was enraged, and hustled her son into a strictly utilitarian alliance. The romance was over. Ten years had passed, and had chilled the King's heart: but

41

Charles Fox could not forget that the girl who was the inspiration of his own youth had kindled a transitory flame in the very King who was now proposing to scrutinise and domineer over the foibles of his remotest dependants.

Many motives—pique, chivalry, sentiment, impatience—went towards his resignation. But consider the circumstances: Fox the ruined rake, the King in desperate need of supporters, the ministry in full retreat, the outside world indifferent. It was an act of real greatness. It was one of those actions so common in life, which if they are right are noble, and if they are wrong are imbecile: there was nothing between. Here Fox's vast experience of games of chance served him well; he approached with apparent nonchalance and real relish a decision to which a calculating man could never have risen. After all, his financial ruin was his own fault: many other men had ruined themselves in the same way, though few to anything like the same amount: and politics was the recognised way to recoup the losses of hazard. But here Fox differed. He had always reciprocated the King's dislike. He knew well enough that to overcome a prejudice as deep-rooted, as strongly based on moral disapproval, he would have to sell his soul. It could be done: there was nobody so odious but the King would buy him if he had any talents to sell: and the Royal Marriage Bill was the Rubicon. If Fox voted for this, his sins were forgiven him: but at the same time he took his place once and for all among the "King's Friends." It was a crisis that brought out all the gambler in Fox. Was he, who had squandered his inheritance many times over for the doubtful joys of faro, to reinstate himself by the safe method of political prostitution? Was his private immorality to be financed by public immorality? Were his friends to say that, however wild he might be with his money, he had an eye to the main chance of his career? He bridled at the thought: at least he would be consistent. There were two things at least that he could never lose. If he lived to the age of Methuselah, he would never lose the ear of the House, or the devotion of a widening circle of friends. With those as his capital, he was happy to put all the rest to hazard.

It was a great action, and it brought with it great opportunities. "Can it signify much," he had said on a famous occasion, "whether faction intimidate us with a rabble, or the King surround us with his guards?" Up to this point in his career he had been defending Parliament, in an equivocal way, against the rabble; now he had the chance of showing that he meant if necessary to defend it against the King. The House knew well enough what sort of speech he would have in favour of the bill—the arrogance, the paradox, the far-fetched but impregnable arguments. What they were not prepared for was the sustained power of his opposition. His resignation had in itself made things more difficult. The first reaction of ministers had been drastically to amend the bill: in the face of loud protests from the King they modified it so as to apply only to members of the Royal Family under twenty-five years of age. When this failed to bring Fox back to his allegiance, there was only one course left to them, and they announced that the bill must be regarded as a stand-or-fall question. The odds from that moment were in favour of the bill.

All through March Fox dogged its footsteps, through all its readings, and on all its clauses in committee. He spoke with a new sobriety and restraint that proved peculiarly telling. He "seized the just point of argument throughout with most amazing rapidity and clearness." He squeezed every drop of advantage out of North's undisguised reluctance. He knocked the heads of the law-officers together on legal points, deriving a particular satisfaction from being once again in opposition to Wedderburn, whose second desertion to the enemy had made him North's Solicitor-General. He made the most damaging attacks upon the Speaker, who for want of better advocates had been induced to descend into the arena. At the end of the month the bill was passed, by a majority of eighteen, every man of the minority knowing that he was not only voting away his own prospects of advancement, but voting the Bedfords more firmly into power.

Though Fox's resignation had ensured the passage of the bill, his opposition to it had immensely enhanced his reputation. Many men thought he had resigned simply in order to show the government how dangerous his attack could be: and though this was certainly not a motive, it was a result. However vindictive the King might be against the rank and file of his opponents, he knew henceforward that there was one of them whom no proscription could touch, and he only waited the chance of buying Fox back at a higher price.

2. *Out of Office, 1772*

Fox had broken new ground: he had shown the world that his moral sincerity and righteous indignation were as formidable as his powers of reasoning. He was quick to improve his new prestige.

Lord Holland, it will be remembered, had in 1744 caused a sensation of the first order by his runaway marriage with Caroline Lennox. Elopements were at that time not merely the basis of most fiction but a very fertile cause of tragedy in real life, though the aspect of this particular elopement with which society concerned itself was the fact that the girl was the daughter of a duke. Nine years later, a measure had been passed, generally known as Hardwicke's Marriage Act, which attempted to put a stop to the practice by bastardising the children of any parents (of any religion) who were not openly married according to the rites of the Church of England after due publication of the banns. This enactment had roused Henry Fox to his full powers: he saw in it an insult to his wife, the manifestation of an inflated social snobbishness, an iniquitous religious discrimination, a fresh weapon in the tyranny of the old over the young. He was a romantic; he believed, as we have seen, that the young are always right and the old wrong: the principle on which he educated his children was the principle on which he fought this law. He fought it as Charles fought the Royal Marriage Act, but from the Treasury bench. The reputation he had made as War Secretary was trebled in a few weeks by the brilliance he showed as the champion of the young, the poor, and the romantic. Fox's opposition to the Marriage Act passed into Parliamentary history as an unprecedented display of generous passion.

Charles inherited all his father's good qualities: his detestation of lawyers (Hardwicke had been Lord Chancellor), his "aversion to all restraints," his young heart, his romanticism, his pugnacity. There was a general feeling of delight when Charles moved for leave to bring in a bill to repeal the Marriage Act of 1753. Already he had shown his chivalry in attempts to modify the bastardy laws and to facilitate divorce. And now his filial piety, and his newly won fame as an opponent of moral restraints, caused Parliament to expect a performance equal to his father's. Fortunately for us, Horace Walpole, who reported the proceedings of Parliament

44

carefully but from a safe distance, was unable to resist the temptation of attending the debate of April the 7th, 1772.

"Though I had never been in the House of Commons since I had quitted Parliament, the fame of Charles Fox raised my curiosity, and I went this day to hear him. He made his motion for leave to bring in a bill to correct the old Marriage Bill, and he introduced it with ease, grace and clearness, and without the prepared or elegant formality of a young speaker. He did not shine particularly, but his sense and facility showed he could shine. . . . Lord North, who had declared that he would not oppose the introduction of the new bill, now unhandsomely opposed it, and spoke well. Burke made a long and fine oration against the motion. . . . Charles Fox, who had been running about the House talking to different persons and scarce listening to Burke, rose with amazing spirit and memory, answered both Lord North and Burke, ridiculed the arguments of the former and confuted those of the latter with a shrewdness that, from its multiplicity of reasons, as much exceeded his father in embracing all the arguments of his antagonists, as he did in his manner and delivery. Lord Holland was always confused before he could clear up the point, fluttered and hesitated, wanted diction, and laboured only one forcible conclusion. Charles Fox had great facility of delivery; his words flowed rapidly, but he had nothing of Burke's variety of language or correctness, nor his method. Yet his arguments were far more shrewd. Burke was indefatigable, learned, and versed in every branch of eloquence. Fox was dissolute dissipated, idle beyond measure. He was that very morning returned from Newmarket, where he had lost some thousand pounds the preceding day. He had stopped at Hockerel, where he found company, had sat up drinking all night, and had not been in bed when he came to move his bill, which he had not even drawn up. This was genius—was almost inspiration. . . . The House dividing, Lord North was beaten by sixty-two to sixty-one; a disgraceful event for a Prime Minister."

That was Fox, just turned twenty-three. First, the contrast between his opening of the debate, which was no more than easy-going, and his reply, which to the end of his life never failed to astonish the House with its grasp and readiness. Then the contrast between him and Burke: the one producing his noble sentences in logical order, the fruit of careful preparation—the other rushing headlong into an impromptu, nervous, repetitive, his ideas fighting for utterance (as one critic said), trusting to providence (in the words of another) to finish his sentences for him. And finally the contrast between his negligence and his success. He can defeat the government, even when it has the rare support of Burke, on a bill which he had not yet drawn up, to repeal another bill which, according to a friend, he had never even read. This monumental idleness was the despair of Fox's family and friends, and in spite of Dr. Newcome's treasured letter it was a source of worry and remorse to himself. "I am afraid," he had written, "it will in the end get the better of what little ambition I have, and that I shall never be anything but a lounging fellow." To conduct a single-handed debate after a heavy day at Newmarket and an all-night session at a road-house is not the achievement of a lounging fellow. On one occasion it has been recorded that he played faro at Almack's for twenty-two consecutive hours, from seven on Tuesday till five on Wednesday, losing on balance eleven thousand pounds; on the Thursday, spoke and voted in an important debate on the Thirty-Nine Articles; sat up drinking at White's from eleven that night till seven next morning; and crossed to Almack's, where he won back six thousand pounds before leaving London for Newmarket on Friday afternoon. This was not an episode in the life of a lounging fellow. But he lacked application, and only with difficulty acquired it when he was in high office. Fox's activities were too wide spread. Every form of sport, every branch of knowledge, made its appeal to him, as well as every species of luxury. Yet his mental appetite was equal to any excess. It is strange to look backwards at Fox's career and see him diffident of his own ambition, after the events of 1783. Idle men are more often ambitious than industrious men. Fox had no love of work: but the effort to concentrate his vast activity of mind developed in him an ambition, and a love of office, that he failed, to his cost, to conceal. His schoolfellows said that he thought he should have been a Privy Councillor while he was still at Eton: at first he hoped to take every thing in his stride: it was the discovery that he could be thwarted at every step by inferior intellects that stirred him to furious ambition.

At the present crisis of his affairs, his idleness served him in good stead. As he had said when he resigned, there was no danger of his going into opposition; which was true enough so long as opposition had no higher aim than to defend the libellers they had paid to lampoon the government. Fox had vindicated his honour with regard to the Royal Marriage Bill in the noblest manner. As for his own Marriage Bill he had given himself no trouble with it: in May it was heavily beaten in a thin house, its promoter arriving from Newmarket too late for the division. There was now no ground of difference between himself and the government. The other opponents of the Royal Marriage Act had been duly punished, but there was no way of punishing Fox: and North was terrified of his potential danger as a freelance. The King was reluctant: he did not choose to have professed gamesters about his person, he said: he had no wish to hear the rattle of the dice-box at the Treasury board-table. Even this prophecy did not deter Lord North, who acquired more leverage with the King the more pressingly he asked to be allowed to resign. He had his way: and in December, 1772, half a dozen loyal King's Friends suffered the humiliation of being shifted from office to office in order to make way for Charles Fox as a Junior Lord of the Treasury at £1,600 a year. The final result of this sensational revolt was a small promotion: "political circles" cynically pronounced the manoeuvre a success. After all, said the wags, whose heavy comments provide such a monotonous undertone to British politics, after all, the Treasury was the place for Charles, for surely he knew as much about the ways and means of raising a supply as any man in the three kingdoms.

3. *Junior Lord of the Treasury, 1772-1774*

It soon became clear that Fox's allegiance, though paid for, had not been bought with £1,600 a year. He was so far beyond the pale of solvency already that the Pay Office itself would hardly have made it worth his while to hold his tongue. A man who owes a hundred thousand pounds is as hard to bribe as a man who has a hundred thousand in the bank: it makes as little difference to either. Fox had come into the ministry on excellent terms: his position was strong, and for the fourteen months of office that remained to him, he abused it to the limit. Lord North was full of equanimity, but Fox's conduct after his reinstatement would have taxed the patience of a saint. If his idea was to make his weight felt, he succeeded to a marvel: but he mistook the King, if he imagined that independence and acuteness of intellect were the qualifications for high office. No doubt he was glad to be back in administration, hating the policy of the Rockinghams as he did: and he was not going to resign until he was forced to, so long as his insubordination was tolerated: but little more than a year sufficed to convince Lord North that the most terrible opponent is less dangerous than an untrustworthy colleague, and to convince Fox that the amusement of keeping the Treasury bench permanently on tiptoes was inadequate compensation for having to endure the company of the Bedford party.

The position of an independent Tory is in many ways the most agreeable that a politician can achieve. When a liberal turns reactionary, he is usually disowned: but when a Tory shows a tendency to liberalism, he is more likely to meet with tolerance and even respect. The peculiarity of Fox's position was that, although on most questions he tended to be more progressive than the government, on others he was more reactionary than any nabob. One day he would horrify his leaders with an invective against Clive (who controlled ten seats) as "the origin of all plunder, and the source of all robbery." The next, he would be hounding some little pamphleteer, whom even his party wished to spare, into prison. So long as he took a more advanced attitude than themselves, the ministers had to endure his provocations in silence, for they were determined not to lose him to the opposition. But if once they caught him in a position too far to the right, where if they repudiated him the Whigs would not acknowledge him, then they were not going to lose the chance of terminating his troublesome career. On this perilous foothold he clung to office all through 1773: it was not until early in 1774 that he made himself wholly insufferable, and then on the old question of Parliamentary privilege.

The Reverend John Horne had made the first of his many appearances in Fox's life as vicar of Brentford at the time of the Middlesex elections. While Fox was canvassing for Luttrell, Horne adjured his willing flock to vote for Wilkes. Horne's admiration for Wilkes had grown into hero-worship, and then turned to envy: and now five years after the election, with Wilkes on the threshold of the Mansion House, Horne, having cast aside his cloth, was setting out to climb the same road to popular favour, for which his acute intelligence and raffish private life qualified him well enough. Horne had a most useful friend in a Mr. Tooke, who subsequently left him a small fortune together with the second name by which he is best known. Mr. Tooke was involved in a land dispute with a neighbour who was also a member of Parliament: the neighbour introduced a private bill to settle the dispute in his own favour: and Mr. Tooke presented a petition against it. Little notice was taken by the legislature either of the Tottington Inclosure Bill or of the petition against the Tottington Inclosure Bill: Mr. Tooke considered himself wronged: he turned with chagrin to his friend Horne. This was a glorious opening for a disciple—nay, a rival—of Wilkes. Horne wrote a letter of immense length, magnificently signed "Strike—But Hear," in which he called the Speaker a liar and a corrupt knave. This document he sent to Mr. Woodfall, the publisher of the *Public Advertiser*, who was never too critical about what he inserted so long as it traduced the House of Commons.

The Speaker did what any Speaker would have done: he complained to the House of Commons. He had been attacked in his capacity as their president: he had been accused of suppressing a petition: partiality on his part must clearly be partiality on their part: if he had been corrupted, it would be by one of them: he threw himself on their protection. This complaint struck the government with perplexity and alarm. They had learnt wisdom in dealing with the press. They could not be sure that "Strike—But Hear" was not "that devil Wilkes" in person, in which case they would be lucky to escape with six months' litigation and the laugh against them. But they did the least they could: they ordered Woodfall to attend. Woodfall came, and testified that the paper had been given him by Horne.

On this there arose a most complicated debate. The majority of the House were heartily sick of the press and the printers and the rules of privilege, on which two years of their life as a Parliament had been unprofitably frittered away: they devoutly hoped that the Speaker would be content with a private action. Charles Fox on the other hand was up in arms, bursting with all the old eloquence about the independence of the House and the menaces of faction. Lord North was divided in his view: sincerely hoping to avoid another squabble such as Fox was thirsting for, he felt that the least the House could do would be to send for Horne, and meanwhile to commit Woodfall, and he promised Fox to vote for such a motion. By "committing" Woodfall, North naturally understood sending him to the Gate House of Westminster under the

49

4

gentle tutelage of the Serjeant-at-Arms: it was a horrible blow, accordingly, when Fox "with the most indecent arrogance" moved to send him to Newgate, which was under the direct jurisdiction of a Wilkite Lord Mayor. He asked Fox to release him from his undertaking to support the motion, and begged the House to vote against it: but Fox was immovable, bent on another trial of strength with Wilkes himself. His motion was heavily defeated, North voting one way and speaking the other.

The conclusion of the affair was as tame as North could have wished. Horne attended the House with the sprightly alacrity of a true Wilkite, and successfully defied them to prove his authorship. But North was still sore from the division: he had no relish for voting in minorities, nor for being hoodwinked by Junior Lords. The King sympathised with his Minister: from a variety of causes, among them the imminence of a general election, he had come to think that the privileges of the House were valued perhaps a little too high: it had penetrated to his intelligence that other people besides Wilkes were "beneath the notice of the House." He gave Lord North his opinion in outspoken terms: "I am greatly incensed at the presumption of Charles Fox in obliging you to vote with him last night, but approve much of your making your friends vote in the majority; indeed that Young Man has so thoroughly cast off every principle of common honour and honesty that he must become as contemptible as he is odious; and I hope you will let him know you are not insensible of his conduct towards you."

After this Fox's ministerial career was a matter of days: but they were days filled with the maximum of provocation. The division on Woodfall's committal was on February the 15th. On the 16th, he tried to get Woodfall on an entirely different and frivolous charge of publishing what he was pleased to call a libel on the glorious revolution of 1688. On the 18th, when Horne was dismissed, to the general relief, he loaded North with reproaches for his pusillanimity in letting the printer go before he was sure of the writer. On the 23rd, he spoke and voted against the government on a dissenter's petition. This was the last straw. "I think," wrote the King, "Mr. Ch. Fox would have acted more becomingly towards you and himself if he had absented himself from the House for his conduct cannot be attributed to conscience but to his aversion to all restraints." On February the 24th, one of the doorkeepers handed Fox a note which ran: "Mr. Fox, His Majesty has thought proper to order a new Commission of the Treasury to be made out, in which I do not see your name. North." At first he thought that this was one of Selwyn's practical jokes, and laughed about it with his friends. But it was authentic. He had been ignominiously dismissed, and dismissed at a moment when he was off his guard.

CHAPTER FIVE

1. *The Financial Crash, 1773*

In 1773, the year during which Fox sat comparatively at his ease on the Treasury bench, a domestic calamity overwhelmed him. His brother Stephen had a son. The blow was unexpected, for Stephen was a bad life, in the expert opinion of Charles' money-lenders. It was deadly, for it cut Fox out of the reversionary inheritance. The birth of that pious Whig, who found a lifetime too short to write an adequate biography of his uncle, was greeted with consternation in every usurer's parlour in London. "Brother Ste's son," Fox remarked, "is a second Messiah, born for the destruction of the Jews." With his inside knowledge of the magnitude of his debts, Fox was sorrier for his creditors than for himself. But even he was staggered by the amount of paper that was duly presented, now that there was no chance of his being able to pay it.

At this point, old Lord Holland stepped in, and asked for a statement of his son's indebtedness. He had already paid huge sums for his children: not altogether well requited, for Charles had latterly neglected his father, and Stephen was almost too devoted to his wife. On the other hand, he could not clear himself from blame: from the time of the five-guinea nights at Spa onwards he had done little or nothing to guide his son into better ways: he had been absolutely consistent to his admirable theories of education, but perhaps those theories were better suited to the bringing-up of a poor than a very rich child. The children of millionaires must gamble deep before they feel the thrill of losing. It was with magnificent consistency that Holland faced the consequence of educating Charles as he had. His old Pay Office clerks were put to the task of sorting out the shoals of liabilities: slowly the full horror of the situation revealed itself. Ruefully Lord Holland sat down and wrote: "I do hereby order, direct and require you to sell and dispose of my long annuities, and so much of my other stock, estates and effects, as will be sufficient to pay and discharge the debts of my son the Honble. Charles James Fox, not exceeding the sum of one hundred thousand pounds." But £100,000 was not enough: the debts were finally paid, or rather funded, at a total of £140,000.

Fox made gestures of penitence: he declared that he would swallow his prejudice against the legal profession and read for the bar. Brooks's was frankly incredulous. "Lord Northington betts Mr. Charles Fox 20 guineas that he is not called to the bar before this time four years." "Mr. Burgoyne betts Mr. Charles Fox 50 guineas that four members of the club are married or dead before Charles Fox is called to the bar." So that even on this meritorious departure he was seventy guineas down.

Lady Holland was horrified. She bombarded Charles with letters of bitter reproach, to be answered with what looked like honest repentance. But from Lord Holland not a bitter word could be extorted; he took the full responsibility; he demanded no guarantee against a repetition of the offence; if he had felt it as a direct nemesis on his own greed he could not have borne the blow with greater calm. "Never," he wrote, "never let Charles know how excessively he afflicts me."

Society regarded this disaster as closely connected with Lord Holland's death the following year, which was followed very shortly by that of Lady Holland. He left Charles a splendid portion for a younger son: £20,000 down, £900 a year, estates in Sheppey and Thanet, and above all Kingsgate itself—the apple of his eye. The whole of it was realised at once. Finally in November of the same year, 1774, Stephen himself died, leaving Charles the Clerkship of the Pells, a sinecure then worth about £2,300 a year. Charles was by then in open opposition to such things as sinecures: so he sold it to the government in return for £1,700 a year for thirty-one years. This just compensated for his pay as a Junior Lord: it began in 1775, and ended by a curious coincidence a month before his death.

The payment of his debts was to Fox merely a paper transaction. It had nothing to do with his leaving the government. He was still as poor as ever: he still played as high and lived as well. Sixteen or seventeen hundred a year would scarcely pay for the candles he burnt at Brooks's. There is no disguising the fact that his incorrigibility, and as they thought insensibility, gave pain to his friends. In taking evidence from Selwyn, it is necessary to discount the smallness of the writer's nature; but the fact is clear that Fox was under something of a cloud. Selwyn was affability itself to Fox's face: but in privacy he writes that he has just managed to "wrench fifty pounds out of Charles' black hands," and that anyone but Charles would have given him a thousand. And he wrote under provocation. Selwyn's correspondent, Carlisle, was Fox's closest friend at Eton; he had lent so much to Fox that he himself found it necessary to live in the country; at the time of the crash he was being urged by Selwyn to sue for £15,000; but he was content with sending a noble letter, stating his claim, to Lady Holland. This was only one of his friends who were also his creditors. Numbers of others were entangled in his misfortunes, and none of them could draw from him more than perfunctory sympathy. It is at once a tribute to Fox's charm, and a reflection on the use he made of it.

A shrewder and more impartial critic was old Mme. du Deffand, and her verdict is the most unfavourable of all. She had no use for him whatever. "No doubt he has plenty of spirit, and above all great talents. But I am not sure that he is right in the head, or that his ideas are properly thought out. He seems to me to live in a sort of intoxication, and I am afraid he will be pretty miserable when this sort of existence comes to an end, and he realises that he is the sole author of all his misfortunes. . . . (Last night) we had a biribi and a pharaon, at which Fox and Fitzpatrick played. I hear that they always lose, and pay up. Where do they get it from? I don't understand it. They are both very wrong-headed, and I fear incorrigible, especially Fox, who takes great pride in his pretended insensibility to his situation. I declare it horrifies me, his future seems to me frightful. . . . At twenty-four to have lost everything, to owe more than one could ever pay, and not even to care about it: nothing is more extraordinary. I could never sympathise with such people or feel any respect for their sort of brilliance. . . . He is not bad at heart, but he has no sort of principles, and pities those who have. I don't understand how he looks forward to the future, he never troubles himself about the morrow. Desperate poverty, impossible debts, all this means nothing to him. Fitzpatrick seems more reasonable, but Fox swears that he is even more indifferent about those matters; this strange feeling of security raises them, so they imagine, above the rest of mankind. They must be very dangerous to other young men. They played a lot here, especially Fitzpatrick; he lost a great deal. Where they get the money, is what I don't understand; I could never care about them, they are absolutely crazy, and without any hope of recovery; I should never have believed, if I hadn't seen for myself, that there could be such madmen. . . . I must have seemed to him an insipid moralist, he seemed to me a sublime profligate. Your Englishmen left a lot of money here; they have started a mania for gambling; people talk now only in thousands of louis; four or five hundred louis is a trifle one doesn't deign to mention; I declare it disgusts me, I don't know what to make of such fools; I don't see how they can be really right-minded. It is such a pity in Charles Fox; he has so much intelligence, goodness and truthfulness, but that doesn't prevent him being detestable, with no principles; I don't say he is dishonest, but I should trust him more if it weren't for this damnable passion. . . . It is true that they are not at all hypocritical or underhand, and although they ruin their friends along with themselves, they are quite good at heart, but they have no scruples or delicacy about the assistance they accept from their friends, and the debts they accumulate, which by all appearances can never be paid."

These were the comments of a woman who knew the world, and had lived dangerously herself. To her, as it happened, Fox appeared without his apparatus of personal fascination, for she was nearly eighty, and blind. No doubt he talked big: no doubt he took an unholy delight in having given such enormous hostages to fortune. But when all allowances are made, both for her disabilities as a critic, and for his temptations as a *poseur*, there is a residuum of disagreeable truth in her remarks. Gambling is of all pleasures the least substantial. Sponging is of all vices the most difficult to extenuate on any social or moral grounds. Fox, to whom all other pleasures and all other ambitions were open, saw himself first and foremost as a gambler: Fox, the paragon of friendship and good company, was an avowed and unrepentant parasite. Only if we place these heavy items on the debit side of his account will we comprehend what an extraordinary credit balance of intelligence and character he required to live them down.

It was all put down to conceit, the easiest of explanations. There was no hope for him, said Selwyn, "till he is less intoxicated with the all sufficiency, as he imagines, of his parts." Walpole found him guilty of another sort of pride. "If Fox once reflects, and abandons his vices, in which he is as proud of shining as by his parts, he will excel Burke"; but he was "too confident and overbearing." Selwyn also advanced the ingenious theory that he was joining the "patriots" in the hope that they would pay his debts, as they had paid Wilkes's. They were both of them completely baffled. Fox took great pleasure in his own "parts" and vices, but not pride. He had barely enough introspection ever to be ashamed, and far too little ever to be conceited. He was a child of instinct, perfectly unselfconscious. That was the basis of his extraordinary personal charm, as well as the clue to his public life. He always repeated his mistakes, for no other reason than that he was too little interested in analysing his failures. It is always attractive when a man does not know his own strong points: it is dangerous when he does not know his own weaknesses either.

With his father's death in these circumstances, and his own dismissal from office, 1774 is the most important turning-point in Fox's life. In the result, it was the start of a new and glorious career: but at that time, his position could scarcely have seemed less promising. Financially at the end, not only of his resources, but of his prospects: politically isolated, not by any attraction to the Whigs, but by being too Tory even for the King—well might Walpole declare that Fox was at the bottom of the wheel, with Wilkes at the top, and nothing between. The prospect was melancholy: but what a retrospect! Barely twenty-five years old, Fox had lived a dozen lives already. He had spent about a quarter of a million at a time when a hundred yearly was a competence and five thousand a noble income. He had sensibly lowered the morals of the period. He could fill the House of Commons at a time when Burke was known as the dinner-bell. He was a scholar in five languages. He was a member of that club of clubs where Johnson, Burke, Reynolds, Goldsmith, Gibbon, Boswell, and Garrick foregathered. If he had not enjoyed his first quarter of a century, no man ever has. If he had died before his father, he would still have been sure of his place in English history.

2. The Transition to Whiggism, 1774

"Charles Fox is turned patriot,"* exulted Gibbon, "and is already attempting to pronounce the words 'country,' 'liberty,' 'corruption,' with what success time will discover." There was room for scepticism. He had resigned before, on a question where he took a more liberal view than the government, and his opposition had lasted ten months. Now he had been dismissed, because the government took a more liberal view than he did. On the previous occasion he had considered himself "very safe from going into opposition, which is the only danger." It was hardly very likely that he would now be received with open arms by the "patriots," from any sympathy for a man who was too reactionary even for George the Third. "Time will discover," said Gibbon, and time discovered that there is no devotee so fanatical as a convert: like Gibbon's Clovis, Fox adored the cross which he had burnt, and burnt the idols which he had formerly adored.

Fox himself was the last person to consider his change of party as a change of mind. He had a curious passion for consistency in small things. Eight years after he had joined the Whigs, Wilkes, by then a sedate and respectable City Chamberlain, moved to expunge from the journals of the House the discreditable record of his expulsion: and Fox, by then the Man of the People, both spoke and voted against the motion, which was carried by a sweeping majority. Again, even when he was leading the campaign against corruption and sinecurism, he would never hear a word against his father's record at the Pay Office, taking his stand on the strictly legal character of those extortions. Like many wayward politicians, he fancied himself as a man of consistent views and continuous principles, around whose adamantine figure the opinions of parties had ebbed and flowed, leaving him at one moment high and dry, the next moment surging back to cluster round his base.

This view was tenable to a limited extent, in that the question to which he practically confined his attention after he left the ministry had never been mentioned before he left it. The one and and only political issue from 1774 to 1782 was America, and Fox

* The word "patriot" in eighteenth-century political slang signified an opponent of the court. When Dr. Johnson observed that patriotism was the last refuge of the scoundrel, what he said was very funny, but what he meant was very trite.

had never yet opened his mouth about America. His hands were free: he was entitled to claim that, even if he had not been dismissed, he would have resigned on the question of America. Hitherto he had made his name by his fanaticism on questions of privilege, and his liberalism on questions of marriage law: no foreign issue had been raised during his term of office. And foreign issues were Fox's native element. It was on foreign politics alone that he could rise to his full height, and unfold the whole power of his mind. That chance had come: from now onwards he could leave the Wilkeses and the Hornes and the Crosbys behind him, and devote the rest of his life to fighting the bogey of national prestige. In home affairs he was always following someone else's footsteps and fighting someone else's battles: in foreign affairs he was the leader, the originator, the first great internationalist.

Another coincidence accentuates this dividing-point of his life, and has some causal relation to his future course. Though his father, as his letters show, would have approved of Fox's taking a liberal line on the American question, he would never have approved an open alliance with the Whigs; and while his father was alive, Fox would never have ventured it. He carried filial piety to a fault. Lord Holland detested Shelburne, so Charles detested Shelburne. Lord Holland regarded the Wilkites as assassins, so Charles called them assassins to their faces in the House. "Though my sons," said Lord Holland, "have as much honesty and good nature as comes to anybody's share, I think I am myself an example of how little use that may happen to be to them." Charles, accordingly, had kept his good nature in the background, and had echoed his father's belief that honesty is the worst policy. That strange education that Lord Holland had contrived for him, by treating him in every way as an equal, while it had allowed his private life to blossom into every variety of excess, had kept his public views in leading-strings. By continually deferring to his son, Holland had actually enslaved him. The young man seemed to take the lead, but he led in exactly the direction his father had intended. Brought up to believe that the world was created for the enjoyment of the rich, the cynical, and the proud, Fox had never faltered either in the pursuit of pleasure or in the defence of the narrow world within which pleasure could be attained. Toryism, as the wisest of critics has said, is enjoyment. The sagacious man never commanded his son to be a Tory: he simply told him to enjoy himself.

CHAPTER SIX

1. *The American Question, 1774*

The American dispute had its roots in the controversies of ten years back, and a very extraordinary and squalid story those ten years had to show. Into the spiritual causes of the quarrel this is no place to enter. The disparities of ancestry, of religion, of temperament, the delinquencies of colonial governors, the litigious spirit of the colonists; all these have been described in numberless books, though nowhere half so well as in the speeches of Burke. Here it is necessary to confine attention to the sequence of events and the personalities of the English politicians who had a part in them.

The Seven Years' War, undertaken largely on behalf of our American possessions, had landed England in 1763 triumphant but deeply in debt. Parliament rebelled against the obligation of meeting the full cost of the war. The Bedfords were in power: their Chancellor of the Exchequer, George Grenville, was a man of ability, but a man whose views did not extend much beyond the immediate objects of sound finance. He proposed two methods for obtaining some compensation from America. In the first place the old regulations of the Navigation Act, which had fallen into the utmost decay, were to be tightened up, and smuggling suppressed; in the second place, a small Stamp Duty was to be imposed on a variety of legal documents, to yield £100,000 a year. These measures were enforced in 1764 and 1765 respectively. The first of them, which amounted to a revival of indirect taxation, was alarming to the colonists, for it was only the practical atrophy of the Navigation Acts which had rendered our theoretical commercial supremacy in the least tolerable: the second was more than alarming, for it was actually the first precedent ever established for direct taxation to be levied in America by authority of the British Parliament.

The colonies were soon in a flame: English manufactures were boycotted: the administration of justice was suspended until the stamps should be removed: open violence broke out. It was all a very familiar process. By the time London heard how America had reacted, Grenville and the Bedfords were gone, and the Rockingham Whigs were in office. They responded to the crisis in a curious, half-hearted way. The Stamp Act was repealed: but at the same time a Declaratory Act was passed, for the express purpose of establishing the right of Great Britain to impose direct taxation on the colonies. The wound was healed, but the right to reopen it at any time was reserved. From this policy Chatham, who was resisting all Rockingham's pleas that he should join the Government, differed violently. "This country has no right under heaven to tax America," he said: in his view the Declaratory Act was a foolish provocation, a futile threat which utterly spoiled the effect of the repeal: he pinned his faith to commercial regulation: whatever was required from America could be obtained through the rusty machinery of the Navigation Acts. Chatham was backed up by his lieutenant, Shelburne: Rockingham was nose-led by his secretary, Burke. The Whigs were split from top to bottom on the abstract side of the question.

The Rockingham Whigs did not remain in office long: not the least among the King's grudges against them being their equivocal policy towards America. Chatham resisted all entreaties to support them: "Confidence," he said, "is a plant of slow growth in an aged bosom"; in his view, these hesitant patricians were merely playing at politics. He waited till they were gone, and formed his extraordinary coalition. Great things were expected of Chatham: by opposing the Declaratory Act he had won for himself all the popularity of the repeal of the Stamp Act, with which it was so absurdly coupled: the country, deeply concerned for the American trade, looked forward to a policy of wisdom and leniency. But Chatham was carried off by the gout: his disappearance left Shelburne in a minority in Cabinet: and his Chancellor of the Exchequer, Charles Townshend, was too clever by half. Townshend, casting around for a revenue, struck on the brilliant notion of two years back. In 1767, he imposed duties on glass, paper, lead, paint and tea—to be levied at American ports.

The effects were what might have been foreseen: boycotts, petitions, a miserably poor yield, and the imminent ruin of the East India Company, the great monopolists in tea. The cabinet had once more to give way: in 1770, the duties on glass, paper, lead and paint were voted away: but the tea-duty, yielding

£16,000 a year, barely sufficient to pay for its own collection, was retained.

It is worth while to examine how the Cabinet came to this decision. Chatham and Shelburne had resigned: Townshend was dead. Grafton had become Prime Minister and North, Chancellor of the Exchequer. A vote was taken on the tea-duty alone. Grafton with three others was for repealing it along with the rest: North, prompted by the King, voted with four others for retaining it: it was retained. Why then did Grafton not resign? The answer is not entirely to be found in the weakness of his character. We find stronger Prime Ministers swallowing worse rebuffs than this. The fault lay in George the Third's conception of the cabinet system. The doctrine of collective responsibility had been gradually building up in the previous reigns: Walpole had brought it near to perfection: George the Third smashed it at a stroke. He wished his Cabinets to be heterogeneous: he wished to choose men of all parties for his purposes. His confidence was by no means necessarily given to the First Lord of the Treasury: on the contrary, a revolt in the cabinet might well be instigated by the King himself, as was this one. In a word, the policy of "measures not men" was in operation. The Prime Minister must defer to the tea-duty, not the tea-duty to the Prime Minister. Well might the King describe Grafton as the most pliable of all his ministers, for almost any other statesman would have realised that a Cabinet disunited in allegiance as well as in opinions was ultimately bound to disappear into the same limbo as the Privy Council.

The tea-duty alone annoyed the Americans almost more than the tea-duty along with the rest. The others had afforded some distant hope of a revenue: this was undisguisedly retained, like a peppercorn rent, to keep the claim alive. To make matters even worse, the East India Company was being ruined by the loss of almost its best customer. The double taxation in England and America, together with the boycott, was crippling its staple trade. Here was a change of face-saving if ever there was one: take off the American tax, not as a concession to the colony, but to the company: pacify America by an action ostensibly aimed at saving the Indian trade. The chance was not taken: instead, the company was given a rebate of the English duty. This cost the Treasury far more than the American duty brought in, and so underlined the penal nature of the tax, as the Americans were quick to see. A colonial boycott of tea by moral pressure had been making great progress: but the new arrangements with the India Company provoked an attempt to prevent even the landing of the obnoxious stuff. In December, 1773, some clippers in Boston harbour were boarded by a party of men dressed as Red Indians, who threw the tea-chests into the sea.

2. *The King and Lord North, 1774*

With the arrival of this news in London, the history of American taxation ends and the history of the American War begins. No hope lingered in the thickest head of ever getting a revenue from America. The only question now was between surrender and punishment, and on this matter opinion was much more clearly divided than on taxation.

The justice, and the feasibility, of the American War are two of those rare subjects on which posterity is unanimous. It has been easy, therefore, to whitewash its opponents and blacken its supporters in an indiscriminate manner. Both for the satisfaction of getting near to the truth and in order to illuminate the theory of parliamentary government as it was then held, it is necessary to probe a little closer into the varieties of opinion. Let us first hear the extreme view, the much ridiculed opinion of the King himself, as he put it to North.

"I owne that let any War be ever so successful if persons will set down and weigh the Expences, they will find as in the last that it has impoverished the State, enriched individuals, and perhaps raised the Name only of the Conquerors, but this is only weighing such events in the Scale of a Tradesman behind his Counter: it is necessary for those in the Station it has pleased Divine Providence to place me to weigh whether expences though very great are not sometimes necessary to prevent what might be more ruinous to a Country than the loss of money. The present Contest with America I cannot help seeing as the most serious in which any Country was ever engaged it contains such a train of consequences that they must be examined to feel its real weight: whether the laying a Tax was deserving all the Evils that have arisen from it, I should suppose no man could alledge that without being thought more fit for Bedlam than a Seat in the Senate; but step by step the demands of America have risen—independence is their object, that certainly is one which every man not willing to sacrifice every object to a momentary and inglorious Peace must concur with me in thinking that this Country can never submit to; should America succeed in that, the West Indies must follow them, not independence, but must for its own interest be dependent on North America; Ireland would soon follow the same plan and be a separate State, then this Island would be reduced to itself, and soon would be a poor Island indeed, for reduced in Her Trade Merchants would retire with their Wealth to Climates more to their Advantage, and Shoals of Manufacturers would leave this Country for the New Empire; these self-evident consequences are not worse than what can arise should the Almighty permit every event to turn out to our disadvantage; consequently this Country has but one Sensible, one great line to follow, the being ever ready to make Peace when to be obtained without submitting to terms that in their consequence must annihilate this Empire, and with firmness to make every effort to deserve Success."

This Teutonic logic was at least arguable, but it did not find an adherent in the Prime Minister. For the eight years of office that remained to him, North was torn between his thorough disbelief in the royal policy, and what he saw as his duty to the King. Almost daily, often many times a day, he implored permission to resign. It was not the sweets of office, of which he was abstemious, that kept him to his post; it was his refusal to leave his master to the mercy of the opposition, until his master would consent to his going. Unlike a modern Prime Minister, whose duty it is to consider that the King's honour is in his hands, North thought that his honour was in the King's hands. The King became the keeper of the Premier's conscience. He stayed in office, but under protest. Sometimes he pleaded ironically: "The nation may yet be saved, but much time is not left to do it in, and it cannot be saved without a change of men, and particularly of the First Lord of the Treasury." Sometimes he pleaded with anguish: "Let me die disgraced, for that I cannot now avoid, but let me not go to the grave with the guilt of having been the ruin of my King and Country." But always he pleaded in vain. The King's determination was an easy winner in a contest with North's misgivings. Every plea for release was checkmated by the threat of abdication. The King knew well enough that without North the war could not be continued for a month: only North could ride the House of Commons at a time like this, and only North could hold together within one cabinet such a rascally reactionary as Sandwich on his right and such a saintly Liberal as Dartmouth on his outside left. What weighed on North's mind was that he was equally aware of his own indispensability: his staying made the war possible: he must take the blame, as much as the King himself, of measures for which he had never concealed his aversion. When Gower left the Cabinet, prophesying ruin to the country, North blandly reported to the King that he had been unable to argue with Lord Gower, having himself held the same opinion for the last three years. Many years later, when he was old and blind, one of Burke's philippics was read aloud to him; after the last of the terrible periods had rolled over its victim's grey head, "Mr. Burke," said North, "did not know that year after year I entreated to be allowed to resign. But I was not allowed." Not that North's view was right. In practice, it played into the hands of as dangerous a bigot as ever lived: in theory it paved the way to the perilously inverted theory that the Prime Minister can do no wrong. In other words, it shook the foundation on which the throne rested—the irresponsibility of the King—at the same time as it put immediate power into the hands of the throne's occupant. By deferring to the King, North handed him a sceptre: but by disowning responsibility for what the King commanded, he undermined the throne. North's conception of his public duty was utterly mistaken. But there is this to be said for it: it was not lax.

Grafton's acquiescence in an internal cabinet revolt engineered from outside, and North's acquiescence in a policy imposed from above, illustrate between them the whole weakness of eighteenth-century Toryism. The long Whig oligarchy had had its good points, and Walpole's cultivation of the cabinet system was one of them. He had evolved the Cabinet to a point where, if the Prime Minister resigned, his colleagues resigned with him: and with this weapon of collective resignation he had contrived to make the Cabinet more dependent on parliamentary than on royal support. North and Grafton allowed George the Third to put the clock back: a retrogression that would have been less disastrous if George the Third had been anything but what he was. North's attitude is comparable to that of Wellington, who would no more have surrendered an office without the royal consent than he would have surrendered a command in the middle of a battle. He allowed himself to be made the instrument by which America was lost: but he stands exonerated by the volumes of his protests which remain on record. And in him the Tory party is exonerated too. A few Tories here and there may have honestly agreed with the King: but American taxation and the American war neither found their roots in Tory tradition, nor cast their shadow upon it.

3. Burke

While this tug-of-war went on both in the Cabinet and in the closet, the Whigs had quarrels of their own. The rift between the Rockingham and the Chatham sections of the party was not healed by the outbreak of war. Though there was now no public issue between them, though the advocates of abstract taxation, and the advocates of no taxation at all, united in opposing the war their personal enmities kept them apart. Chatham had nothing but contempt for Rockingham and his trepidations: "I am resolved," he said, "to be a scarecrow of violence to the gentle warblers of the grove, the moderate Whigs and temperate statesmen."

It was necessary for Fox to identify himself with one or other section of the opposition. He had a free choice between the party which had repealed the Stamp Act and passed the Declaratory Act, and the party which had opposed both. And here is one of the great failings of Fox as a public man—his decision was to be made on a public issue, and he made it on private grounds. He had been brought up by his father to regard Shelburne as a wicked man. Shelburne had tried to induce Holland to leave the Pay Office by what looked like sharp practice: "Young man," Holland had said, "you have begun your career with an act that has ended many, a falsehood." Shelburne had described his action as a pious fraud: "I see the fraud," was Holland's comment, "but not the piety." Such was the family legend about Shelburne, and Fox had swallowed it without question, as he accepted all his father's views on every matter. How far the prejudice against Shelburne was justifiable, will be very fully considered at a later stage. At present, it is enough to notice that his mistrust of Shelburne was sufficient to prevent Fox from working with the Chatham half of opposition.

On the other hand were the Rockinghams. Their head was not

an imposing figure: a "poor dumb animal," terrified at the sound of his own voice. The best that could be said for him was said by Burke in a fine epitaph: "His virtues were his arts." But honesty is not enough for a leader of opposition in stormy years: Rockingham's diffidence, idleness, and gullibility were an incalculable handicap to his party; while a strain of intense respectability in him repelled Fox, and drove Shelburne to distraction. It is characteristic of the old territorial Whigs, and shows how little they had adapted themselves to the conditions of the new reign, that they consented to be led by a man whose only qualifications were that he was a marquis and immensely rich: and similarly that his principal followers were two immensely rich dukes. The Duke of Portland was not a politician of any importance; and in any case, Fox would hardly be drawn to ally himself with a man whom he had come near to dispossessing of the cream of his estates. The Duke of Richmond was of very different mettle, both able and ambitious; if it had not been for his advanced ideas on parliamentary reform, which were not at all to the liking of the old Whigs, he would have made a far better leader than Rockingham. As it was, he soon sickened of their incompetence and their hidebound conservatism, and threw in his lot with Shelburne, with whom his new ideas and active mind had their scope. In the meantime, he was doing what he could to galvanise the noble dotards of his party into life; and in that effort he was only too glad of the services of Fox, who was his nephew.

Such were the three leaders of the orthodox Whig party at the time of its second childhood—two of them nonentities, and a third whose enthusiasm was so consistently frustrated that he soon gave up; all three chosen on account of their rank and their fortune, in the bad old way. Fox's adhesion to this sinking crew is so far unexplained. The explanation lies in Burke.

The paradox of Burke's strange ill-balanced mind has often been laboured. The root fact is that he was much more than a politician. His equipment for politics was supreme, but his judgment was often swayed by his poetical instincts. His career is a series of battles against great wrongs. The American war, political corruption, misrule in India, Jacobinism—these were the wrongs he fought with the tenacity, the fanaticism, the single-mindedness of genius. The hard work, the logic, the wit with which he fought his battles were prosaic qualities: but he was at heart a mystic.

Each of his causes was embodied for him in some person, some ritual, some institution for which he could feel a passionate devotion. All his efforts were sacrifices in the temple of antiquity. The mainspring of his opposition to the Jacobins was not his rational dislike of their new institutions, but a crusader's vow to avenge the desecrated chivalry of ancient France. The guiding light which led him to spend ten years of his life in the thankless task of prosecuting Hastings, was not the reforming zeal of a Macaulay or a Mill, but a romantic challenge to destroy the man whose narrow commercial greed had pillaged the gorgeous accumulations and violated the timeless religions of the East. He clung to the detail, and exposed the facts better than any man before or since: but when he came to his mystical theme he was transported with eloquence, and spoke with inspiration. Continuity, tradition, prescription, antique right: those were the themes that moved him to language Shakespeare would have envied.

One of the altars that Burke had set up in his mind was the British constitution. Deep study of its history had convinced him of its merits: its haphazard intricacy fascinated his sense of texture: but its continuity alone would have sufficed to make him love it. He loved its very faults; he would not part with a jot or a tittle of it, or level out one solitary inequality. He invested it with Miltonic grandeur, and credited it with a legendary influence on our history. If it was his chosen task to keep the constitution free from the stain of corruption, he must also keep it safe from the experiments of a meddling generation. So he discriminated between one reform and another. He abominated change, but loved decay. Economical reform was the removal of a blot on the constitution: but parliamentary reform was a detestable innovation. The corruption of Parliament by the King was new, and must be stamped out: but the antiquated system of franchise was hallowed by centuries of steady deterioration, and no impious hands must be laid on it. To the common people, and to the leaders of their thought, it was clear that the state of the representation was intimately connected with the corruption of Parliament. The former made the latter possible, and the latter created a vested interest in the continuance of the former. But to Burke they were poles apart. He was the life and soul of the movement for economical reform: against Parliamentary reform he slammed the door.

This suited the Rockinghams' book to a nicety. As the great

land-owning party they had a large stake in the existing state of the representation: under the present system they returned members to a Parliament out of all proportion to their following. For a generation and a half they had had things all their own way. And now they found themselves in competition with the Treasury. The public purse was outbidding their private resources, great as they were. The royal favour was becoming a surer road to success than the patronage of the Whig magnates. Corruption came from above instead of from below. The Whigs were furious, but they found little sympathy. It was difficult to go to the people of England with the complaint that if politicians were to be subverted it should be by themselves alone. When a man of the calibre of Shelburne stood boldly for both economical and parliamentary reform, when the outside public firmly believed that either reform was useless without the other, it was difficult to discriminate openly between the policy which furthered their private interests and the policy which knocked them on the head.

It was by this curious chain of events that Burke found his spiritual home among the Rockingham party, and hitched his star to their wagon. To him they stood for the ancient aristocracy, fighting to maintain the constitution in its integrity. To them he was an adventurer, to be utilised rather than promoted, but a heaven-sent spokesman, who not only positively believed what they wanted him to believe, but could clothe it with all the oratorical pomp and circumstance of a holy war. Was a new pension to be granted on the Irish civil list? Burke would rush into the fray, calling all history to witness to the new-fangled abomination. Was some rotten Cornish borough to be disfranchised? Only over Burke's dead body would the suffrages of past generations be snatched away.

Fox had known Burke when he was still a boy. The friendship was made to succeed. Love of literature, love of art, a deep understanding of politics, and mutual appreciation of each other's minds had drawn them close together. Much as Burke disliked Lord Holland's politics, he adored the filial piety of his son. When Fox had been in office, often attacking Burke in the most virulent way, they had remained on terms of intimacy. It was a joy to escape from the Attorney-General's hectoring wit, or the First Lord's insolence, or the Privy Seal's stupidity, to stretch his mind with Burke's at a table presided over by Johnson. The two of them formed a society of their own: Fox would respect Burke's right to oppose his Marriage Bill, and Burke would respect Fox's right to embroil Parliament with Wilkes: each of them knew that he was dealing with a first-rate mind.

On American questions they were in absolute agreement: but their methods of attack were antithetical. Burke was an orator, Fox a debater. Burke was as masterly with the written as with the spoken word: his speeches were the labour of weeks, as finished as his pamphlets: he owed everything to his material, his arrangement, his command of language: his manner was lamentable, turgid and forced. Fox never prepared a speech, and only once in his life published one: "I always hated the thought of any of my speeches being published," he said, and with good reason. They depended on the juncture of the debate, and without their context are often meaningless. They were repetitive, ill-arranged, and crudely expressed: they are barely readable. With Fox everything depended on the manner. A Frenchman once asked Pitt how it was that Fox, with what was by that time a murky political record, retained his personal influence: "Ah," said Pitt, "you have not been under the wand of the magician." Fox's vehemence and passion were irresistible: he spoke at headlong speed, he screamed, sometimes he wept. He held his audience entranced. He was always ready: nothing could catch him unawares: his fluency seemed sometimes to suffocate him, but he was never in danger of running short. "Others may have had more stock, but Fox had more ready money about him than any of his party." So said an experienced witness: Burke even more emphatically declared that Fox "rose by slow degrees to be the most brilliant and accomplished debater that the world ever saw." He was now in his meridian.

Such was the combination by which the American War was opposed. To open the debate, an exhaustive and classic orator, in perfect command of all the facts and of all the arts of expression, a man whose speeches will die with the language. To reply to it, a debater armed at all points, witty, adaptable, inexhaustible, and magically persuasive. With Burke for artillery and Fox for cavalry, the Whig army had no reason to despair.

CHAPTER SEVEN

1. *Fox and Burke, 1774-1775*

The news of the Boston Tea Party came to England early in 1774: the King lost no time. Parliament was presented with three punitive measures, directed specifically against the town of Boston—suspending its privileges as a port, fining it, and limiting the jurisdiction of its courts. To anyone so misinformed as to suppose that Boston was alone in its recalcitrance, or so feather-headed as to ignore the principles at issue, these measures must have seemed efficacy itself. The penalties imposed were insupportable: the population on whom they were imposed, tiny. Forget about the feelings of the rest of America, and you would have applauded a smart piece of resolute government. Fox took his stand against it at once: "I take this to be the question, Whether America is to be governed by force or management?" He could not swear that the rest of America would make common cause with the Bostonians: he had no superior means of information to refute those who held that America could be conquered in a couple of short campaigns. On such questions he could only exercise his commonsense, and make lucrative wagers as to the stoutness of the American resistance: but on the question of principle his decision was unqualified. "The noble lord said that we were in the dilemma of conquering or abandoning America: if we are reduced to that, I am for abandoning America."

The principle was clear enough: it needed no more than a sentence: it was a matter of right feeling as much as of clear thinking. The details presented a far wider front: the solidarity of the Americans, the feasibility of war, the future value of a conquered colony, the danger of foreign intervention, the efficiency of our war preparations—all these afforded unlimited scope for debate. But the first object was to make a final effort to remove the cause of the quarrel. In April, 1774, Burke delivered his American Taxation speech on a motion to repeal the Tea-Duty. Burke's record was open to criticism: he had been an ardent supporter of the Declaratory Act: he had defended the *principle* of taxing America.

Here is an important clue to Burke's mind. The taxation of America was being continued, not for revenue, but on principle: Burke admitted the principle as a legal point, while he tore to bits its expediency. On the other hand, the war with America was a war of expediency: yet Burke fastened on the principle of it. Both political parties are in the habit of pointing to Burke as the originator of their beliefs, or, at the least, as their first articulate exponent; while it is a common gibe that a good quotation on either side of any question can be culled from Burke. All this is loose thinking. One school of thought prides itself on adherence to principles, on willingness to apply any question, no matter whose interest may be involved, to the yardstick of its accepted dogma. The other school of thought relies upon devotion to hard facts, upon stern practicality, upon its sense of expediency. Burke belonged to neither school: his mind was equal to the application of both tests, to every question. The French Revolution, the Nabob of Arcot, Catholic disabilities, what you will—Burke, before he had mastered the subject, had submitted it not only to the Conservative test, What are the chances? but to the Liberal test, What is the principle at issue? The principle of American taxation might be unexceptionable, but the chances of a revenue were slender: the chances of subduing America might be considerable, but the principle at stake forbade the attempt. He condemned the Tea-Duty on Conservative grounds, and the war on Liberal grounds. It was this double approach to political thought that made Burke the Colossus that he is. He strides the gulf between the reactionary and the progressive, between the empiricist and the doctrinaire.

The American Taxation speech was an attack on the expediency of a policy: Burke was for the moment the conservative, the pragmatist, weighing facts and assessing odds; it was in this role that his wit found its greatest opportunities. He described with gorgeous clarity and sparkle the whole process of mutual blunders for ten years past by which it had come about that "so paltry a sum as threepence in the eyes of a financier, so insignificant an article as tea in the eyes of a philosopher, have shaken the pillars of a commercial empire that circled the whole globe." He elaborated the insignificance of the legal issue beside the issue of mutual interest: "the question with me is, not whether you have a right to render your people miserable, but whether it is not your interest to make them happy? It is not what a lawyer tells me I *may* do;

but what humanity, reason, and justice tell me I ought to do. Is a politic act the worse for being a generous one?" He pointed to the unreality of the issue, which had left the safe ground of finance, and had become a face-saving struggle of contending dignities: "you are at this moment in the awkward situation of fighting for a phantom; a quiddity; a thing that wants, not only a substance, but even a name; for a thing, which is neither abstract right nor profitable enjoyment."

The American Taxation speech was delivered in April, 1774: actual bloodshed had not yet begun when, in March, 1775, Burke followed it up with the Conciliation speech. This time he dropped the empiricist, and became the man of principle, laying down the law of nations in one undying sentence: "I do not know the method of drawing up an indictment against a whole people." That was a first principle, not a calculation of the event nor a weighing up of merits. It was a declaration of war against civil war.

When Burke was speaking on the same side it is unnecessary to pay much attention to the fragments that remain of what Fox said in his support. These two speeches, so different in their approach to an identical conclusion, exhaust their subject: and not their immediate subject only, for they comprise the whole canon of political wisdom. For any crisis of affairs, for any crucial public decision, somewhere in their depths an oracle is to be found. They are our Sibylline Books.

The Taxation speech commanded forty-nine votes: the Conciliation speech seventy-eight. Of the mentality and status of those who voted in the majority we can judge from a passage in Gibbon's autobiography. "I took my seat," he says, "at the beginning of the memorable contest between Great Britain and America, and supported, with many a sincere and silent vote, the rights, though not, perhaps, the interest, of the mother country." Unabashed by this confession, he goes on. "The cause of government was ably vindicated by Lord North, a statesman of spotless integrity, a consummate master of debate, who could wield, with equal dexterity, the arms of reason and of ridicule. . . He was upholden on either hand by the majestic sense of Thurlow, and the skilful eloquence of Wedderburn. From the adverse side of the House an ardent and powerful opposition was supported by the lively declamation of Barré, the legal acuteness of Dunning, the profuse and philosophic fancy of Burke, and the argumentative vehemence of Fox, who in the conduct of a party approved himself equal to the conduct of an empire." Such was the Parliamentary scene, through the eyes of one who chose his epithets more carefully than his politics.

2. Rockingham Secedes, 1776

"The Opposition seemed to have lost all spirit," writes Walpole of the state affairs in January, 1776. "What little life there was, existed in the Duke of Richmond and Charles Fox. The latter bustled, tried to animate both the Duke and the Marquis, conferred with Lord Shelburne, but neither abandoned his gaming nor rakish life. He was seldom in bed before five in the morning, nor out of it before two at noon." To animate the Marquis (of Rockingham), whom Walpole elsewhere describes as a wet dishclout, was a labour of Hercules: but Fox had one or two successes elsewhere. It was after a conference with Fox at Newmarket that Grafton, that well-meaning man, resigned the Privy Seal and came into open opposition.

It is hard to blame Rockingham for his futility, for the prospects of the opposition were almost desperate. A cleverly timed dissolution in the summer of 1774, before the country could grasp the implications of American repression, had given the ministry another comfortable majority of about three to one: incidentally obliging Fox to quit Midhurst for Malmesbury, a more democratic constituency where the ratio of members to voters was two to thirteen. While the Whigs' exertions in Parliament seemed to be thrown away, they had every reason for wishing to turn their backs on politics. Most of the leaders of the party were landowners on a big scale, in Ireland as well as in England. They were sportsmen too. It is no easier to blame them for preferring the hoarfrosts and falling leaves of their beloved shires to the fug and bustle of an autumn session, than it is to blame Howe for dancing and drinking the winter through in Philadelphia instead of starving in four foot of snow at Valley Forge. But it is a discreditable reflection all the same, that the one occasion during these critical years when the Whig magnates were stirred to real activity was when North proposed a tax which would fall almost entirely on themselves, namely a tax on Irish absentee landlords.

When the spring session of 1776 ended, completing two years of nugatory resistance, the Dukes and Marquises decided among themselves that the game was hardly worth the candle. They talked of not coming up to London that autumn. Indignation was wasted on an impregnable ministry: it would be better to work it off on their pheasants and foxes. They proposed to sulk in their tents for the next few sessions, until the public came to their senses and began to feel their loss. It was all very well for Lord Chatham and Lord Shelburne, professional politicians, to be continually in attendance at Westminster: but a Rockingham or a Portland had other things to think about—their own exchequers and their own revenues were occupation enough for any man.

It was a plausible impulse, and one by no means uncommon in parties whose moral indignation is great and numbers small. But it was, and always is, an impulse to be scouted. It stultifies the two-party system: it is the negation of Whig principles. It was particularly perilous at a time when the King was experimenting with a Bolingbroke constitution. It cut no ice with Fox. He was fully as versatile a sportsman as any of his party; his moneylenders and their annuities were fully as troublesome as all Lord Rockingham's rents; but he had energy and to spare for a losing battle. When Fox drew his sword, he had thrown away the scabbard. His spirits rose as his cause declined: the more hopeless the struggle the greater figure he made. When he got wind of the proposal to secede from Parliament, at Newmarket—that Mecca of the Whigs—he was up in arms against it. His letter to Rockingham survives. It is written as from an equal to an equal, not from a follower to his party leader. It is plain that two years of opposition had brought Fox to an independent position somewhere between the Rockingham and the Chatham sections of opposition, an inference confirmed by Walpole when he speaks of Fox "conferring with Lord Shelburne."

"A secession at present," Fox writes, deriving strength for his argument from the recent British victory in Long Island, "would be considered as a running away from the conquerors, and we should be thought to give up a cause which we think no longer tenable . . . Above all, my dear Lord, I hope that it will be a point of honour among us all to support the American pretensions in adversity as much as we did in their prosperity, and that we shall never desert those who have acted *unsuccessfully* upon Whig principles, while we continue to profess our admiration of those who succeeded in the same principles in the year 1688." These pleas were reinforced by some plain speaking from Burke. "This is no time for taking public business only as a part of the scheme of life, which comes and goes at its proper periods, and is mixed in with occupations and amusements. It calls for the whole of the best of us; and everything else, however just or even laudable at another time, ought to give way to this great, urgent, instant concern." But neither Burke's insistence that he should give all his time to politics, nor Fox's insistence that he should at least attend to business during the session, could move Rockingham from his incurable diffidence.

Rockingham's views on the usefulness of opposition would have been considerably modified if he could have seen a note addressed by the King to Lord North just a month later. "I learnt from Lord Weymouth that Charles Fox had declared at Arthur's last night that he should attend the business of the House this day, and either tomorrow or Sunday should set out for Paris, and not return till after the recess: I think therefore you cannot do better than bring as much forward during the time Parliament shall be assembled as can with propriety be done, as real business is never so well considered as when the attention of the House is not taken up by noisy declamation." The King knew what Rockingham never guessed, that Lord North in his heart of hearts believed that it was only a matter of time before Fox's scalding oratory culminated in his own impeachment. Fox believed it too; he saw that the ministry's easy majorities were no safeguard against a loss of nerve; sooner or later his words would batter down all their defences. Comfortable cynics like Selwyn might go on voting against the cowardly colonists: gentlemen of the mentality of Gibbon might continue to support "the rights, though not, perhaps, the interests, of the mother country." But on men of less intellectual pretension, the merits of the case would some day weigh heavier than bribes. "I am clear the *opinion* of the House is now with us," Fox writes. "I cannot help flattering myself that *opinions* will, in the long run, have their influence on *votes*." Some day North would fall before a blast of Fox's trumpet, as Grafton had crumpled up in face of Chatham. It was only a matter of time.

3. Burke Secedes, 1777

Aware as he was of the shortcomings of the Whig potentates, Fox was no less alive to the charms of their society. After a spring session in which the Whig vote had fallen, owing to the secession, to between thirty and forty, he spent almost the whole summer of 1777 at Chatsworth. The fifth Duke of Devonshire had married the reigning beauty of the day, and fallen out of love with her. Georgiana found her inspiration in Fox: to the end of her life (and they died in the same year) her devotion to him was unfaltering and unquestioning. When Fox was in his deepest disgrace, "Would I were a man," she wrote, "to unite my talents, my hopes, my fortune, with Charles's; to make common cause, and fall or rule with him." This friendship was still young in 1777. "Mr. Fox came in the evening from town—Charles Fox *à l'ordinaire:* I have always thought that his great merit is his amazing quickness in seizing any subject. He seems to have the particular talent of knowing more about what he is saying, and with less pains, than anybody else. His conversation is like a brilliant player at billiards: the strokes follow one another, piff! paff! And what makes him more entertaining is his being here with Mr. Townshend and the Duke of Devonshire; for their being so much together in town makes them show off one another. Their chief topics are politics and Shakespeare. As for the latter, they all three have the most astonishing memory for it. I suppose I shall be able in time to go through a play as they do." So his hostess wrote, and it would be difficult to decide whether she shows herself or her guests in the more attractive light. As a guest, Fox found the atmosphere of defeatism depressing: he wrote to Burke, full of his despondency. "I have been living here some time, with very pleasant and very amiable people: but altogether as unfit to storm a citadel, as they would be proper for the defence of it."

From Chatsworth he went for a round of visits in Ireland, taking Townshend with him. There he assured his popularity by going for a swim in the Devil's Punch Bowl at Killarney, the waters of which were reputed to be fatal; he attended a debate in the Irish Parliament, where he was with difficulty restrained from speaking; and he struck up an enduring friendship with Grattan. In the midst of oceans of wine and talk in Dublin, he got an answer to his letter to Burke, page upon page of it. To Fox's intense disappointment,

Burke had come round to Lord Rockingham's view and had decided to secede from Parliament, but from a diametrically opposite reason. Rockingham abstained because he cared too little about public affairs: Burke because he cared too much. Burke's abstention could never by anyone be attributed to idleness: it merely gave him opportunities of increasing his prodigious industry at home. But he was not fitted to this sort of struggle: his rage became uncontrollable, sometimes depriving him of his voice, sometimes betraying him into unpardonable conduct: the dread of England's ruin, contempt for the men who were ruining her, and the sense of his own impotence drove him almost out of his senses. There are some people who think that Burke died mad, on account of the transports of rage with which he opposed the French Revolution. Certainly he came near to insanity, and his anger at the American War was almost as great as his anger in the nineties: his secession from Parliament was most likely wise.

Burke's answer to Fox's complaints was an attempt to persuade him to join the Rockingham party openly, and to unite with them in their protest against the ministerial policy by leaving Parliament. He praised the character of Rockingham and his friends, and his infatuation with their rank is manifest in every word. "Some faults in the constitution of those whom we most love and trust . . . are intimately connected with honest disinterested intentions, plentiful fortunes, assured rank, and quiet homes. I am quite convinced that they are the honestest public men that ever appeared in this country, and I am sure that they are the wisest by far of those who appear in it at present . . . God knows whether this citadel is to be stormed by them or by anybody else." He expatiated on the impetuosity and unwisdom of his own youth. "If *you* should grow too earnest, you will still be more inexcusable than I was; your having entered into affairs so much younger, ought to make them too familiar to you to be the cause of much agitation, and you have much before you for your work. Do not be in haste. Lay your foundations deep in public opinion. Though (as you are sensible) I have never given you the least hint of advice about joining yourself in a declared connection with our party, nor do I now; yet, as I love that praty very well, and am clear that you are better able to serve them than any man I know, I wish that things should be so kept as to leave you mutually very open to one another."

Burke was the last person to deprecate earnestness and agitation,

and Fox the last person to listen to him. This loyal attempt to defend the Rockinghams, written by a man whose earnestness and
agitation had driven him speechless into retirement, was exquisitely
calculated to defeat its own end. A fig Fox cared for plentiful
fortunes, assured rank and quiet homes. The impatience with which
he read this panegyric may very probably have led him to overlook
that trenchant piece of advice: "Lay your foundations deep in
public opinion." For this was a thing Fox had never begun to do.
Not many public men at that time, when many seats in Parliament
depended on a landowner's influence, and most promotion on the
royal favour, had any foundations at all in public opinion. Chatham
was the only man who had learnt and availed himself of that wasted
force, which for want of better leaders was perverted by such men
as Wilkes. That was what Fox learnt in the next five years, to such
effect that he inherited for a time almost the whole of Chatham's
popularity. How he abused that popularity, and who succeeded to
it, will form the core of his history. In the meantime, we shall see
how deep he laid his foundations in public opinion, and what
miserable help the Rockinghams afforded him to that end.

4. Fox Carries On, 1777

Fox returned to Westminster for the autumn session of 1777
abandoned by his friends. He had only to wait a fortnight before
his decision to persevere was abundantly rewarded. Early in
December, the news reached London that Burgoyne had surrendered at Saratoga six weeks before. Burgoyne was Fox's
personal friend; in sending home his account of the surrender, it
occurred to him that he might be made the scapegoat for a defeat
for which he was not to blame; as a safeguard, he sent a copy to
Fox as well as to the Gazette. The event was exactly what Burgoyne
anticipated. Fox read Burgoyne's papers with rising anger: "There
are passages in them," he said, "which our governors will not much
like to make public." He went down to the House well primed, and
struck with terrific force exactly where the government was most
vulnerable.

Lord George Germaine, the Secretary for War, was accurately
described by Fox as an "ill-omened and inauspicious character."
Originally known as Lord George Sackville, he had disgraced

himself early in life at the Battle of Minden: whether it was cowardice or disobedience is a point still undecided, but the fact remains that he had been dismissed with ignominy, struck off the Privy Council, and declared unfit to serve the King in any military capacity whatever, a sentence which by George the Second's express command was read aloud to every regiment in the army and entered in their books. Such was the man whom George the Third employed, under a different name, in no less military a capacity than that of Secretary for War. Fox had no intention of letting the House forget the Secretary's past history: when the news from Burgoyne arrived he let fly. It would soon be necessary, he said, to bring the noble lord to a *second* trial; the House could surely not submit to see this nation disgraced by him in *every* capacity. He moved for the production of Germaine's instructions to General Howe.

The plan of campaign had been that Burgoyne and Howe were to join forces on the Hudson River: Burgoyne would not have been forced to surrender if Howe had moved northwards in good time: Howe would have moved in time if he had received his instructions from Germaine: and Germaine (the story goes) would have sent those instructions in time, if he had not been unwilling to postpone his Saturday to Monday at Knole. Such was the sequence of events, if only Fox had known it. But he had guessed much. A determined effort was later made by the government to shift the blame upon Burgoyne, but Fox's intuition had saved him in advance. At each successive stage of the inquiry, the government was more and more deeply discredited by the mysterious non-arrival of Howe's instructions. In his withering attack on Germaine, he had found the Achilles' heel of the government. What is more, he had brought his friends back to town: they divided eight-nine: the secession had yielded to his single example.

CHAPTER EIGHT

1. *War with France, 1778*

The visit to Paris at the end of 1776, which had filled the
King with such relief, was not all vingt-et-un and biribi and
pharaon, in spite of Mme. du Deffand's shrill disapproval.
Fox had friends in high places in Paris, as well as in low: he
returned to England firmly convinced that French sympathy with
the Americans would soon take the form of military alliance. There
was indeed every reason to fear it. Every section of the French
nation wished us ill. The intellectuals saw in the American colonies
a community, founded and nurtured on the true principles of
Rousseau, being forced into the mould of an effete monarchy—a
nation born free, on which the chains were being riveted before
their very eyes: they gushed over Franklin, and some of them even
crossed the Atlantic to gush over Jefferson. The non-intellectuals,
on the other hand, saw what mattered more, that England was engaged in an attempt to subdue a country many times its own size,
with three million inhabitants, at a distance of six weeks by sea, by
means of an army of 35,000 men. She had left herself defenceless,
and all the disasters inflicted on France by Chatham fifteen years
before could be avenged by sending a few troopships across the
Channel on the first favourable breeze.

Fox lost no time in drawing attention to the danger. Immediately
after his return, in February, 1777, he spoke out in Parliament.
He affirmed from his own knowledge that we were on the eve of a
war with France. The administration, he said, were extremely
negligent in respect of home security and national defence, particularly in not calling out and embodying the militia, when it was
well known in what a defenceless state we stood. He enlarged on
the disposition of the French nation, and pointed out that Franklin
was being received in Paris as the representative of an independent
nation.

His warning fell on deaf ears, but all through 1777 events moved
steadily in the direction of a French war. The dismissal of Turgot
in the previous year had paved the way for it, and open prepara-

tions were being made throughout France for a war which could only have one object. A magnificent fleet was being assembled at Brest, and what was even more undisguised, an army of 25,000 men was encamped beside it. All who had eyes to see could point to the certainty of a new Armada: and the number of regular troops in England at the time had fallen below 10,000.

If the outbreak of war with France had been in doubt, the raising of Hessian and Brunswicker mercenaries would have made it certain. The King's negotiations with the heads of those and other petty German states had brought disasters in their train. The troops were expensive and mutinous; when they arrived in America, they failed to distinguish between loyalists and rebels, and by looting both alike they lost us what allegiance remained in every province through which they passed. But these were minor drawbacks: in the realm of policy the consequences were calamitous. In the first place, the employment of these boorish huns, coming on top of the incitement of the Red Indians to scalp and disembowel their masters, removed the last ounce of compunction that such men as Washington, who had won fame in fighting the French at Fort Duquesne, could feel at the thought of enlisting the French against the mother country. In the second place, it exposed our weakness to the gaze of all Europe. Catherine of Russia bluntly informed George the Third that she would not send a single soldier to help him make a fool of himself: Frederick the Great sarcastically levied a cattle-toll on those of the mercenaries who passed through Prussia: France exulted.

In the teeth of all these considerations, the ministers, on adjourning the House for Christmas of 1777, blandly announced that our relations with France had never been better. But there was one member whose recess was not brightened by these smooth words. Fox came back to Westminster in a fighting mood. On February the 2nd, 1778, he rose to move that no more of the regular troops leave the kingdom.

It was a full-dress occasion. A vast multitude, we are told, filled the galleries, and by way of signalising their sense of the importance of the debate, ministers ordered the galleries to be cleared. A stubborn resistance was put up by the ladies, including the Duchess of Devonshire, who contrived to hold up business for two hours before Fox could begin his speech. He spoke with restraint: he recapitulated the sequence of events during the last four years "with astonishing memory and method"; he described the initial folly of supposing Massachusetts to be the only discontented colony; he deplored the manner in which the American petitions had been put aside; he dwelt upon the incompetence with which the war had been directed from home, and the scanty prospect that remained of making any further headway now that all thirteen colonies were up in arms. And so he came to his conclusion: in the present situation of things it would be folly to send any more troops out of the kingdom. There was the greatest reason to prepare for a foreign war. There was an actual deficiency on the peace-establishment of 6,000 men. It appeared from this that it would be madness to part with any more. He hoped it was not intended that the safety of this country was to be left to the new levies.

He sat down after a speech of two hours and forty minutes, all of it in a tone of moderation entirely new to him. There was the usual buzz of conversation and the usual coming and going, during which the next speaker's opening sentences are usually drowned. But there was no next speaker: the government sat like deaf-mutes: not a syllable was forthcoming, until someone called for the question, and the House divided. In the division Fox had the reward denied him in the debate: even Gibbon on this occasion wearied of assisting the decline and fall of the British Empire: the figures were 259 for ministers to 165 for opposition.

This brilliant division bore its fruit soon enough. A fortnight later, North introduced a series of conciliatory proposals, of a drastic character. All the penal laws were to be repealed, taxation and even the right of taxation to be renounced, free pardon to be granted, and a commission sent out to treat with Congress, as if it were a legal body, on these terms. In other words, everything was to be conceded but independence, and even independence was to be admitted until a treaty should be ratified.

This was not the first time North had tried concessions. Three years before, when Fox had been in opposition less than a year, the government had put forward some conciliatory bait with the express purpose of tempting him back to their side. He had been flattered, but not deceived. He had laughed at the proposal, and turned the debate upside down in such a way that in order to save North from being beaten by his own side, it had to be publicly explained that the proposals were not seriously intended, and that the concession was more to Fox than to America.

North had been badly stung on that occasion in February, 1775: but that was nothing to the punishment in store for him in February, 1778. The previous triumph had been due to the presence of mind of a born debater: this now was due to good luck. About an hour after the debate began, Fox was informed that the treaty between France and the rebel colonies had already been signed the previous week. Horace Walpole had heard of it from his cousin. As they both, in his words, "distrusted Burke, and feared the childish fluctuations of Lord Rockingham," they agreed to tell Fox. They were abundantly justified. Burke would have blurted it out before the debate began, in deathless sentences: Rockingham, "whose virtues were his arts," would have taken the Prime Minister aside and informed him, as one gentleman to another: but Fox saw that the news was dynamite for the Treasury bench, and held his peace. Lord North made his motions with complacency: "a dull melancholy silence" ensued, as the Tories digested the full extent of the proposals: then Fox got to his feet. He complimented the noble lord; he welcomed the propositions, and would give them his vote; he was particularly pleased by their striking resemblance to Mr. Burke's propositions of three years ago, except that those had been timely; he could not describe these as timely; they were in fact eleven days too late, Mr. Franklin having signed a treaty with France on the 6th. The noble lord was unaware? Indeed, it was no trifling matter. He wished the ministers would give the House satisfaction on this interesting point, whether they knew anything of this treaty, and whether they had not been informed previously to the making of their proposition, of a treaty which would make that proposition as useless to the peace as it was humiliating to the dignity of Great Britain.

North could brazen out most situations, but he was unequal to this. He was brought up by loud and angry cries of "Answer!" He owned he had heard a report: it was possible, nay, it was too probable: but our ambassador had not authenticated it. It was a pitiful display.

The report was all too true. The conciliatory proposals were passed unanimously: the commission went out, and was snubbed by each of the American leaders in turn. In March, our ambassador was recalled from Paris, and the militia were called out—a measure for which Fox had vehemently called in February of the previous year.

2. *Proposed Coalition, 1778*

There was to be a war with France: and there was one Englishman alive who had punished France as they had not been punished since the Middle Ages. The King, the Tories, the Whigs immediately bethought themselves of Chatham: the entire outside public, who had never quite lost faith in him, turned to Chatham: and North himself, jubilant at the idea of quitting office, joined in the cry for Chatham. The King made his position quite plain at the start. He was prepared to reinforce his ministry by taking in Chatham and Shelburne, together with two of their followers, Barré and Dunning. He was also prepared to make Fox Treasurer of the Navy, sarcastically remarking that he would probably be more glad of a lucrative than a responsible post. Of the existing ministers, Germaine, whose position had been shaken by Fox's attacks, was to quit, but as few others as possible. The Rockingham party was not so much as mentioned. Finally, there was one most characteristic proviso: if Chatham came in the King would welcome him with open arms, but until he came in there must be no direct intercourse between the King and him.

North negotiated under this authorisation. First, as to Fox. Fox "stated himself to be unconnected and at liberty"; he would be satisfied to be Treasurer of the Navy: he could work with any of the present ministers except Germaine. It was a most satisfactory interview. Fox was clearly desperately keen for office: his unbridled language in Parliament had not marred his personal friendships with ministers: and best of all, he was not yet openly bound to the Rockingham party.

Lord Shelburne was then approached, and was less helpful. He said that Chatham must be dictator, but that Rockingham would have to be brought in as well. This suggestion was reported to the King, and met with no response. If Chatham's being dictator meant North's accepting a secondary position, the King would have none of it. He soon discovered, however, that North had started the negotiations primarily in the hope of securing his own release from office. He deluged his unhappy minister with protests. "Are you resolved, agreeable to the example of the Duke of Grafton at the hour of danger, to desert me?" "Rather than be shackled by those desperate men, I will rather lose my Crown rather than wear it as a disgrace." The King's emotions were always accurately reflected in his grammar.

As for "those desperate men," the Rockinghams, it was obvious that Shelburne was right—that if Chatham came in they must come in too. They had the pocket-boroughs and the votes. Chatham had only his prestige and a mere handful of followers. So the Rockinghams got in touch with Chatham and discussed terms. They soon found something to disagree about, as they had disagreed about the Declaratory Act.

It seems an academic question, but it was not, whether if a coalition were formed, and if America were evacuated, as Chatham would insist that it should be, the independence of America should be recognised, or her renewed allegiance sought. Both parties agreed that if they came into the government the American war must be stopped, and the war with France fought out. But the Rockinghams wished to let America drift, to give her up for lost already. From this view, both Chatham and Shelburne dissented violently. Shelburne, the diplomatist, looked to the future, to the bargaining value of independence in case the war continued: he hoped to have the making of the peace, and in that case to have his hands free. Chatham, the war minister, looked to the past. America was his child: he had wrested it from the French: in every American province there was a Fort Pitt or a Pittsburgh or a Pittville: ten Americans read his speeches for one Englishman: his prestige in America stood second only to Washington's. "My heart," he said, "is garnered in America." Chatham *knew* that America would not desert England while he was at the head of her affairs, and directing her once again in a war against France. He rebelled vehemently against the craven suggestion to cut America adrift.

There was much to be said on both sides, and while it was being said, Chatham heard that Richmond was about to introduce a motion in the Lords on this very subject, a motion calling for the recognition of independence. Infuriated by what looked like an attempt to queer the pitch, he rose from his bed, in spite of entreaties and commands, and went up to the House, racked with gout. He spoke of the unwisdom of surrendering America without an attempt at reconciliation: but he did not speak well. "His speech faltered, his words were broken, and his mind not master of itself." Before he could finish his speech, he fell back in a fit. A few weeks later he died.

That was the end of the negotiations. There was no public call for the Rockinghams, except as voters for Chatham: there was no chance of Fox coming in on his own. The King regained the whip hand over North. "May not the political exit of Lord Chatham incline you to continue at the head of my affairs?" All was as it had been: both France and America were to be fought by exactly the same ministry as before.

A heavy responsibility lay with Rockingham and his friends. Their inability to agree with Chatham was temperamental. Years before, they had alienated him by their insistence on the Declaratory Act, as worthless a measure as ever passed: now they alienated him by their insistence on American independence, an issue which in any case could not arise for a year or two, and was far better left open until it did. In the first case they had stickled for retaining a useless right, and in this case they stickled for throwing away a precious one. It is not merely that in each case they were wrong, but that they were obstinate about matters that allowed of adjustment. If Chatham had lived, the Rockinghams would bear the responsibility of frustrating a coalition which would have withdrawn our troops from America, left the way open for a reconciliation with America, fought France with a full complement of men and ships, and that under the greatest war minister in this country's history. It is lucky for their good name that Chatham died when he did.

From this indictment Fox is free. He was delighted to serve with Chatham: as we have seen, he was still unconnected and at liberty: he had no part in his friends' disastrous scruples. But Chatham's death had one serious consequence for Fox. Chatham's mantle fell upon Shelburne, a man well worthy of it, and long trained for it by mutual confidence and respect. Against Shelburne Fox still felt the groundless prejudice he had inherited from his father. Shelburne was anathema to Lord Holland: so inevitably he was anathema to Fox. Having wavered long between the two branches of the Whig party, "conferring with Shelburne" one moment, and "animating the Marquis" the next, he now openly identified himself with the latter out of simple bias against the former. It was not the least lamentable outcome of the Great Commoner's death.

Fox was not ashamed of his willingness to join mini
contrary, he blamed his new friends for their reluctance
combination which might have stopped the war, and begged
them to hold themselves open to another offer, if it came. Some
time after Chatham's death he reopened the subject in an important
letter to Rockingham: "What you considered as a step of the
most dangerous tendency to the Whig party, I looked upon as a
most favourable opportunity for restoring it to that power and
influence which I wish it to have as earnestly as you can do. . . .
You think you can best serve the country by continuing in a
fruitless opposition; I think it impossible to serve it at all but by
coming into power, and go even so far as to think it irreconcilable
with the duty of a public man to refuse it, if offered to him in a
manner consistent with his private honour, and so as to enable
him to form fair hopes of doing essential service. . . . All that I
desire is that you will give me explicit answers to two questions;
and this I think I have a right to, from the very open conduct I
have always held towards you. The first of these questions is,
Whether you persist in the opinion you had of rejecting, if again
proposed, the offer formerly made? . . . My next question is,
Supposing an Administration should be formed partly of those
who now act in Opposition, and partly of the present people
(always understanding the most exceptionable to be removed,
particularly North, Sandwich, and Germaine), whether you
would give such a Ministry any countenance whatever?" It was a
long and angry letter, but abundantly justified, for Fox now led
the opposition in the Commons, and he completed his thirtieth
year on the very day he wrote it. He had a right to an answer; but
Rockingham was incapable of an explicit answer to these or any
other questions. Helplessly, he turned the letter over to Richmond,
who replied to it with all the evasiveness of an uncle. He explained
that the terms offered were not good enough; that not enough of
the old ministers were to go, and that those who did were to be
loaded with honours instead of ignominy; that "as to measures,
none were proposed, except to withdraw the troops in general
from North America, as from necessity or prudence, and to carry
on a vigorous war against France." From that he went on in a true
avuncular tone to say: "You have many of those social virtues

which command the love of friends. You have abilities in abundance, and your confidence of late years has done much to regain that public confidence which is so necessary to a public man. By a steady perseverance you may accomplish so essential an object. Once more pardon the effusion of a sincere heart, and believe me, ever yours, Richmond."

The advice was as excellent as the explanation was miserable. The measures proposed, to evacuate America and fasten on France, were the only measures for which Fox lived. He would have given North or Sandwich or Germaine a dukedom to make way for these measures, he would have thrown every internal reform to the winds for the sake of these measures, which Richmond sedately belittles as the only measures proposed. What can Fox have felt, as he read this exasperating letter, except that to its ducal supporters the Whig party was more important than the lives of thousands of Americans and Englishmen?

However, there was nothing for it now. The opportunity was gone past recall, sacrificed to the punctilios of the dukes and the marquises. You would never have guessed from Fox's language in the House that he had been the foremost in his eagerness to join the Government. "What! enter into an alliance with those very ministers who had betrayed their country, who had prostituted the public strength, prostituted the public wealth, prostituted what was still more valuable—the glory of the nation. The idea was too monstrous to be admitted for a moment. Gentlemen must have foregone their principles and given up their honour before they could have approached the threshold of an alliance so abominable, so scandalous, and so disgraceful."

Hansard at this period is strewn thick with the scenes that Fox created. He used terrible language about North, continually harping on impeachment, sometimes reducing him to tears, and even—what was much more difficult—to a loss of temper. But his language to North was buttermilk compared with his language to Germaine, at the time when Germaine was trying to save his reputation at the expense of Burgoyne's. Torrents of abuse about Germaine's "well-known cowardice" brought the members crowding into the House day after day. After one of the most violent of these philippics, he went over to the Treasury bench for a talk. "I am glad you did not fall on me to-day, Charles," said North, "for you were in full feather." While such was the temper inside the House, the outside public formed a wrong impression. They were tired of politics being treated as a game, between two cliques of aristocrats who were dining together within an hour of the debate. When they heard the reports of Fox's speaking, they decided (though slowly) that the man they wanted had come at last—an uncompromising man, an outsider, a man who would have no truck with the family compacts and gentlemanly alliances inside politics. In 1774, Fox was known as the Black Boy: in 1780, as the man of the people. He achieved that metamorphosis principally on the strength of his vehement sincerity. He *was* sincere, but little the people knew to what shifts and compromises he would stoop to gain his ends, little they knew that, with the solitary exception of Germaine, "he was prepared to act with present ministers." It is vitally important to remember the discrepancy between the Man of the People, as he appeared on the hustings, and that good fellow Charles as he appeared in Parliament, when we come to consider the causes of his downfall.

Parliament was sometimes described as the best club in London. They knew their Charles Fox, and liked him all the better for his vitriolic tongue. "Such good humour," said a Tory, "is at the bottom of all that pretended acrimony." And they knew too that if he did happen to overstep the limits, he was always prepared to be shot at from fourteen paces by the injured party. By no means the most unkind of his invectives was aimed at one William Adam, who had left the opposition and joined the ministers. He subsequently became one of Fox's most unflinching supporters, and in his old age he kept open house for the Blair Adam Club where Walter Scott spent the week-ends of his tragic years. This excellent man took exception to Fox's derisory remarks, and a duel followed in Hyde Park. Fox—a massive target—was slightly wounded. "I should infallibly have been killed," he observed, "if Mr. Adam had not been using government powder."

4. Fox Rises to the Occasion, 1778

The French war made matters difficult for the opposition. In all wars the opposition has the choice of opposing the war or not opposing the government. In this war they were handicapped by having on every vote to discriminate between the American and the French wars. And they were handicapped by much more than that. They were confronted once again with their own past record. For more than a century it had been the Whigs who were the war-mongers; the Tories who were the pacifists. We must see how this had come about.

Cromwell's New Model had been the first taste of a regular army that England ever had: and it may well be imagined how the country gentlemen felt about that army, with its psalms and pillage, its prayers and plunder, its Colonel Zachariahs and Major Obadiahs, its sermons and drumhead law. When England had been saved from that reptile rule, it was the chief preoccupation of the Tory party to prevent it ever from recurring. The Tories pinned their faith to two defences—the navy and the militia. The navy was safe enough so long as that stout Tory, the Duke of York, had charge of it. The militia was safe enough while every Tory squire rode at the head of a body of local apprentices and farmhands, every man of whom he knew by name. And England was safe from the only two things she dreaded: an invasion and a second military tyranny. But as soon as the Duke of York became James the Second, and tried his hand at establishing a military tyranny by the importation of Irish troops, the Tories disowned him, and played their part—an honourable, a decisive, but a reluctant part—in the sad events of 1688.

William came as a deliverer, but not with that primary intention. He was not disinterested; he did not come to England in any altruistic or missionary spirit, to save us from error and darkness. He wanted England as a recruiting-ground, as a weapon in his fight with France, and once his authority was secure he made no bones about his ambitions. The navy he left in charge of a drunkard: the militia he insulted and ridiculed. England was garrisoned by Dutch troops, while every Englishman he could conscript was bundled off to Holland to fight in the hottest of his battles with the least reward. The first Mutiny Bill was passed, though by the efforts of the Tories it was only passed for a year:

and from that day to this, England has never been without a regular army under martial law. The old militia, whose discipline was maintained, and not so ill maintained, by the ordinary civil courts, fell beneath the displeasure of a would-be Continental conqueror. The Whigs, both Dutch and English, exulted in a return to standing armies and applauded the fruitless campaigns against France: the Tories, robbed of their safeguard against tyranny and of their beloved territorial army, could only bide their time.

The Whig passion for standing armies and French wars was justified, so far as it could be justified, by Chatham's success in the Seven Years War. The Great Deliverer in a lifetime had taken and lost and retaken a handful of fortified towns: the Great Commoner in a few campaigns secured India, America, Canada and the West Indies, and made us the richest and most powerful nation under the sun. By the end of George the Second's reign, the Whigs could at least point to practical results: but the Tories were unconvinced. They were the little Englanders of the day; they still opposed the estimates, and hated the sight of a red coat. Within a few days of his accession, George the Third was presented with a King's Speech for signature. He read it with approval till he came to a reference to the present "just and necessary" war. He struck out the adjectives: "bloody and expensive," he wrote. The Tories had come into their own.

With such a record, it was out of the question for the Whigs to criticise the French war. Violently Gallophobe, they had to make a sharp distinction between the American war and the French. The one was aggressive, and just as much a civil war as if it had been undertaken against Bristol instead of Boston. The other was defensive, and against our old and natural enemies. To fight the French war with any hope of success, it was essential to stop the American war that instant. The Whigs were on strong ground again: here was their chance.

Fox, coming into the Whig party with a fresh mind, accepted the prejudice against the Bourbons red hot, fond as he was of French culture and Parisian life. He rose to the occasion superbly. "Attack France," he cried, "for she is your object. The nature of the war with her is quite different. The war against America is against your own countrymen: that against France is against your inveterate enemy and rival. Every blow you strike in America is against yourselves, even though you should be able, which you never will be, to force them to submit: every stroke against France is of advantage to you. The more you lower her scale, the more your own rises, and the more the Americans will be detached from her as useless to them. Even your victories over America are favourable to France, from what they cost you in men and money: your victories over France will be felt by her ally. America must be conquered in France: France never can be conquered in America."

With this splendid outburst of authentic patriotism, Fox cast off at the same time the prejudice against the militia and the navy, which had been the cause of so much unpopularity and reproach against the Whigs. England was facing a grave risk of invasion, unprepared: a crisis unthinkable while Chatham was in power. The country was swept with sudden alarm and enthusiasm. The greatest living soldier and the greatest living sailor, Amherst and Keppel, had both flatly refused to serve against the Americans, in company with whom they had won their fame. On the outbreak of war with France, Amherst took the home command, and Keppel accepted the grand fleet. The country at last had its heart in the war: the King was cheered instead of hissed when he appeared. In all this the Whigs played their part, for which they had been prepared by Fox's demand as early as February of 1777 that the militia should be called out. Grafton, Richmond and Devonshire abandoned political life for the militia camps. London was full of uniforms. Sheridan wrote *The Camp*. Johnson slept under canvas. Mr. Tasker inscribed his little-known *Ode to the Warlike Genius of Britain*, in which he made his genius feminine: which being pointed out to him—"Palpable, Sir (cried the enthusiast); I know it. But (in a lower tone) it was to pay a compliment to the Duchess of Devonshire, with which Her Grace was pleased. She is walking across Cox Heath, in the military uniform, and I suppose her to be the Genius of Britain. . . ." It was time for a wise man to forget his politics.

CHAPTER NINE

1. The Keppel Trial, 1778-1779

One uniquely discreditable feature of the American War was the friction between the fighting services and the executive ministries. With an attainted coward at the War Office, and an army asked to fight against Englishmen with whom they had fought shoulder to shoulder twelve years back, perfect harmony could hardly be expected. Amherst refused to serve; Carleton in Canada was not on speaking terms with Germaine; Cornwallis risked his career at Westminster as gladly as he risked his life in America; Burgoyne and Howe both served under protest; and when Burgoyne was brought back to England to face an inquiry obviously designed to save Germaine's face, Howe threw up his command as well, loudly declaring that his honour was not safe in the hands of the Secretary for War.

General Howe had a brother, Admiral Lord Howe, who was commanding the fleet in American waters. At the outbreak of war with France, the Toulon fleet set out for America, while the Brest fleet continued its preparations for invading England. Lord Howe was not informed by the Admiralty of the departure of the Toulon fleet, of which he was totally unaware until they hove into sight off Sandy Hook. Not without reason, Lord Howe decided that his honour was unsafe in the hands of the First Lord of the Admiralty, and joined his brother in England.

Fox had made endless political capital out of the Burgoyne inquiry, conducting his friend's defence in a most damaging way. In 1778, a parallel case arose in the navy, which gave Fox the chance of adding another personal enemy to Germaine. Lord Sandwich, at the Admiralty, was a credit to no government. He was the very man to whom Wilkes had thought fit to confide the bawdiest morsels of his *Essay on Woman*, the very man who had signalised his horror of that performance by having it filched from Wilkes' rooms and read aloud to the House of Lords, an action by which he had earned the nickname of Jemmy Twitcher. This cold and arrogant man had won the King's confidence by an appearance of ability, a confidence he soon betrayed. He had managed the navy well enough in peace-time, but for war he was entirely unfit. Having let the Toulon fleet cross the Atlantic without informing our admiral in those waters, he then neglected to inform himself of the strength of the Brest fleet. Admiral Keppel, who had consented to command so long as it was against the French, sailed with twenty ships of the line to meet what he was told was a fleet of seventeen. Meeting the French fleet, he found that instead of seventeen they had thirty-two sail of the line and a more than proportionate superiority in frigates. After a hasty return for reinforcements, Keppel engaged the French off Ushant, and fought an indecisive action, which would have been victorious but for a very unexpected miscarriage. Sir Hugh Palliser, commanding his rear, deliberately and openly disobeyed a signal; the French fleet were in retreat and Palliser refused to chase them. The fleet returned and London buzzed with the extraordinary story. Palliser, in danger of disgrace, decided that attack was the best form of defence, and started attacking Keppel's conduct of the battle in the press; and finally, having prepared the ground, applied to the Admiralty that Keppel should be court-martialled. Now Palliser was a Tory M.P., and Keppel was not merely a Whig, but belonged to that innermost circle of the Whig aristocracy, whose forebears had come over to England with William (the Third). Sandwich, not in the least put out by the precedent of a sub-ordinate officer denouncing his admiral, decided in his swash-buckling way that here was a godsent chance of discrediting a Whig grandee, and getting back on the party who had shot Admiral Byng for political motives. He granted the court-martial with alacrity.

For the first time since the Irish Absentee Tax the Whig patricians showed signs of animation at the prospect of one of themselves being tried for his life. Five dukes and unnumbered lesser lights went down to Portsmouth for the trial, and so raised the cost of living in the town that the unhappy naval men were almost ruined. Dunning, Chatham's brilliant Solicitor-General, conducted the defence, and led an even better advocate in Erskine, who was to figure largely in the history of Fox's party. At first it was difficult to find any naval men who were prepared to sit in judgment on their admiral: while the common sailors made no pretence of impartiality—Keppel was the hero of the day. As soon as it came out that all mention of the disobeyed signals had been torn out of the log books of Palliser's ship, the prosecution collapsed. The court found that the charge against Keppel was malicious and ill-founded.

Keppel's trial had been watched by the whole nation. If there was one man the common people hated it was the ruffianly earl who had peached on their favourite Wilkes: if there was one man they loved, it was the gallant admiral whose image still swings outside a thousand public-houses. The news of his acquittal was celebrated as the acquittal of the Seven Bishops had been celebrated. Shiploads of Pallisers were burnt in effigy: and England over, the night of February the 11th was turned into day. The Whigs came pelting back to London: it was a bumper night for Mr. Brooks. Just before dawn, Fox, Lord Derby, and a Major Stanley sailed forth from Brooks's into the midst of a window-breaking crowd, among whom they found a drunk Tory duke throwing stones with the best. Led by this imposing quartette, the crowd made their way to the Admiralty, forced the gates and broke the windows, while "Lord Sandwich, exceedingly terrified, escaped through the garden with his mistress, Miss Ray, to the Horse Guards, and there betrayed most manifest panic."

Fox had wagered that Sandwich would not survive Keppel's court-martial a month, and he was not so far from winning. Just under a month later, he moved a vote of censure on the conduct of the Admiralty. The division was terrific: 204 to 170. The government majority of 34, in a full House, was a number Fox would have been thankful to muster in the opposition lobby a couple of years before. He then gave notice of a personal vote of censure on Lord Sandwich.

Here fate intervened. One night in April poor Miss Ray was shot dead at Covent Garden Theatre by a clergyman whose advances she had spurned. There was a trial, and a tedious scandal as the whole story of the First Lady of the Admiralty came to light. Sandwich's distress was unfeigned. The House of Commons felt that this was not the time, nor Fox the man, to censure him: the second motion fell flat.

2. Danger of Invasion, 1779

From the time of the Keppel trial onwards, Fox had the Admiralty on his hands as well as the War Office. Inquiries into the state of the navy and motions to remove Palliser from Greenwich Hospital followed each other thick and fast, and were tolerably sure of a hundred and fifty votes. By the end of the session Fox's was a name to conjure with among the navy, for in this war as in no other, to be really popular with the services it was necessary to be a member of the opposition.

By the end of the session, moreover, the navy needed what encouragement they could get, since so little was to be had from Whitehall. Spain had joined France against us in accordance with the Family Compact, and the combined fleet of both countries was approaching our shores. Sixty-six sail of the line appeared off Plymouth, while 50,000 troops and 400 transports waited to follow them up: the position of this country was that the channel fleet comprised only thirty-five sail of the line, while in all England there were no more than 10,000 regular troops to supplement the not excessively formidable militia. In the middle of August the situation was momentarily saved by a violent gale which blew the new armada out to sea. Before it could return, Fox, whose friends were mostly busy in their various counties drilling militia, had rushed down to Torbay to be in the thick of the excitement. "The fleet was a most magnificent sight. . . . Faith, when one looks at it and thinks there is a possibility of its coming to action in a day or two, *on se sent ému beaucoup*. If some things were otherwise at home and the fleet was commanded by Keppel, one should feel very eager indeed; when even in the present damned state of things, who cannot help feeling something at the sight of it?" The combined fleet did return, though a virulent epidemic of small-pox on board again forced it to retire. But the lesson of what he had seen was not lost on Fox. "Between this and next campaign there is time for increasing the navy incredibly, or for, what would be much better, making a peace which we should dare to do, and these poor devils dare not."

So wrote a pacifist of no ordinary discernment.

3. The Economical Reform Movement, 1779-1780

The opposition had been attacking the war for five solid years, without any better vote than their 170 against Sandwich, when in the last month of 1779 they discovered a new tunnel through which to mine the government, and one which promised well. The discovery was Burke's. Ever since the secession Burke had been speaking less than his wont in Parliament: he had been more at home, conducting an immense correspondence, looking after the affairs of Bristol, and keeping his ear very close to the ground. So little was public opinion studied or regarded by the old-fashioned Whigs, that they found with surprise that the war was unpopular, less because of its infraction of the first principles of statesmanship than because of its cost. The common herd thought little of drawing up an indictment against a whole people, but they did object to dear beer, and traced its dearness to the actual cause. This original discovery in the realm of public opinion was exploited by Burke to its full implications.

The public had a strong case. They paid the taxes, and out of those taxes came not only the reasonable cost of a war of which they disapproved, but the immense profits of the Paymaster and of the Treasurer of the Navy, the profits on contracts given to government supporters for war supplies which were not too closely checked either as to quantity or quality, the premiums of 10 or 12 per cent. on government loans which were allotted privately to government supporters instead of by tender, and a hundred other forms of bribery. Moreover, the King was granted a lavish civil list, which the public would have been delighted to see him spend as his predecessors had spent theirs, on palaces and mistresses: instead of which it was notorious that he stinted his breakfasts and went without fires in order to buy up rotten boroughs at from £5,000 to £10,000 a time, and was constantly asking Parliament to pay his debts even at that.

How efficaciously this money was spent it needs only one simple squalid instance to point out. Gibbon, having voted for four years against his country's interests, had finally summoned up moral courage enough to vote for Fox's motions of February, 1778, against sending any more regular troops to America, and enhanced this noble deed with the sentiment that North, whom he had supported so long through thick and thin, was undeserving of "pardon for the past, applause for the present, or confidence for the future." This swagger was short-lived. His solitary act of rebellion had given him a price. As Fox put it:

> "King George in a fright
> Lest Gibbon should write
> The story of Britain's disgrace,
> Thought no way so sure
> His pen to secure
> As to give the historian a place."

Not only his pen, but his vote, was secured by a seat at the Board of Trade, which never met. The pay was £800 a year: the duties, as Gibbon sniggers, "not intolerably severe." Henceforward he did for cash what he had previously done for lack of better lights.

It was clear that here was a prime example of a vicious circle. The war created contracts: the contracts bought votes for the war. The war created loans, on a market where the stocks had fallen from 89 to 54: the allotment of those loans at a gratuitous discount bought votes for the war. The war created jobs, whose recipients voted for the war. The public might elect whom they pleased: while the war lasted there would be a dozen ways of buying their representatives. The machinery of corruption was even in peace time a formidable structure: in time of war it was almost irresistible.

There were two ways to break this vicious circle; either the reform of Parliament or what Burke called "economical reform." The one was a radical, a casual reform. Cornwall would lose her forty-four members, Manchester and Birmingham would get them: the suffrage would be widened: the responsibility of members would be tightened up by triennial, or even annual, elections. The other remedy was ramal, a reform of effects. According to Burke's plan, 39 jobs in the Commons, and 11 in the Lords would be abolished: public contractors would be prohibited from sitting in the House: and revenue officers, 11,500 of them, all under government's mercy, who turned the scale in seventy constituencies, would be disqualified from voting at elections.

Here was a disagreement at the outset. Burke and the Rockinghams wished to perpetuate the bad old system of election: they wanted to keep the rotten boroughs in their own pockets, and to stop the King from buying up more boroughs than they could afford: they wanted to see to it that their nominees in Parliament, elected at so much expense to themselves, were not subsequently bought out of the Treasury's bottomless purse. They only hated corruption in so far as it competed with their own resources: so they went for economical reform. Shelburne, on the other hand, hated corruption under any guise. Years past, his master, Chatham, had propounded the germinal idea of parliamentary reform, though he had his own way of putting it. "Allow a speculator in a great chair," he wrote, "to add that a plan for more equal representation, by additional Knights of the Shire, seems highly reasonable." Shelburne had followed that illustrious lead.

Fox was in agreement with Shelburne: so was Richmond. Ultimately Richmond sickened of the Rockinghams and joined Shelburne: but Fox was still, now and always, kept apart by his petty and tragic personal prejudice.

Crippled at the start by this lameness in one leg, the Whig party set out on the first popular political campaign this country ever saw, and the last until the Reform Bill agitation. On December the 29th, 1779, a great meeting was held at York of the freeholders of the county, where a stringent petition was agreed to, calling upon the Commons "to inquire into and correct the gross abuses in the expenditure of public money." This was a most heartening event: but it struck panic into Lord Rockingham. The meeting was respectable in the extreme, summoned officially according to ancient practice by the sheriffs: it was held in a town that virtually belonged to Lord Rockingham; it was attended by a body of Whig grandees who could have paid the civil list annually out of their own pockets: and it had passed a resolution unexceptionable even by Rockingham's self-interested standards. Yet such was his incorrigible flabbiness that he wrote to Shelburne, of all men the least likely to be fussed by such misgivings, that he greatly feared that "discretion and correctness had not predominated."

Though the old Whigs might tremble at the movement they had set on foot, the country took it up with fervour. In county after county meetings were summoned according to the same forms to pass the same resolution: an association was formed to keep it alive: and we find, with delight, Fox going down to Shelburne's own county, and from the same platform as Shelburne, telling an ecstatic audience at Devizes that they were the first uncorrupt assembly he had ever had the honour of addressing.

The movement gained impetus every day. By the time Parliament met it was country-wide, and still proceeding from strength to strength. On February the 2nd, 1780, only thirty-five days after the Yorkshire meeting, Fox presided over a meeting in Westminster Hall, again officially summoned by the Sheriffs, of 3,000 Westminster electors. Portland and Burke supported him; but the principal attraction of the day was the presence of no other than Wilkes. Middlesex and Westminster were two of the very few constituencies which then had freehold suffrage; the member for Middlesex now had the pleasure of seeing his old antagonist rouse the audience to such enthusiasm that they chose him as candidate for Westminster then and there.

Six days later, in Parliament, Fox supported the Yorkshire petition, in a speech of exquisite wit. "I will put the controversy between the ministry and gentlemen on this side of the House, on the same issue on which the wisest of men, Solomon, rested the determination of the dispute between the two women, each of whom claimed the living child. We say to ministry, you misapply the public money—nay, you do worse, you apply it to bad purposes. Ministry say to us, you want our places; and thus the charge of corruption is given and retorted. Come now, let us see whose child Corruption is. Opposition are willing, are desirous, that it should be sacrificed: ministry have often made similar professions. The time is come to prove the sincerity of both. See who will now acknowledge, see who will father this dear but denied child, Corruption."

Three days after that speech, the House of Commons had another feast of wit on the same theme. Burke introduced his plan for the Better Security of the Independence of Parliament and the Economical Reformation of the Civil and Other Establishments, on which, as on the Yorkshire petition, ministers thought it best not to take a division.

All through February the government was in full retreat. On a motion to lay the Pension List on the table they had a majority of two. Burke's plan, served up as an Establishment Bill, got its second reading unchallenged, and started off swimmingly in committee, where the Board of Trade was voted away by eighty votes, to Gibbon's horror, after Burke had kept the committee in roars of laughter for a solid day. A Bill for disqualifying contractors was accepted. An obsolete Accounts Commission was revived.

Inside the government there were signs of disintegration. The Bedford party, still its backbone, was rent with quarrels: one member had resigned, another was dismissed. Wedderburn, horrified to find his recent friends gaining so fast on his new friends, began to negotiate for a safe refuge as Lord Chief Justice. Most extraordinary of all, North appears to have sought a clandestine meeting with Fox. Why when they met every day in the House, they should have chosen to confer behind the scenes of the Haymarket Theatre, accompanied only by two of the greatest gossips in town, is hard to say. But according to more than one witness, North, Fox, Brummell (North's secretary and the Beau's father), and a successful young playwright friend of Fox's called Sheridan, did meet there in the early days of April. Possibly it was a duel—shots rang through the theatre—Sheridan acted for once as a second: more probably it was a green-room party after a performance of Sheridan's latest recruiting play. At all events, they met, and the town talked.

Finally, after two months of rising fortunes, the Whigs scored a crowning victory on April the 6th. That morning, Fox had another meeting in Westminster Hall, which overflowed into Palace Yard: he came out strongly in favour of annual parliaments and an additional hundred members for the unrepresented towns. Meanwhile, inside the House, Dunning, the principal lawyer of the party since Wedderburn went, and a follower of Shelburne, opened the historic motion "That the influence of the Crown has increased, is increasing, and ought to be diminished," which was carried by 233 votes to 215.

Never has an opposition beaten down heavier odds. The work of six years had culminated in a downright defeat of government on a crucial debate. Two hundred votes had been added to what used to be the minority's strength. Everyone knew who had contributed most to that result. But Fox was found wanting when the victory was won. It is hard to blame him, but off he went to Newmarket. He was worn out. "Though I like the House of Commons itself," he said, "I hate the preparatory business of looking at accounts, drawing motions, etc., as much as you could do." Which, seeing he was writing to Fitzpatrick, the embodiment of lethargy, was saying a lot. "No wonder," said Burke, "that my friend Charles is so often more vigorous than I in the House, for when I call upon him in my way thither, jaded by the occupations of the day, there he is, just out of bed, breakfasting at three o'clock, fresh and unexhausted for the contentions of the evening." Though he claimed to have spoken for two sessions on every night but one, he was still inclined to wish for the palm without the dust.

The opposition tide ebbed from this moment. As luck would have it, the Speaker got the gout, and the House adjourned at a critical moment. The Court got busy with the recalcitrants: they defeated the Contractor's Bill in the Lords: the Establishment Bill began to make heavy weather in committee and was abandoned. Finally, to complete the series of reverses, the Whig dissensions on parliamentary reform, which had been kept silent so far, broke out into open squabbling. A section of the party, encouraged by their recent success in lopping off some of the branches of corruption, began to wish to pull it up by the roots. "I am sorry," wrote Burke, "that the committee turned their thought towards a change in the constitution, rather than to the correction of it in the form in which it now stands." A bill being brought in for triennial Parliaments, Burke declared strongly against it, and Fox supported it: the result being a two to one defeat. The movement was thus declining of its own accord, by bad luck and by the intransigence of one-half of its supporters, when it was killed dead by one of the most extraordinary calamities of the century.

4. The Gordon Riots, 1780

For some time past there had been a growing feeling in Parliament, a feeling wholly divorced from party divisions, in favour of the relief of Catholics from their disabilities under old and scandalous laws. An Act to that end had passed two years before, supported, according to Burke, by "the whole House of Commons, the whole House of Lords, the whole bench of bishops, the King, the ministry, the opposition, all the distinguished clergy of the establishment, all the eminent lights of the dissenting churches." But there was one man, and a member of Parliament at that, who was irreconcilable to any measure of toleration, though it might have passed the synod of the saints.

Lord George Gordon, the Kensit of his day, was well enough

versed in black arts to know that among the ignorant and the superstitious he could create a panic by calling out "Popery!" as easily as in a theatre by calling out "Fire!" It had happened so often before, with Titus Oates, with Irish Night: it can happen still. It happened in June, 1780. From the 2nd till the 9th, this maniac held London in his power. Like a Thames flood, the population of the miserable quarters to the east rolled up into London, filled with blind panic by a word. Drink completed what Protestant fervour had begun. The chapels of the Catholic ambassadors were burnt: the Houses of Parliament were threatened: while Newgate was in flames and the Bank was standing a regular siege, Alderman Wilkes sat in the Mansion House and broadcast warrants. The houses of the opposition leaders were particularly marked out for destruction: Fox and Fitzpatrick spent their time fingering muskets in Lord Rockingham's hall. The constabulary broke down entirely: the Guards contented themselves with digging trenches in Hyde Park. The only branch of the executive power to distinguish itself in the least was the King: by his good sense and moderation, the tide was stemmed and finally rolled back, with three hundred deaths and untold damage in its wake.

If the government had been disgraced by their incapacity to cope with the riots, they were immensely fortified by the terror and disgust of law-abiding citizens, and the fine behaviour of the King.

The Gordon riots had various results. Wedderburn began his career as Lord Chief Justice by sending twenty-nine of the rioters, mostly children, to the gallows. Gordon was charged with treason and acquitted, and, after a flirtation with Methodism, turned Jew. The Ministerial press spread the story that the whole thing had been financed by the opposition. Others affirmed that Burke was really a Jesuit. A golden opportunity was provided for a general election on the crest of the reaction. All parties distinguished themselves equally by an absolute refusal to go back on the repeal of the penal laws: but for the second time in two years the progress of the opposition had been cut across by a national issue on which their attitude was suspect. The stars in their courses seemed to fight against Fox.

His private correspondence during these years displays a chastened but still an undaunted determination. "People flatter me that I continue to gain, rather than lose, my credit as an orator; and I am so convinced that this is all I ever shall gain (unless I choose to become the meanest of men), that I never think of any other object of ambition. I am certainly ambitious by nature, but I really have, or think I have, totally subdued that passion. . . . Great reputation I think may acquire and keep, great situation I never can acquire, nor, if acquired, keep without making sacrifices that I never will make." That is the frame of mind in which public men make their greatest strides, a frame of mind in which they gain the respect of Parliament and the confidence of the people. English politics have remained to a large extent patrician, only because this blend of self-confidence and resignation is seldom found except in men who have great private positions to fall back upon when politics fail them. It is the poise of a Grey or a Cavendish. If Fox could have held that course his story would have been far different.

CHAPTER TEN

1. *The Whigs Despair, 1780*

It was one of the maxims of the Leicester House school of politics always to negotiate with the opposition when they were down, both in order to damp any incipient pride in the majority, and to extort humiliating terms from the minority. July, 1780, was a well-chosen moment for such overtures. The opposition's progress had been arrested by the Gordon riots: the No Popery scare had suddenly fastened on the Whigs for its victims. The King took his opportunity of laying a trap in front of Lord Rockingham's feet, and into it Rockingham fell, head over heels. An insincere proposal for a comprehensive ministry was put before the Whigs, and from their reactions the King was able to take the exact measure of their strength and of their solidarity.

First, as to the men Rockingham proposed to bring into the suggested coalition. Fox was on the list: but the King was cynical about him. "As to Mr. Fox, if any lucrative, not ministerial office can be pointed out for him, provided he will support the measures of government, I shall not object to the proposition, he never having had any principle can certainly act as his interest may guide him." Burke was on the list; "a real acquisition," said the King. Keppel was on the list, and Fox's friend Townshend. And there was the inevitable tail of Whig dukes: Richmond, whom the King would not accept owing to his radicalism; Portland, a nonentity after the King's heart; and Manchester, a figure of unfathomable obscurity, though doubtless of great wealth. Such was Rockingham's proposal. Nothing was said about including Shelburne. Only two years before, Shelburne, at a moment when opposition was strong, had refused to come in without Rockingham: now when opposition had never been weaker, Rockingham proposed to come in without Shelburne, or even one of Shelburne's followers. Not a word about Dunning or Barré, those stalwarts of debate: not a word about Grafton or Camden. The whole of the Shelburne section of the Whigs was excluded, and excluded in favour of such men as Portland and Manchester. That was Rockingham's idea of statesmanship to come into office with a compact family party; and his idea of gratitude, to veto the man who (to his cost) had refused to veto him.

So much for the personnel: the policy propounded by Lord Rockingham was more extraordinary still. As a first condition, Sandwich was to leave the Government: nobody else, not even Germaine. How this troupe of little-known dukes was to be accommodated without displacing anyone but the First Lord, was not suggested: all that is certain is that he was to go, because Keppel was to come in. Some—an unspecified proportion—of Burke's proposals for economical reform were to be passed: a condition which delighted the King by its vagueness. Parliamentary reform, of course, was to be shelved. But the most important stipulation was in connection with the war.

In March, 1778, when Chatham was urgently needed at the head of affairs, and could more or less make his own terms, the Rockinghams had prevented him from coming in by their insistence on the policy of declaring America independent, without either attempting to reclaim her, or extorting any concession in return for recognition. Now, in July, 1780, the Rockinghams, hoping to shuffle into the government without any of Chatham's disciples, entirely jettisoned the very scruples to which Chatham had been sacrificed. Chatham had risked much to bring Rockingham in, but Rockingham risked even more to keep Shelburne out. The independence of America was *not* to be recognised: the troops so urgently needed on this side of the Atlantic were *not* to be withdrawn from the other. Everything for which Fox and Burke had fought for six years was to be thrown overboard in order that one ministerial earl might give way to three Whig dukes. That was the unblushing proposal of Lord Rockingham: if his virtues were his arts, he cannot pass for a very artful man.

The King's purpose was served as soon as the negotiations had revealed this abject surrender among the higher ranks of the Whig party. A body of men so downcast as to offer to come in at the expense of all their vaunted honour, could hardly constitute a very formidable opposition, still less a very powerful accession to the ministry. Having gauged the full weakness of his enemies' forces, the King withdrew his flag of truce, and proceeded to dissolve Parliament. There is a story of George the Third looking at a list of the British commanders in America, and remarking that whatever the enemy might feel about such a list of names, they made *him* tremble. Fox might have said the same of his own party leaders. In estimating Fox's achievement between 1774 and 1782, it would be doing him an injustice to forget that the official leader of the Whigs during all those years was a man so stupid as not to know when he was doing a disingenuous thing.

The election was a foregone conclusion. In some places the Whigs were denounced for having truckled to the papists: in others for having instigated the anti-papist riots. Everywhere the terrified electorate, equally afraid of the riots and of the concessions which had provoked the riots, voted for the existing powers. That was how Burke lost Bristol, and had to retire to a pocket borough of Lord Rockingham's. At Westminster the King spent £8,000 to keep Fox out; but he was elected, with Admiral Rodney as his senior member. Most important of all, William Pitt, having failed for the University of Cambridge, was presented with a seat at Appleby by the very Sir James Lowther who had tried to increase his vast electoral influence at the expense of Portland. Altogether, the ministerial majority was virtually unimpaired at about 70: but the contest had cost the King some £80,000. As he was never tired of remarking in later years, he got poor value for his money. The 1780 Parliament lived four years, but saw enough vicissitudes for forty.

2. Financial Interlude, 1781

"My old game faro, is lately revived," writes Horace Walpole and, needless to say, it was Fox who had revived it. "Mr. Fox is the first figure in Parliament, at the gaming table, at Newmarket. Last week he passed twenty-four hours without interruption at all there." But his extravagances nowadays, after his father had been dead six years, were harder than ever to support: we read of his "having levanted every soul at Newmarket," and that "he has not now, nor has had for some time, one guinea, and is happier on that account." His health suffered as well as his finances: towards the end of 1780 he was seriously ill, and had to go to Bath for "waters and regularity": but when he told Selwyn that he was living with the regularity of clockwork, all Selwyn said was "Tick tick, tick."

One night at White's he announced that he had found a way to make good. He was going to embark on "a kind of itinerant trade, which was to go from horse-race to horse-race, and so, by knowing the value and speed of all the horses in England, to acquire a certain fortune." An intrinsic lack of originality about this proposition somehow brought it to grief, though he pursued it so far as to achieve the reputation of being the best handicapper in the south of England. His bets were often good bets, but they were always much too large, and he appeared to think that Whig horses were necessarily faster than those that belonged to Tories: his own horses were often good horses, but he had far too many, and the best of them were apt to be seized by his creditors.

It was to retrieve this situation that Fox opened a faro bank at Brooks's in the spring of 1781. Most of his contemporaries, when their losses pressed too hard, were in the habit of laying enormous wagers that they would not bet again for a stated length of time. Fox had an even more drastic method: he exchanged the role of punter for that of banker, and with Fitzpatrick and Lord Robert Spencer as partners and Brooks as financial backer, he flew at higher game. And, what is more, he had a considerable success. In May, Selwyn met him "in a new hat, frock, waistcoat, shirt, and stockings; he was as clean and smug as a gentleman, and upon perceiving my surprise, he told me that it was from the Pharo bank." When Fox sported clean linen, the whole world knew that his luck must have turned. "His success at faro has awakened his host of creditors; but unless his bank had swelled to the size of the Bank of England, it could not have yielded a sop apiece for each." He was sold up: his furniture—"such furniture I never saw"—was hauled out into St. James's Street by the bailiffs: his library was sold including a presentation copy of Gibbon with some venomous remarks about the author on the title-page. But still the Pharo bank went on winning. Most of his books were bought in: his horses were re-entered in Lord Derby's name: his rooms were not merely re-furnished, but actually cleaned. "Charles, from paying his debts, proceeds to make presents; he is now quite *magnifique avec une abondance de richesses.*"

The fame of these transactions spread far beyond Brooks's. From the other side of St. James's Street one can get quite a good view into the Subscription Room on the first floor, and the spectacle of the Man of the People acting as a croupier to a circle of gullible young peers until far into the night was not a spectacle his Westminster constituents could resist. "The Pharo bank is held in a manner which, being so exposed to the public view, bids defiance to all decency and police. The Opposition, who have Charles for their ablest advocate, is quite ashamed of the proceeding, and hates to hear it mentioned." So it went on for nearly the whole of the year. It was a curious occupation for a man on the threshold of high office, but it seems to have left Fox and Fitzpatrick comparatively solvent. Spencer, who started from scratch, bought a large country house on the proceeds.

3. *William Pitt, 1781*

In February of 1781 Burke reintroduced the proposals for reforming the civil list, which had met with so much success in February of 1780. On that occasion they had not even been challenged: now they were defeated by 43. But the setback in numbers was more than compensated by two maiden speeches, which showed the opposition that the general election had not been held in vain. Sheridan was known to the whole House as a man of thirty who had already written some of the best comedies in the language: but his presence in the House was felt to be an intrusion on aristocratic preserves, and his maiden speech was marred by the effort not to sound like an actor's son or a singer's husband. It was very much otherwise with Pitt. Pitt was the House of Commons' adopted child. His father, who held the Commons in the palm of his hand, had educated Pitt to the solitary aim of achieving the same mastery. An orator almost in the nursery, the young man had never cherished a moment's ambition apart from the Commons. He entered it at twenty-one, and spoke after six months, amid the breathless expectation of a crowded assembly. He did not disappoint them: his speech, strong in favour of Burke's reforms, was the speech of Chatham's son in every word. "He is not a chip of the old block," said Burke, not perhaps very happily, "he is the old block itself." Others "doubted whether he would not prove himself superior even to Charles Fox." Fox had rushed up to congratulate him in his fervid way when an old member remarked that he hoped to live to see the two of them battling away at each other as he had seen their fathers before them. "I have no doubt," said Pitt, "you hope to attain the age of Methuselah." In token of this new and indissoluble alliance between the sons of Chatham and Holland, Pitt was elected on Fox's nomination to be a member of Brooks's.

Fox was just ten years senior to Pitt. Thirteen years before, when Fox had been rollicking about the Continent, Lady Holland had written a letter to her husband full of implied reproach of the methods adopted for the education of her son. "I have been this morning with Lady Hester Pitt, and there is little William Pitt, *not eight years old*, and really the cleverest child I ever saw, and *brought up so strictly and so proper in his behaviour*, that, *mark my words*, that little boy will be a thorn in Charles's side as long as he lives." If Lord Holland had needed any inducement to continue to demoralise his son, he would have been encouraged by the thought that Lord Chatham's son was being brought up in the opposite way. Charles continued to do exactly as he pleased; William continued his course of strict and proper behaviour. The time had come to mark Lady Holland's words.

Sheridan, elected to Brooks's at the same time, found there his spiritual home, a paradise of wine, talk and high play. Pitt seldom if ever visited the place. Faro banks and betting books had no place in Pitt's scheme of life: hard work in Parliament and hard work at the bar were his youthful dissipations. He was no prig: he loved wine as much as he loved work, and cared as little for money as for women. But to be tarred with Fox's brush, to be associated in the public mind with Fox's hard-living cronies, was not his notion of an auspicious outset to a great career. As between the Rockingham and the Shelburne sections of the Whig party, he belonged to the latter, both by descent, as the disciple of his father's disciple, and by inclination. He had no use for Rockingham's position and wealth: he had great respect for Shelburne's intellect and seriousness. And on the issue that Pitt put first of all, the issue of Parliamentary reform, the Rockinghams were selfishly opposed to him, and only Shelburne was sincere.

Pitt kept his own counsel. "He is at the head of half a dozen young people, and it is a corps separate from that of Charles's; so there is another Premier at the starting-post, who as yet has never been shaved." These young men constituted a club of their own, Goosetree's, where they could enjoy each other's talk without winning each other's money. Whether or not they consciously suspected that Fox was the wrong horse to back, they deliberately renounced the joys of his companionship which to most young Whigs was the only consolation for being in opposition. Agreeing on most policies, Goosetree's and Brooks's pointed different ways. Brooks's was the citadel of old-fashioned Whiggery—aristocratic, influential, hard-living, and totally indifferent to public opinion. Pitt's club was the nucleus of a party which based its hopes, not on bought constituencies and family solidarity, but on a reformed Parliament and a free expression of the popular will. It was Pitt who was slowly laying his foundations deep in public opinion: Fox might be the popular hero of the moment, but to Fox popularity was a thing to be won in a moment and lost the next, a gambling counter like everything else he had.

4. The Fall of North, 1781-1782

In October, 1781, almost all that remained of the British army in America surrendered to Washington at Yorktown. For the last three years our efforts had whittled down to a process described by the King as "distressing America," but after Yorktown, it was unlikely that we could continue to cause even much distress. As the City of London grimly put it in a remonstrance to the King: "Your armies are captured. The wonted superiority of your navies is annihilated. Your dominions are lost." The war, if it was to be maintained at all, could only be maintained on principle, without hope of success.

The news reached London just two days before the opening of Parliament, but the King's Speech made it quite clear that the war was to go on, and a furious debate ensued. The blame for the loss of Yorktown was about equally due to the Admiralty and the War Office, and, to Fox's delight, his old antagonists fell out with each other in violent recriminations. He declared that he would impeach Sandwich, and call Germaine as chief witness. He trusted that, by the aroused indignation and vengeance of an injured and undone people, ministers would hear of their misdeeds at the tribunal of justice, and expiate them on the public scaffold. He saw a learned gentleman smile at the word Scaffold. What! did not the learned gentleman think that it was *yet* time for punishment? Had they in his imagination not done *enough*, or had they *more* calamities to

inflict, *more* negligence to exemplify, *more* treachery to complete?
What was the learned gentleman's opinion? When did he think
the fit moment would arrive, when suffering would be supineness
and retribution be just?

The division was disappointing—a defeat by 89. But Fox's
vehemence had gone home. The ministerial garrison, apparently
impregnable from outside, began to wonder about the terms of
capitulation. Dundas, that very same learned gentleman who had
smiled uneasily at the word Scaffold, after one night's sleep upon
it, made a speech the next day in favour of the opposition.
Germaine himself, who had hitherto shown none of his "well-
known cowardice" in Parliament, began to think discretion the
better part of valour. He contrived to quarrel with North about
the appointment of a new commander-in-chief in America, and
carried his objection so far as to resign. The King insisted on his
having a peerage, so that "no one can then say he is disgraced,"
and so Germaine went to the Lords, in the teeth of a stiff protest
from his fellow-peers.

Germaine's pretext for resigning, and his promotion to the
peerage, deceived nobody. Germaine had gone, and everybody
knew it, because he was afraid of Fox and his threats. There was
some difficulty in finding a successor, and the office finally
devolved upon a hardened placeman, whose pliability and incompetence were a standing joke. The ministry faced Parliament after
the Christmas recess with an ugly gap in their ranks, clumsily
patched. The first stone of the arch had fallen.

With Germaine gone and his successor not worth attacking,
the full blast of Fox's fire was directed at Sandwich, who had just
committed another major blunder in sending out only twelve ships,
when more were available, to intercept a French fleet of nineteen
sail. This, coming on top of the Keppel episode and many others,
made an unanswerable case for Sandwich's removal. On the 24th
of January, 1782, Fox moved for a committee of the whole House
to inquire into the ill-success of the navy. The motion was accepted;
the committee sat. Fox presented an indictment of Sandwich that
took three hours to read, and moved, on the 7th of February, that
there had been gross mismanagement of His Majesty's naval
affairs in the year 1781. That motion was defeated only by 22 votes,
and Fox gave notice that he should move it again in the House,
and not in committee, so that it might be recorded in the journals.

Accordingly on February the 20th, he repeated his motion, and lost it this time by no more than 19.

Fox's attack on Sandwich was real beheading matter. When the Secretary for War had run away, and angry minorities were rising against the First Lord, the most faithful Tory wanted all his courage to stick to his post. It only needed a frontal attack, and success was certain. On the 22nd of February, a Whig of great respectability and moderation, General Conway, was put up to move an address to the King that the American War be no longer pursued for the impracticable purpose of reducing the inhabitants of that country to obedience by force. Fox suited his language exactly to the occasion. Ministers were in a panic, and Fox made their flesh creep. "He was glad to have discovered who the infernal spirit was that conducted all our mischiefs: it was a person higher than the noble lord, for the noble lord was only his puppet and acted as he was told." Ministers knew well enough how much use it would be to shift their responsibility on to the King when Fox was impeaching them in Westminster Hall: the irony was not lost on them: Conway's motion was defeated by one vote. This was equivalent, in the circumstances, to an actual victory: on the 27th a similar motion, moved by the same man, was carried by 19 votes, and a most unwelcome address from his faithful Commons sent up to the King.

For the next three weeks all was chaos. The King sent a tart and ambiguous answer to the Commons, and sent for the royal yacht to take him back to Hanover. North resigned several times a day, only to be told that he was never more badly needed than now, that the budget was not ready, that as *he* had borrowed the money *he* must introduce the taxes. The Lord Chancellor was sent on crafty missions to Shelburne and Rockingham. Pitt, now approaching his twenty-third birthday, surprised the House of Commons by announcing that, whatever arrangement might be made, he for one would never accept a subordinate position. The political underworld of Rigbys and Jenkinsons and Robinsons was in a frenzy of activity. And Fox was most active of all. The "black patriot" rushed about the Subscription Room at Brooks's, "giving audiences in every corner of the room," "closeted every instant with one or the other, so that he can neither punt nor deal for a quarter of an hour." Whatever befell, Fox was sure of a front place, for he had done more than any other ten men to overturn the ministry and to stop the war.

The ministry was already mortally wounded, but the opposition gave it a few more stabs in Parliament. On March the 8th, a stringent censure was lost by ten votes; another on the 15th by nine votes; a third was down for the 20th, but North forestalled the mover of it by announcing that the adminstration was at an end.

North was as blithe as a lark at his ultimate release from twelve years of servitude. It had not been an agreeable period for him, nor a creditable period in his country's history. Dr. Johnson, the stoutest of Tories, judged North's ministry on its results. "Such a bundle of imbecility never disgraced a country. If they sent a messenger into the City to take up a printer, the messenger was taken up instead of the printer, and committed by the sitting Alderman. If they sent one army to relieve another, the first army was defeated and taken before the second arrived." Incompetent they certainly were, but the real indictment against them is something more grave than that. North was misled by his well-meaning Toryism into regarding himself as the servant simply of the King. After the first two Georges had been used by the Whigs as the tools of a party, George the Third was enabled by North's pliability to reign almost as a Stuart. But in this country, the executive must always be responsible. If North was responsible (as he imagined) only to the King, then it was the King who was responsible to the people and their representatives. It followed that the King must be removable: and about 1780 it looked very much as though he would be removed.

Fox had stopped the American War. In doing so, he had arrested the last attempt in our history at arbitrary government— an attempt which was leading straight to the expulsion of the Hanoverians. He had vindicated the fundamental principle, which the impeachments of Danby and Somers had laid down, that no minister may ever shelter himself behind the royal prerogative. He had proved that "government without faction" was impossible. "In the conduct of a party," Gibbon had said, "he approved himself equal to the conduct of an empire." That remained to be seen.

CHAPTER ELEVEN

1. *Cabinet-Making, 1782*

The King's approaches to the opposition were made through the agency of his Lord Chancellor Thurlow, to whom he gave *carte blanche* to negotiate with any individuals he pleased, but not to negotiate with any organised group. A Whig administration was clearly unavoidable, but the King would not recognise the existence of what he called the Phalanx. He still clung forlornly to his tenet of "measures, not men": he still hoped to reconstruct his fabric of personal government on the jealousies and stupidities of the Whig leaders. With these instructions Thurlow first got into touch with three men who had left North's government—Grafton, Gower, and Weymouth. Getting little help from them, he then went to Shelburne, as the next least objectionable Whig leader: but Shelburne once again pointed out that the section of the Whig party led by himself was insignificant compared with Lord Rockinghham's following, and again deferred to the man who had tried to wriggle into office without him. "My lord," he said, "you could stand without me, but I could not stand without you."

Thurlow, thus reduced to treating with Rockingham, tried a stratagem which shows how little he thought of his intelligence. He asked Rockingham to come into office unconditionally, and brushed aside his terms, "treating them as inferior and subsequent considerations, to be settled after the formation of a ministry, and not as conditions of acceptance." This, as Walpole says, was a very silly device to have failed "though a man of so great talents was the messenger, and a man of so slender parts the receiver." It did fail, and Rockingham got his terms. They were the following: power to accede unconditionally to the independence of America; a large abolition of offices along the lines of Burke's plan; the bill for excluding government contractors from Parliament to pass; and the bill for disfranchising revenue officers to pass.

These were high terms to obtain, as to measures: as to men, the King had more of his own way. Clearly, most of the "phalanx" would come in, but, wherever he could, the King counterbalanced them with members of Lord Shelburne's party. The result was a government very evenly weighted. Rockingham was First Lord of the Treasury: Thurlow, as a concession to the King, remained Lord Chancellor. The Secretaries of State were Fox for Foreign, and Shelburne for Home Affairs. So far there were two members of the Phalanx to two outsiders: it is important to see how the other offices were apportioned. Shelburne got offices for both his followers in the Lords, Grafton and Camden; but he had less luck with his followers in the Commons. Dunning, who might have been Lord Chancellor fifteen years back, got a cabinet post, to the fury of the Rockingham party; but they had their revenge on Barré, to whom they refused to give the Paymastership, long promised and well deserved; while Pitt, to whom Shelburne wished to offer a cabinet post, they would not have on any terms; and Pitt would take nothing less. Against Shelburne's four, with whom Thurlow could be relied upon to vote, the Phalanx were five strong—Rockingham, Fox, Cavendish, Keppel, Richmond. But there was one other member of the cabinet who belonged neither to Shelburne nor to Rockingham: the new Commander-in-Chief. "That innocent man, General Conway," as Shelburne said, "never perceived that he had the casting vote of the cabinet."

The same bickering that went on inside the cabinet arose over the distribution of the minor offices. If the Rockinghams behaved meanly to Shelburne and his followers, whom they regarded as enemies, they behaved more meanly still towards the greatest of their own supporters. Burke was left outside the cabinet in the Pay Office. The Rockinghams were admittedly a hierarchical party, but this was carrying the aristocratic principle to monstrous lengths, to pass over a man who had been the motive force of the party when Fox was still at Oxford, a man without whom Fox would never have been tempted to join the party. Burke's claims were irresistible: the King himself admitted in 1780 that he would be a "real acquisition" to the cabinet. If the Rockinghams were outvoted in the cabinet, they had only themselves to blame for their childish jealousy towards the one man who was greater than them all.

2. Lord Shelburne, 1782

"I see," said Fox, when the cabinet was formed, the "administration is to consist of two parts, one belonging to the King, the other to the public." It was a groundless assumption. Thurlow, to be sure, belonged to the King: but it was ridiculous to insinuate such a thing of Shelburne, whose language about royal influence had been stronger than his own; or about Camden, the judge who incurred the King's undying resentment by acquitting Wilkes; or about Dunning, the mover of the resolution that the influence of the crown had increased, was increasing, and ought to be diminished.

Fox had made up his mind to dislike Shelburne, and succeeded disastrously in disliking him very much. It is worth while investigating whether there was any basis for this prejudice. Lord Holland had started the notion that Shelburne was radically dishonest, with his famous repartee about the "pious fraud": and the world greedily accepted this estimate. The King called him the Jesuit of Berkeley Square; the newspapers nicknamed him Malagrida; Horace Walpole said that he was as fond of insincerity as if he had been the inventor of it. He is invariably caricatured as a sinister and Machiavellian figure, admitting dark emissaries by secret doors to Lansdowne House, and creeping disguised to clandestine meetings with the enemies of his party or his country. Such was the legend, originated by Lord Holland, and accepted without question by Fox.

What was the reality? Shelburne was a great nobleman, who lived magnificently, and gave splendidly, on a fraction of his income. His ability was of the first order, and was matched by his industry. He was happily married to a sister of Richard Fitzpatrick's. Bowood and Lansdowne House were princely houses, and Shelburne filled them, not with fashionable gamesters and rakes, but with the first brains of the time. Price, a financial theorist second only to Adam Smith, was an inseparable companion: Priestley, the great scientist, was his librarian and his son's tutor: Bentham lived for years at one or other of his houses. All that was best worth patronising he patronised: he lived on terms of intellectual equality with the cleverest thinkers in science, in eonomics, in political theory. He maintained a regular intercourse with well-informed correspondents of many countries: he kept his own staff of clerks at Lansdowne House to analyse and examine the public accounts. He was a government department in himself; he knew more about the revenue than the Chancellor of the Exchequer, and more about diplomacy than the Foreign Secretary. He was armed at all points, a professional among amateurs.

His manner, at once insinuating and reserved, was partly responsible for his evil reputation. He was a little too anxious to please; he protested his candour overmuch; in a word, he was "smooth." Among the offhand young bloods of Brooks's he appeared incongruous and alarming. There was nothing he didn't know, except possibly the rules of faro. He would never have dreamt of laying fifty guineas on a card. When he should have been calculating odds and pedigrees, he was poring over the civil list arrears: he would be opening his private dispatches from Paris at an hour when Fox and Sheridan were half seas over. He was not a good fellow, not at all clubbable, always a little outside the pale. Brooks's regarded him rather as they would have regarded Peel or Gladstone descended in their midst: the higher ranks of the party, the Portlands and Rockinghams, regarded him as a boy who wins scholarships is regarded by boys who do not. Fitzpatrick was amused by the assiduity and distinction of his brother-in-law: Fox was openly and sullenly mistrustful.

Out of this cloud of jealousy and mistrust grew the legend of Shelburne's duplicity. So far in the story his honesty has been such as to put the Rockinghams to shame, and honest he remained to his dying day. Some historians have accepted and some have rejected the fashionable view: there was so much smoke that the fire has been taken on trust. To anyone whose first aim is to write a panegyric on Fox it must rank as a cardinal article of faith. But it does not happen to be true.

3. Retrenchment and Reform, 1782

The composition of the new government was only one of its handicaps. An even heavier disadvantage was the extravagant expectation with which it was awaited by the outside public. After twelve years of personal Government, the advent of the Whigs seemed like a millennium to all the worthy freeholders who had flocked to the county meetings. They had too many well-wishers possibly to succeed. Wonders were expected of them:

peace with America, France, Spain and Holland; reform both of the franchise and of the duration of Parliament; economical reform; and retribution on the Tories. It was a great deal to demand of a government divided by such crippling jealousies within itself.

Parliamentary reform was the most complete and final disappointment. No government with Rockingham at its head would initiate it, and Shelburne had too much prudence to press it after he had raised the matter in cabinet and been outvoted. But Pitt had no reason to love the Rockinghams, who had elbowed him out of their cabinet: to their great embarrassment he moved outright for a committee on the state of the representation. On this the Whigs were split from top to bottom. Fox prevailed on Burke, as the most violent enemy of reform, to stay away from the debate, but the motion was defeated all the same. That was the first major disappointment. It was followed the next week by a motion for shorter parliaments, when Fox failed to persuade Burke to hold his tongue. Burke "attacked W. Pitt in a scream of passion, and swore Parliament was and always had been precisely what it ought to be." Here was a mortifying situation, when that half of the government which preened itself on "belonging to the public" was directly opposed to the one reform the public most desired, while those whom they sneered at for "belonging to the King" had only to mention the matter in Parliament for Burke to rise like a fish.

Economical reform had a more successful, but a chequered, career. Shelburne thought it good policy to humour the King in small matters, and turned the blind eye to several sinecures. A very bad impression was created by the pensioning of Barré, who had long been promised the Pay Office. Barré was a pillar of the Shelburne party, and accordingly the Rockinghams were determined that he should not get the Pay Office: they were equally determined that Burke should have it, as the only post outside the cabinet that they had the face to offer him. But even the Rockinghams could not deny Barré any reward at all. He had sat in Parliament for twenty-one years, and had become a first-rate speaker; although he was one of Chatham's favourite officers, he was deprived of his regiment in 1763 for voting against the Court in a debate on Wilkes; he had been promised restitution by the Rockinghams, and, like Wilkes himself, had been betrayed when they came to power; he had had to wait another seventeen years to obtain justice. Though he was neither a duke nor a millionaire nor a Cavendish, the Rockinghams could scarcely ignore Barré's existence altogether. So while Burke became Paymaster, Barré was bought off with £3000 a year for life; the public realised that a Whig plant could be quite as expensive as a Tory plant.

Apart from these difficulties, a great deal of solid reform was achieved. The Contractors Bill was passed, in spite of a violent attack on it by the Chancellor from the Woolsack. The Revenue Officer's Bill was passed. A large part of Burke's plan became law, by which some forty jobs were abolished, and about £72,000 a year saved to the public. Finally, Burke justified his appointment to the Paymastership by reforming the Pay Office to the tune of £50,000 a year, more than half of it at the expense of his own legitimate emoluments.

The public expected, from Fox's language just before he came into power, that North would be impeached: North expected it also. Here again they were disappointed. Shelburne proposed it in cabinet, but again was outvoted. It was characteristic of him to propose it, and characteristic of the Rockinghams to quash it. He was a politician before he was a gentleman: they were gentlemen before they were politicians. But the public had been promised retribution: they had no liking for this loyalty among the upper classes.

Among this catalogue of lost causes one curious and irrelevant episode deserves a place as a beautiful example of the pitfalls that surround a young government. Admiral Rodney, who commanded in the West Indies, was at one and the same time a magnificent seaman, a popular hero, a Tory member of Parliament, and Fox's senior colleague in the representation of Westminster. But the Whigs had censured his conduct in allowing a West Indian island to be sacked: and when they came to power they recalled him. The rights of the question are not ascertainable, though a man of Keppel's honour was not likely to recall a fellow-admiral for nothing. Clearly, if the recall was necessary, it was courageous, for everything combined to make it appear like a mean partisan device, on a par with the Tories' treatment of Keppel. Fate had a nasty trick in store for the government. Five days before they decided on the recall, Rodney had won one of the great battles of naval history: a month later the news arrived and the

Tower guns were booming for the victory of the Saints. What were the cabinet to do? Every course was objectionable, and they chose the worst. They moved him a vote of thanks. They stuck to their supersession, and sent out a much inferior sailor, to whom the newspapers did not fail to insinuate that Fox owed money. And, worst of all, they made him a peer, in this way creating a by-election at Westminster at the moment most unfavourable to themselves. The affair is unimportant, but its combination of bad luck and bad management is typical of Fox's ministerial history.

4. Peace-Making, 1782

Far the most important of the government's undertakings was the conclusion of peace, which fell to that inharmonious couple, the Secretaries of State. This was where the hopes of the nation had been most confidently aroused, and where the administration must succeed or fall. Fox had always spoken as though he had a treaty in his pocket, as though only an imbecile could fail to end the war. Now came the unkind test of events.

Fox rose admirably to the duties of a departmental chief. After his first month in power, Walpole (who really knew about the Foreign Office) writes that "Mr. Fox already shines as greatly in place as he did in opposition. He is now as indefatigable as he was idle. He has perfect temper, and not only good humour, but good nature, and more common sense than any man, with amazing parts that are neither ostentatious nor affected." Again, after his ministry was over, he says that Fox "displayed such facility in comprehending and executing all business as charmed all who approached him. No formal affectation delayed any service or screened ignorance. He seized at once the important points of every affair, and every affair was thence reduced within a small compass, not to save himself trouble, for he at once gave himself up to the duties of his office. His good humour, frankness and sincerity pleased, and yet inspired a respect which he took no other pains to attract. The foreign ministers were in admiration of him: they had found few who understood foreign affairs, or who attended to them, and no man who understood French so well, or could explain himself in so few words." He never touched a card while he was in office, seldom if ever went into Brooks's, and is even said to have taken lessons in handwriting. If he failed, then, it was not through indolence or lack of grasp.

The Secretary of State's office had long been divided into a Northern and Southern Department. The Southern Department in the course of its development had come to cover what is now the Home Office and the Colonial Office; and Shelburne was accordingly Home, Irish, and Colonial Secretary. The Northern Department was what is now the Foreign Office; Fox was Foreign Secretary. From this arose a swarm of complications. Was America a colony or a foreign country? Its independence *de facto* was unquestionable: but did this entitle Fox to negotiate with its representatives? Again, was there to be a joint treaty with France and America, or two separate treaties signed by the respective Secretaries of State? It was a situation in which two men who trusted each other perfectly would have found it hard not to quarrel: and Fox mistrusted Shelburne so malignantly that Shelburne would have been more than human if he had not mistrusted Fox. "Shelburne is ridiculously jealous of my encroaching on his department," he complains, "and wishes very much to encroach on mine." Suspicions, complaints and accusations fill his correspondence. If Shelburne had been an angel of forbearance, he would have found it hard to work against such a querulous prejudice: and he was nothing of the kind: he was an impatient and contemptuous man, with an uncommonly sharp tongue.

Shelburne, moreover, had one incalculable advantage over Fox: he was not committed to American independence. In the spring of 1778, when a Chatham coalition was in the air, Shelburne had stood out against the clamour for the abandonment of America. He had done so because he visualised just such a situation as he now held, of negotiating with an America that was free in fact, but would make very great concessions to have its freedom recognised. Shelburne was the first free trader, and had set his heart on a commercial treaty with the new United States; he wanted to make sure that the loyalists were compensated and protected; he believed too that France was sufficiently interested in our recognition of America to moderate her Indian claims in return. All these were ponderable concessions that could be extorted in return for the recognition of independence and the abandonment of New York, which we still held. The Americans were distracted with party divisions; their armies were melting away; their government was rudimentary; either party would have bid high for an honourable settlement. Fox, on the other hand, could not stipulate for these advantages: his hands were tied: he was pledged to evacuate New York and to grant unconditional independence. This was another of the countless disadvantages of having attached himself to the wrong wing of the Whig party.

The first move in the negotiations was that Benjamin Franklin, then the American agent in Paris, wrote to Shelburne, who was a friend and a kindred spirit, to suggest a parley. Shelburne sent out a man after Franklin's heart, one Oswald, an intelligent Scotch merchant of great foreign experience. At the same time Fox sent a messenger to M. de Vergennes, the French minister. Fox's selection was equally characteristic—a smart twenty-six-year-old Guards officer of no experience at all, Tom Grenville. Oswald and Grenville were born to disagree: and the latter, as a son of the author of the Stamp Act, was not immoderately welcome to Benjamin Franklin.

It at once appeared that Fox was less anxious for peace than Shelburne. He held tenaciously to the old Whig theory that France was the inevitable enemy, and the Bourbons the curse of Europe. They had come into this war unprovoked, except by our vulnerability, and, unless they could be reduced to concluding a treaty on the lines of the 1763 treaty, Fox would prefer the war (against France alone) to go on. He was fortified in this resistance by finding from our ambassadors that he personally was extremely well thought of both by Catherine of Russia and Frederick of Prussia. Even George the Third was bound to admit that his relations with his great fellow-monarchs noticeably improved when Mr. Fox was in power. Fortified by the support of the Northern Powers, he put up a strong resistance to French pretensions, all the stronger after Rodney's victory of the Saints. Vergennes, who had expected to make a fool of this pacifist demagogue, groaned with vexation: "c'est un fagot d'épines que ce M. Fox."

From these complicated premises Fox came to have a strong position *vis-à-vis* France and a weak position *vis-à-vis* America. But his evil genius would not let him rest content until he had both negotiations in his own hands. He could not bear to leave Shelburne the American treaty, and in order to secure it for his own department he was indefatigable in trying to get independence openly declared, after which America as a foreign country would fall to his province. In the midst of fighting this issue in the cabinet he discovered a new and absurd provocation against Shelburne in the following way.

When Franklin first met Oswald he was naturally inclined to pitch his demands pretty high. He gave Oswald a paper for Shelburne, suggesting that Britain should cede Canada to the United States, the undeveloped lands to be used to indemnify the large body of American loyalists. There is no evidence that Shelburne took this preposterous suggestion seriously, and he certainly did not trouble the cabinet with it. It was not until six weeks after that Oswald, who was as communicative as Shelburne was secretive, casually informed Grenville of it. Grenville was up in arms at once, and wrote off to tell Fox that he had unearthed a secret conspiracy. Fox took the whole thing *au grand sérieux*. "Pressing as the thing is," he wrote back to Grenville, "and interesting as it is both to our situations and to the affairs of the public, which I fear are irretrievably injured by this intrigue, and which must be ruined if it is suffered to go on, we are resolved not to stir a step till we hear again from you, and know precisely how far we are at liberty to make use of what you have discovered. If this matter should procure a rupture, and consequently become more or less the subject of public discussion, I am sensible the Canada paper cannot be mentioned by name; but might it not be said that we had discovered that Shelburne had withheld from our knowledge matters of importance to the negotiation? . . . Do pray, my dear Grenville, consider the incredible importance of this business in every view, and write me word precisely how far you can authorise us to make use of your intelligence. It is more than possible, that before this reaches you, many other circumstances may have occurred which may afford further proofs of this duplicity of conduct, and, if they have, I am sure they will not have escaped your observation. If this should be the case, you will see the necessity of acquainting me with them as soon as possible. You see what is our object, and you can easily judge what sort of evidence will be most useful to us. When the object is attained, that is, when the duplicity is proved, to what consequences we ought to drive, whether to an absolute rupture, or merely to the recall of Oswald and the simplification of this negotiation, is a point that may be afterwards considered. I own I incline to the more decisive measure, and so, I think, do those with whom I must act in concert."

No more foolish letter can ever have travelled in a Foreign Office bag. Fox, it is clear, was merely spoiling for a quarrel: and he got it, a swift, sudden and disastrous quarrel. For some time the forces in the cabinet had been evenly matched. Conway had wavered; "quite with us in the general view," Fox describes him, "but unfortunately *doubts* in almost every particular instance." Still, it had been fairly even. Then Rockingham was taken ill with influenza, and had to absent himself. As a result, Fox was twice outvoted in cabinet. In the touchy state of his nerves it was more than he could tolerate. On June the 30th, he announced his resignation. It was a hazardous move. All resignations are unwise, but Fox's—so overwhelming was his personal prestige—carried a possibility of success. But not for long. Fate called his bluff. Next morning, on the first of July, Rockingham died.

CHAPTER TWELVE

1. *Resignation, 1782*

Almost before the breath was out of Rockingham's body, the King had sent for Shelburne, who accepted the post of First Lord of the Treasury. Fox, if he withdrew his resignation, was left with three followers in a cabinet of ten. If he did not withdraw it, he stood guilty of a grossly unstatesmanlike action. He could hardly object to Shelburne's promotion, seeing that Shelburne had already stood down once in Rockingham's favour. He could hardly pretend that Rockingham was missed on account of his sagacity in council, or for anything but his vote. In fact, there was no disguising the fact that he was resigning for personal reasons, because he could not and would not work with the new Prime Minister.

If he was going to adopt this course, it was essential to take as many as possible of his colleagues with him. The more he could weaken Shelburne, the sooner he would be back himself. This he failed to do, by making the cardinal mistake of choosing the wrong successor to Rockingham.

According to the ideals of the old-fashioned Whigs, the party leader had to be a man of the highest rank and wealth. Rockingham's death left two such, the Dukes of Richmond and Portland, of whom the former was a front-rank public figure and the latter a dummy, who had been relegated to Dublin Castle when the Rockingham ministry was formed. Fox accordingly approached Richmond about the leadership, but made it clear that he would follow no man who remained in the government. Richmond observed that it would be time to quarrel with Shelburne when he had done something wrong. Fox, infuriated by this, offered the leadership to Portland, who took it. "It did not," says Walpole, "redound to the credit of his faction that in such momentous times they could furnish their country with nothing but a succession of mutes." The results were calamitous. An unheard-of duke was set up as a rival to a man of Shelburne's qualifications; and Richmond was finally alienated. Richmond had long been drawn towards Shelburne, finding that he was sincere about Parliamentary reform, to which the Rockinghams only paid lip-service: now he openly broke away, and henceforward pursued his radical aims beneath the standard of Pitt, with results that Fox was bitterly to regret.

Having selected Portland as a worthy successor to Rockingham, Fox then propounded a theory that Shelburne's promotion was unconstitutional. Since Shelburne's right to accept the Premiership was incontestable, Fox adopted the more desperate course of impugning the King's right to offer it. The cabinet, he said, was entitled to elect the Prime Minister. This astonishing dogma was, always had been, and still is in direct variance with the English constitution, though it is a feature, and a very bad feature, of some others. Moreover, even if it had been put into practice on this occasion, Shelburne would still have been chosen by six to four. But that Fox should ever have promulgated such a figment was a sign that his rage had supplanted his better judgment. The general verdict on his behaviour at this crisis was that "Charles is mad and ruining himself."

His fury was increased by the refusal of so many of his colleagues to come out with him. He summoned a party meeting on the matter, where Richmond stood out against "a monstrous scene of violence on the part of Mr. Fox." He abused Shelburne in an unpardonable manner, and swore "he would have no managements in his language." But he carried no conviction. Keppel refused to resign, and explicitly said that "the share of power offered by Lord Shelburne was equal to anything that could in justice be required, or with propriety granted." Conway felt no call to throw up his job because one of his colleagues disliked another. Only Cavendish within the cabinet followed him: with Burke, Sheridan and Fitzpatrick outside the cabinet. The complete failure of the manoeuvre was only made more bitter by Shelburne's turning to Pitt for help. "They look to you," Fox said to Pitt, "without you they cannot succeed: with you I know not whether they will or no." He was right. Shelburne, finding himself absolute, chose the young man whom the Rockinghams had refused to let him have before, to be Chancellor of the Exchequer at twenty-three. He proved a pillar of strength. Pitt's long career as "a thorn in Charles's side" had begun.

It would be difficult to exaggerate the chorus of reprobation which greeted Fox's resignation. There was nothing to be said for it. Gibbon from a safe distance was amused: "Three months of prosperity has dissolved a phalanx, which had stood ten years' adversity." A wary politician, Lord Temple took this favourable opportunity of deserting him, observing that "Fox has undone himself with the public, and his most intimate friends seem of the same opinion." The public indeed were furious. He had promised them peace, and in the very act of making peace he had run away from his post, from no better reason than pique that a distinguished colleague whom he happened to dislike was promoted over his own nominee. The idea of his depending on a Rockingham or a Portland for moral support was ludicrous: it was obviously to a personal feud, and nothing else, that Fox had sacrificed his public duty.

Let him speak for himself, in a letter to Tom Grenville: "I have done right, I am sure I have. The Duke of Richmond thinks very much otherwise, and will do wrong; I cannot help it. I am sure my staying would have been a means of deceiving the public and betraying my party; and these are things not to be done for the sake of any supposed temporary good. I feel that my situation in the country, my power, my popularity, my consequence, nay, my character, are all risked; but I have done right, and therefore in the end it must turn out to have been wise. If this fail me, the pillared firmament is rottenness, and earth's base built on stubble. Adieu. Your brother disapproves too."

It is clear from this that Fox realised the whole calamity of his mistake. He had not written like that when he resigned over the Royal Marriage Bill. That had been a gambler's throw, but he got back his stake intact. This was a gambler's throw, but he lost. And how much more had he risked: the position it had taken eight years to consolidate, that unbounded confidence in the Man of the People, those roots in public opinion. It was only the first, and by no means the most serious, of Fox's political mistakes. But it was the mistake of his whole life which cost him dearest. It was the initial side-slip, without which the subsequent nose-dive would never have begun.

2. The Prince of Wales and Perdita, 1782

On the day that Fox resigned, the Prince of Wales dined with him, and assured him that he would always consider Lord Rockingham's friends as the best friends of their country. The Prince had the best possible excuse for being a Whig, for his father had ruled him exactly as he ruled the Bostonians, and with as little success. The Prince knew by heart all the petty obstinacy and Teutonic literalism of that small mind; and the first act of his emancipation was to attach himself heart and soul to the man of all his father's subjects who was most notorious for his "aversion to all restraints."

"The Prince of Wales," says Walpole, "had of late thrown himself into the arms of Charles Fox, and this in the most undisguised manner. Fox lodged in St. James' Street, and as soon he rose, which was very late, had a levée of his followers, and of the members of the gaming club at Brooks's—all his disciples. His bristly, black person, and shagged breast, quite open and rarely purified by any ablutions, was wrapped in a foul night-gown, and his bushy hair dishevelled. In these Cynic weeds and with Epicurean good humour, did he dictate his politics, and in this school did the heir to the throne attend his lessons and imbibe them."

This friendship was spontaneous and disinterested: but if Fox had been at all a wise politician he would have avoided the Prince like the plague. There was little enough chance that Fox would ever be in favour with the King, but as soon as he had given the King an excuse to suspect that he was corrupting his son with women and wine, there was no chance at all. Fox became at once the leader of the King's personal, as well as of his political, enemies: and he assumed a reversionary interest in the King's death. He relied less on the support of public opinion, and more on the support of the heir to the throne. The outside world disliked being ruled from Buckingham House, but they fancied being ruled from Carlton House even less. Carlton House constituted yet another clique, of which Sheridan became the chief. It was a deep-drinking, high-playing, practical-joking clique, very much to Fox's taste. But it was anathema to the middle classes, who were prepared to forgive the King much for the simplicity of his private life. It was a barrier between Fox and his public: it was unworthy of the Man of the People to be hob-nobbing with the future King. It is an attractive thing about Fox that his best friendships were his worst mistakes: this was the most fatal friendship of them all.

The first service Fox was able to do for the Prince was to relieve him of an unwanted mistress. At the age of sixteen, while he was still under his father's supervision, the Prince had fallen deeply in love with an actress, the lovely and obliging Mary Robinson, whose performance in *The Winter's Tale* had earned her the name of Perdita. So far as he could elude the bevy of bishops to whom his welfare was entrusted, he maintained a connection with her: and the instant he obtained his own establishment, at the age of eighteen, he set her up in the greatest splendour in Berkeley Square. But Perdita was impossible: her extravagance knew no bounds: and after eighteen months of bliss, she was paid off with a bond for £20,000 to be redeemed when he came of age. What could be more natural than that she should occupy the intervening months by consoling the fallen Secretary of State, from whom she could certainly not be suspected of taking money? Sarah Lennox, who saw little of her nephew now that he had quarrelled with her brother Richmond, writes to Susan Fox-Strangways: "I hear Charles saunters about the streets, and brags that he has not taken a pen in hand since he was out of place. *Pour se désennuyer* he *lives* with Mrs. Robinson, goes to Sadler's Wells with her, and is all day figuring away with her. I long to tell him he does it to show that he is superior to Alcibiades, for *his* courtesan forsook him when he was unfortunate, and Mrs. Robinson takes *him* up." Perdita's windows commanded a fine view of Lansdowne House: and when someone reproached Fox with deserting his friends at Brooks's, who had paid up arrears of subscriptions to enjoy his company again, "you see," he said, "I have pledged myself to the public to keep a strict eye on Lord Shelburne's motions."

3. Junction with North, 1783

During the six months after Fox resigned, he spoke little, and it would have been better if he had not spoken at all. The House of Commons was in no mood to listen patiently to tirades of unsubstantiated abuse against a Prime Minister who had so far done nothing that was unworthy either of a statesman or of a Whig. They might not trust Shelburne very far, but they certainly trusted him further than Fox. Shelburne, however, was making heavy weather inside his own cabinet. Though he had left the Secretary of State's office, he kept the business of peace-making very much in his own hands: and, indeed, he tended to monopolise the business of every department. Never did a man suffer fools less gladly, or rely more confidently on his own omniscience and versatility. His triumph over Fox had endeared Shelburne to the King, and Shelburne misused this strong position by ignoring and domineering over his colleagues. Pitt was the only one of them whom he troubled to treat as an intellectual equal; the others he treated as conveniences. To a high-spirited Whig nobleman this triumph of youth and brains over age and rank was treason against the hierarchical organisation of the party. Twenty years before it had been old Pitt and Shelburne who had run the party; now it was Shelburne and young Pitt under whom they chafed. Finally, in January, 1783, Keppel resigned: while Richmond and Grafton announced that they would keep their posts, but not attend the cabinet.

The government had its troubles in Parliament as well. Gibbon cryptically notes the state of the parties thus: "Ministers, 140; Reynard, 90; Boreas, 120." If Reynard and Boreas ever happened to agree, the ministers would be out by 70. But of course it was unthinkable that they should ever agree. Why, the most scurrilous of the many scurrilous things Fox had said about Shelburne was that he believed him to be capable of forming a coalition with North.

All the same, it was touch and go for the ministry, and they looked forward with apprehension to the reception of their peace preliminaries, which were signed in January. With so much apprehension, in fact, that Shelburne finally decided to make overtures to Fox to return, thinking innocently that there was still no ostensible cause for their separation beyond personal spite, which might have cooled. He despatched Pitt to make the invitation to Fox. The interview was a short one. Fox asked if it was proposed that Shelburne should remain First Lord of the Treasury. Pitt said it was. Fox said: "It is impossible for me to belong to any administration of which Lord Shelburne is the head." Pitt said: "Then we need discuss the matter no further. I did not come here to betray Lord Shelburne." It was the last recorded interview between Fox and Pitt; it was the first recorded occasion on which Fox was snubbed. Seven months of disgrace had taught him nothing.

Pitt and Fox met on the 9th or 10th of February: on the 14th, Fox had an interview with Lord North, at which they came to a close and explicit agreement. It seems that Loughborough, who as Wedderburn had served with both of them, was the prime mover in this *rapprochement*, and that Adam (the duellist) and George North provided the necessary personal links. But little assistance was needed: it is obvious from the lightning speed of the arrangement that both parties were enthusiastic for a reconciliation. The motive is clear. It was Fox's only chance of ever getting back to power. Shelburne was closely supported by the King: Pitt had proved himself a success: if the old Whigs, the Keppels and the rest, left the government, North's followers, if not North himself, would take their places at the King's insistence: when that happened, Shelburne would have a majority in Parliament. There were three fairly equal parties in Parliament: it was clear that soon there would be only two. Fox had a choice of three courses. Either to remain by himself, and watch North join Shelburne: or to make his peace with Shelburne: or to join North. The first would be foolish without being public-spirited; the second would be (by now) humiliating, but wise and statesmanlike; the third was madness.

Three days after their meeting, the preliminaries of peace were put before Parliament. The peace between England and France was discussed at great length, but the peace between Fox and North at greater. Fox had a difficult task. He had to show, first that his reconciliation with North was within the rules of political honesty, and further that it was necessitated on public grounds. It had to be condoned first, and justified afterwards. The former was the simpler task. "I am accused of having formed a junction with a noble person, whose principles I have been in the habit of opposing for the last seven years of my life. . . . It is not in my nature to bear malice, or to live in ill-will. Amicitiæ sempiternæ, inimicitiæ placabiles. I disdain to keep alive in my bosom the enmities which I may bear to men, when the cause of those enmities is no more. When a man ceases to be what he was, when the opinions which made him obnoxious are changed, he then is no more my enemy, but my friend. The American war was the cause of the enmity between the noble lord and myself. The American war and the American question is at an end." So much for his apologia, which did not answer the question whether it was North who had been made a Whig, or Fox who had been made a Tory, by the conclusion of the American war. The defence was unconvincing, but the attack was pathetic. In order to give his coalition with North some semblance of public necessity, and a veneer of principle, it was necessary to pretend that they had been drawn irresistibly together by their common horror at the proposed terms of peace. "It is proclaimed, as an unanswerable argument against everything I can say, that some months ago I declared that any peace would be good and desirable, and that we must have peace on any terms. . . . You call for peace, says the noble lord, you urge the necessity of peace, you insist on peace: then peace you shall have, but such a peace that you shall sicken at its very name. You call for peace, and I shall give you a peace that shall make you repent the longest day you live that ever you breathed a wish for peace. I will give you a peace that shall make you and all men wish that the war had been continued—a peace more calamitous, more dreadful, more ruinous than any war could possibly be." All this was just forcible-feeble. Nobody sickened at the very name of Shelburne's peace: it was neither calamitous, dreadful, nor ruinous. The fact is, it was rather a good peace. If Fox had thought it a bad peace, he would hardly be going to such lengths of intrigue to obtain the office of making it a better one. He was not so inexperienced as not to have learnt that in England any peace, good or bad, is fatal to the career of the man who signs it.

However lame Fox's excuses might be, his numbers were now irresistible. He carried an amendment by 16 votes; and four days later a vote of censure by 17. On the 24th of February, Shelburne resigned.

For the entire month of March, the country was kept under an interregnum, while the King beat about for an administration to stave off the hated coalition. There was hardly anyone he didn't try—Pitt, Thurlow, Mansfield, Gower, Stormont, Temple, Northumberland, one and all had the Treasury pressed upon them. He sent for North and asked him point-blank what were his objections to the treaty, without eliciting any rational reply. He conducted a long and comical correspondence with Portland, in which neither party summoned courage to mention Fox by name. He declared in answer to a suggestion that he would gladly try "Mr. Thomas Pitt or Mr. Thomas Anybody." His despair was pathetic. Towards the end of a harassing month, he made a final effort to persuade the man whom he had tried first of all— William Pitt. "Mr. Pitt," he wrote, "I am much hurt to find you are determined to decline at an hour when those who have any regard for the constitution as established by law ought to stand forth against the most daring and unprincipled faction that the annals of this kingdom ever produced." The King was notoriously a persuasive talker: Pitt was twenty-three, and a bundle of ambition: it is not everyone who is offered the ultimate prize of life, the government of his country, on his own terms, within three years of coming into Parliament. But Pitt had excellent reasons for refusing. He had the same advantage over all other politicians that his father had had—he was aware of the existence, the weight, and the direction of public opinion. He saw that Fox had no idea that opinion outside Parliament existed or mattered, that his popularity was already gone, and that this new coalition would make him the best-hated man in the country. He had lost his pristine admiration for Fox; he saw that he could never ally himself with a man of so little foresight or balance: there was no room for them both in one party: yet he realised the difficulty of "conducting great and difficult affairs with such abilities to criticise them." With that view, he decided to give Fox rope to hang himself. Most probably, he imparted this line of reasoning to the King. At all events, immediately after his second refusal, the King capitulated. On April the 2nd, Fox and North kissed hands as Secretaries of State, and Portland as First Lord of the Treasury.

At this ceremony the King, it is said, "turned back his ears and eyes just like the horse at Astley's, when the tailor he had determined to throw was getting on him." He made no attempt to conceal his anger: "It was impossible he could wish that such a government could last," he declared openly. "I hope many months will not elapse before the Grenvilles, the Pitts and other men of abilities and character will relieve me." If there was any distinction, he was perhaps less angry with Fox, whom he had always hated, than with North, with whom for twelve whole years he had worked so smoothly—"that *grateful* Lord North!" "Did I ever think, my Lord Guilford," he exclaimed to North's father, "that Lord North would have delivered me up in this manner to Mr. Fox?"

For the first time in twenty-three years, the people of England agreed with their King. Just a year and a week before, Fox had come into power on a wave of extravagant popularity: and now hardly a word was said in his defence. Out of volumes of contemporary comment, the best that can be extracted is a little half-hearted palliation. The general opinion was well expressed by the verdict that the coalition "had the vices of both its parents; the corruption of the one, and the violence of the other." It was remembered how, six months before, he had taunted Shelburne with being a man capable of the very same sacrifice of principle for place which he was now making. It was remembered how, just thirteen months before, he had spoken about North and his followers. "From the moment when I shall make any terms with one of them," he had said, "I shall rest satisfied to be called the most infamous of mankind: I could not for an instant think of a coalition with men who in every public and private transaction, as ministers, have shown themselves void of every principle of honour and honesty; in the hands of such men I would not trust my honour even for a minute." This, and much more recrimination of the same sort, was gathered into a slender volume called *Beauties of Fox and North*, which went to stimulate the fury of an insulted electorate.

Fox's plea that he was by nature easily reconciled to his enemies was not found convincing. "I am a bad hater," Fox once said: and so he was, for he hated the wrong people. It was ridiculous to strain at Shelburne and swallow North, to declare that all his differences were at an end with the Tory, at the same time as he was execrating the Whig leader. If there was one thing the public deplored, it was the mutual *bonhomie* among their rulers. Family attachments, class solidarity, good fellowship between Whigs and Tories were constantly leading to concessions and compromises (as Grafton's career illustrates) by which the public was befooled. The root cause of Fox's short-lived popularity had been the belief that he was an uncompromising man. With impeachments and scaffolds always on his lips, he struck them as a man who would fight to win a popular cause in the teeth of any loyalty, no matter what friendships he might traverse. His unprecedented vehemence of language had taken them in: and now he turned round in his course, all affability, and assured them, with irresistible charm, that everybody who knew him at all knew that he was the most easily reconciled of men. They had been hoodwinked: he was not the remorseless tribune they had taken him for; he was like all the rest, a gentleman first and a demagogue second. All his acrimony was just the ammunition of the moment: at heart, he felt that a Tory was just a good as fellow as a Whig. Better the agreeable Toryism of a kindred spirit like North than the repellent Whiggism of the cold and uncongenial Shelburne. Shelburne was not one of Fox's set: North's friends, if not North himself, were very much in his set. His first loyalty was to the friends whom his matchless charm had gathered round him. He made a present of his political principles to Shelburne and Pitt, in return for a fresh lease of North's agreeable company, and for North's assistance in ousting the outsider from power.

Fox's immediate circle—Brooks's, in other words—would have followed him if he had coalesced with the devil. But they had few illusions about this move. Even Fitzpatrick, the closest friend of all, gloomily remarked that it was "an unnatural alliance." From Fox himself the best encouragement that could be had was that "nothing but success could justify it." The same could be said of any gamble: but Fox had gambled once too often. He had little left to lose, and this particular horse scarcely started. The best that can be said for the coalition is that the folly of it was even more egregious than the infamy. Fox deserved to be ruined by it: but perhaps he was ruined by it a little more thoroughly than he deserved.

CHAPTER THIRTEEN

1. *Troubles of the Coalition, 1783*

The history of the coalition ministry is a sequence of unendurable humiliations. Its composition, in the first place, was a makeshift. Cavendish came back with Fox, and so did Keppel. Richmond flatly refused, saying that he had signed too many protests against North to shake hands with him now. Thurlow was ousted: but the King had his private spy in the cabinet in the person of Lord Stormont. There was no Lord Chancellor: the seal was put in commission, Loughborough presiding. Sheridan, Fitzpatrick and Burke (still outside the cabinet) returned. Perhaps the most galling feature of all was that a small sinecure had to be found for Sandwich, who was to have been beheaded.

The King was "very civil, but no more." He made no pretence of intending to confide in them. He refused to grant any honours, even to those to whom they had long been promised: so that ministers had to make pensions do the work of peerages. This was not pettiness on the King's part: it was policy. He took the measure of his ministers very accurately. North, he said, "was a man composed entirely of negative qualities, and actuated in every instance by a desire of present ease at the risk of any future difficulty. As for Fox, he allowed that he was a man of parts, quickness and great eloquence; but he wanted application, and consequently the fundamental knowledge necessary for business, and above all, was totally destitute of discretion and sound judgment." This was fair, almost generous: it was on public, not on personal grounds, that he thwarted his ministers whenever he could.

The two Secretaries of State worked admirably together. North was self-effacing and loyal, and let Fox encroach on his department to his heart's content: North's idea of public felicity was achieved when he was occupied in asking pardons for convicts and small pensions for officers' widows, neither of which the King grudged. But Fox had an uphill task. The first essential of a good foreign minister is a strong position in his own country, and all Europe knew that Fox was clinging to office by his teeth. There was little of the "fagot d'épines" about him now: the foreign ministers could afford to wait till he fell. The French were contemptuous: the Americans were furious at the return of North, the arch-murderer (as they saw it) of their countrymen. Moreover, Fox had come into power on a censure of the peace preliminaries: that had been his platform, that had been the only plausible pretence he had been able to find by way of a public issue between him and Shelburne. He was under an obligation to make good his statement that Shelburne's terms were more calamitous, more dreadful, more ruinous than any war. This he completely failed to do. He very nearly made things worse: for the French minister seriously thought of renewing the war if he should return to power. As it was, he swallowed it whole, the treaty at whose very name he had sickened, the treaty which was to have made him repent to his last day that he had even breathed a wish for peace. It was only to be expected. The King could not refrain from taunting him with his own weakness. "For every difficulty in concluding peace, this country has alone to blame itself; after the extraordinary and never to be forgot vote of February, 1782, and the hurry for negotiation that after ensued, it is no wonder that our enemies, seeing our spirit so fallen, have taken advantage of it." Much more extraordinary, though, and much less to be forgot, was the vote of February, 1783, by which Fox had wantonly condemned the work of a strong Foreign Secretary, and pledged himself to improve upon it, although he well knew that he would come into office, if at all, as a Foreign Secretary feeble, temporary and disowned. This was a disservice to the public. It was unedifying in any event to seize office by an acrobatic trick: but to do so at a crisis when the country desperately needed a strong and well-grounded foreign policy was worse than frivolous. It was not his pacifist antecedents that militated against him: it was his sudden and opportunist conversion to the view that any war was better than a peace negotiated by Lord Shelburne. When it became known that he had altogether failed to improve on the terms he had denounced, the mask was off. The last shred of principle was gone.

To lead the opposition to the coalition ministry was child's play for Pitt. He exposed their weaknesses, and widened their differences, with the relish of an anatomical demonstrator. When the ministers raised a loan by the old method of private allotment at a discount, Pitt had only to remind the House of Fox's previous tirades against the practice, adding the biting comment that it was a practice characteristic of a gambler. He brought forward a resolution in favour of Parliamentary reform, which infallibly drew up North in opposition, and was defeated by 144 votes—a crushing blow to the ministry's credit with the public, since Pitt's previous reform motion, when Rockingham had been in power, was only lost by twenty. He followed this up with a bill for the reform of abuses in public offices, skilfully framed in such a way that ministers had publicly to knock it on the head.

Another heavy liability to this government was Burke. It must be confessed that whenever Burke was in office his leaders slept on thorns. His sense of justice could never adapt itself to any party exigency. If he thought something was wrong, he was not deterred from attacking it by any regard to unanimity or consistency. His countryman Goldsmith saw his weakness best:

> "Though equal to all things, for all things unfit,
> Too nice for a statesman, too proud for a wit;
> For a patriot too cool; for a drudge, disobedient;
> And too fond of the right, to pursue the expedient."

He was, in short, far more than a politician. In this ministry, he committed a blunder which more than undid the good effects of his previous reform of the Pay Office. During Shelburne's government, Barré had had the Pay Office in accordance with his expectations; Barré had found that Lord Holland's accounts as Paymaster, though eighteen years overdue, were still unsettled, and some £100,000 still owing to the public. The clerk responsible, Powell, was an old creature of Holland's, who had managed both his public and private affairs (including Charles's debts) for many years, and made a sufficiently good thing out of it to purchase Kingsgate. Barré dismissed Powell. Burke, returning nine months later, reinstated him, out of sheer kindness of heart. Pitt saw to it that the fullest publicity was given to the transaction, which was acutely embarrassing both to Fox, who wished the public to forget the origins of the wealth he might have had, and to Burke, whose zeal for economical reform in general was not equal to his unbounded kindness of heart in particular instances. Burke actually had to be held down in his seat when the matter was debated. It was a relief to both of them when Powell cut his throat, in May.

The crowning misfortune came in June. In that month, as luck would have it, the Prince of Wales came of age. Fox was already hand in glove with the Prince: he looked forward to his accession as a sort of Whig millennium; for he was always ready for a wager that the King would die, or take leave of his senses, within the next few years. So anxious was he to please the Prince, that he had promised to procure him a settlement of £100,000 a year when he came of age. The question now arose. Fox was at once embroiled with his own Chancellor of the Exchequer, Cavendish: but he was much more deeply embroiled with the King. The King was furious with what he called "my son's ministry," but at the same time he saw that they were delivered into his hands. Now, he exclaimed, "the public shall know how well founded the principles of Economy are in those who have so loudly preached it up." This was the chance he had been waiting for: a dismissal and a dissolution, and Fox would have to go to the country on the programme that the heir to the throne should have a six-figure income. Fox saw that he was trapped: he went to the Prince as a suppliant, and was released from his pledge: and the Prince had to be content with £50,000 a year, the Duchy of Cornwall, and £30,000 down. We know how two-thirds of that sum was earmarked already; Fox was able to do the Prince a favour in return, by inducing Perdita Robinson to surrender her bond for £20,000 in consideration of an annuity of £500.

It was not the Prince's amenability that had saved Fox on this occasion: the King could still have dismissed him and told the world the ridiculous cause. The King had taken counsel on this course from a very clever politician, Lord Temple, one of the friends Fox had lost by resigning from Shelburne's cabinet. Temple agreed that the Prince's settlement would be unpopular, but the peace treaty would be more unpopular still. Treaties are always unpopular, and this one more than most, especially coming from Fox. If Fox were turned out on the treaty, there would be no danger of a successful appeal to the country. But Temple was a far-sighted man. He saw a better rod in pickle for Fox even than the peace treaty, even than the Prince's settlement.

2. Fox's India Bill, 1783

Both parties, in both Houses, as well as the King, had been unanimously of the opinion, for some ten years, that the East India Company stood in vital and urgent need of reform. Resolutions had passed, committees had sat, reports had been presented; while India, and the company, had progressed from bad to worse. This was the Serbonian bog in which Fox now ventured.

Briefly, our interests in India had long outgrown the framework of a chartered company. A legitimate trade in tea and rice might be adequate to produce dividends on India stock and a certain tribute over for the Treasury: but it was not adequate to support the civil government of a continent and the maintenance of a standing army of 60,000 men. No regular taxing power existed, and extortion took its place. From the acceptance of small bribes, the system of extortion had swollen until princes were overset, populations sold, and towns annihilated in the everyday course of the company's business, for money. The company maintained a precarious solvency by these methods, in which its trade was forgotten. But the company was not the real gainer: for every pound that came into its treasury, a hundred went into the pockets of its servants. India became the paradise of the fortune-hunter: a nabob was a synonym for a millionaire: whoever obtained a post under the company was a made man: a job with a nominal salary of three hundred was worth anything up to fifty thousand a year. "What is England?" said Walpole in 1773. "A sink of Indian wealth filled by Nabobs and emptied by Macaronies." The company's patronage was allotted among its stockholders: and in this way the stock, which was worthless as a commercial obligation, was scrambled for as a title to consideration when the next Indian appointment was to be made. As Burke put it, of what interest was it whether the dividend rose to ten, or fell to six per cent., to a man whose son, before he had been in Bengal two months, could sell the grant of a single contract for forty thousand pounds? This divorce between the interest of the company and the interest of its employees had by 1783 reached a point beyond which it could go no further. On the one side were the returned nabobs, fabulously rich, some of them returning as many as ten members to Parliamant, all voting in a bloc for the maintenance of the old system. On the other side was the company, whose liabilities at this date exceeded its assets by eight million pounds, much of which was owed to the Treasury.

The difficulty of coping with the matter, the difficulty which had postponed all action for ten or a dozen years, lay in the immense strength of the company as a vested interest. There were the stockholders, who had bought their shares dear in the full knowledge that any return they could expect was in the form of graft rather than dividends. There were the directors, men of influence and substance, wielding a patronage more sought after than the patronage of the Prime Minister himself. There were the returned nabobs, the poorest of them worth his quarter million, crowding the Tory benches with themselves and their nominees. Fox put it in a sentence: "The influence of the crown, in its most enormous state, was nothing compared to the boundless patronage of the East India government, if the latter was to be used in influence of the House." It was a formidable nettle to grasp.

Burke had for some time past diverted his unceasing industry from America to India. Wherever on the globe an injustice was being done, Burke made it his duty to find it out and track it down. In India he discovered injustices beside which the crimes of the Spanish conquerors were venal. From 1780 to 1793 their avenging became his life's work. It was Burke who inspired Fox to justify the existence of the coalition by introducing an India Bill. Fox gave up the summer recess to a piece of genuine hard work. Parliament was reassembled early. A hint was dropped in the King's speech. The definitive peace terms were almost forgotten in the excitement that prevailed when it became known that the problem four governments had shirked was to be tackled at last.

Fox's remedy was simple and drastic. The whole government of India, and all the appointments that went with it, were to be placed in the hands of seven commissioners. These commissioners were to be appointed in the first instance for four years by the government: subsequent vacancies were to be filled by the King. Another subordinate board in India would perform the executive work of the company: but the seven commissioners, sitting in London, would have supreme control.

The opposition to this measure took three forms. The first was the outcry that the company's charter was being infringed: so it was, but the company had already infringed its own charter at so many points that there was little left of it. Charters are revocable, and the City of London itself would have lost its charter long since if it had committed a tenth of the crimes of the company. But the attack obtained a better hearing than the defence. Charters in those days were important things, intimately bound up with the system of franchise. By tampering with charters, James the Second had upset the whole electoral machinery of the country. Charters took the place of company law. There was a widespread scare on account of the sanctity of charters. From all over England chartered boroughs petitioned against the dangerous precedent. Wilkes led the clamour on behalf of the City of London. The man in the street was informed that if charters could be withdrawn, every constituency in England could be disfranchised at government's desire. The charter argument was the one which appealed most to the panic-stricken stockholders. So much heat was generated by it that one director of the company died of apoplexy during the debates. As a stick with which to beat the Bill it was important: as an argument it was trumpery.

The second and third criticisms of the Bill were mutually destructive. They were that it increased the influence of the crown, and that it increased the influence of ministers. The former was an unimportant argument, a mere sop to the newspapers. Nobody cared who filled the vacancies on the India board years hence: the interesting question was, who was to make the initial nominations?

Patronage was a matter which interested the eighteenth century more keenly than we today can easily conceive. It was the eternal problem of the younger son. In one period he would go to the wars, in another he would enter the church, but in the eighteenth century he would rely on his next of kin in either House of Parliament to make sufficient favour with ministers to procure him a collectorship of customs in the Bahamas, or a receivership in bankruptcy in Nova Scotia, or any other snug appointment of a few hundred a year which did not involve leaving London. America, before we lost her, was honeycombed with petty sinecures of this sort: the Irish pension list, a favourite form of patronage, crept steadily up to £174,000 a year, all of it used in small *douceurs* to government supporters; but nothing the government had to offer could compete with the plums at the disposal of the East India company. An Indian appointment was to an Irish pension as a bishopric is to a curacy. The younger son of a Sir

James Lowther could not hope to be as well provided for as the younger son of an India company director. The transference of this fountain of honour from Leadenhall Street to Westminster was a political revolution of the first order.

Everything, of course, depended on the list of the new commissioners. There was a most aggravating delay in divulging their names. At last they were published: the names of four notorious Foxites and three stalwart followers of North, including his own son. Then the storm burst.

North's practised eye had foreseen it. "A good receipt to knock up an administration," he remarked of Fox's Bill. "Influence of the crown, and influence of party against crown and people, are two of the many topics that will be urged against your Bill." But both Fox and North were taken aback by the howl of execration that arose. They had not foreseen that what they were doing could be construed by the opposition into a constitutional upheaval as serious as, say, the abolition of the Lords. This is how the opposition saw it—Fox had got into power by a trick. His tenure was precarious, and his majority artificial. He wanted to consolidate his position during the few months that were his. Here was a patronage beside which, in his own words, the influence of the crown was nothing. He and North had for the moment a majority in both Houses. They would snatch the opportunity, collar the whole Indian patronage, install seven trusty friends, and Parliament would be theirs. They could outbribe the Treasury with ease. The civil list would be a drop in the ocean of Indian wealth which would shower from the hands of Fox and North. General elections would have no more terrors for them. The coalition, born a sickly child out of ill-mated parents, would wax into a young tyrant before whom they all would have to bow.

There is a curious unreality about the India Bill debates. That any political leader could have been suspected of contemplating a Parliamentary *coup d'état* under the disguise of a better government for India, appears far-fetched and melodramatic. Yet it was all too likely true. The influence of the crown was a powerful factor in politics: it was a magnet that sooner or later drew almost every public man out of his course; it had cost the Whigs twelve years of struggle to pass a resolution with which every man in Parliament agreed, that the influence of the crown had increased, was increasing, and ought to be diminished. "Provided we can stay in long enough to have given a good stout blow to the influence of the crown," Fox had written, "I do not think it much signifies how soon we go out after." The India Bill certainly drew a good stout blow to the influence of the crown, but it achieved that purpose, not by diminishing the King's patronage, but by setting up a counterbalance, by making a good stout addition to the influence of Charles Fox. "Here is a man," said Dr. Johnson, "who has divided the kingdom with Cæsar: so that it was a doubt whether the nation should be ruled by the sceptre of George the Third, or by the tongue of Fox."

Of all the aspects of this extraordinary question, the most baffling is, how far Fox really did intend to combine the reformation of Indian government with the improvement of his own political fortunes. It is unquestionably certain that Fox's first wish was to achieve the reform for which his friend Burke was working himself to death. His heart bled for the condition of India: his nature revolted against the injustice and cruelty that Burke had dragged to light. But he was handling an explosive. The Indian patronage must always be a choice prize. It must be taken away from the company, as a first condition. And given to whom? To the crown? To Lord Shelburne? To whom could it be given, but to a mixed body of Foxites and Tories? What broader basis was there to receive it, and what could be better calculated to cement that arbitrary union than the division between them of such bonus? It is difficult to see what less Fox could have done, and he might have done far more. The appointments were rapidly to revert to the crown, so rapidly as to arouse considerable criticism on that very head. The commissioners named in the Bill were men of some weight, far removed from mere party wire-pullers. On the whole, the job was done as respectably as circumstances permitted: but it was still a job. The King's refusal to grant peerages for the coalition would fade into insignificance beside Fox's power to make any of his followers a nabob. Whether he used his power well or ill, the Bill would make Fox the most powerful commoner in England. It was an unescapable boon. There is no need to assume that he intended to misuse a power, merely because he did not hand it to his enemies. Let him be given full honour for the excellence of his motives. Let him be given honour in its least perishable form, in the language of Burke:

"It will be a distinction honourable to the age, that the rescue of the greatest number of the human race that ever were so grievously oppressed, from the greatest tyranny that was ever exercised, has fallen to the lot of abilities and dispositions equal to the task: that it has fallen to one who has the enlargement to comprehend, the spirit to undertake, and the eloquence to support so great a measure of hazardous benevolence. His spirit is not owing to his ignorance of the state of men and things: he well knows what snares are spread about his path, from personal animosity, from court intrigues, and possibly from popular delusion. But he has put to hazard his ease, his security, his interest, his power, even his darling popularity, for the benefit of a people whom he has never seen. This is the road that all heroes have trod before him. He is traduced and abused for his supposed motives. He will remember, that obloquy is a necessary ingredient in the composition of all true glory: he will remember, that it was not only in the Roman customs, but it is in the nature and constitution of things, that calumny and abuse are essential parts of triumph. These thoughts will support a mind, which only exists for honour, under the burden of temporary reproach. He is doing indeed a great good: such as rarely falls to the lot, and almost as rarely coincides with the desires, of any man. Let him use his time. Let him give the whole length of the reins to his benevolence. He is now on a great eminence, where the eyes of mankind are turned to him. He may live long, he may do much. But here is the summit. He never can exceed what he does this day."

Superb words: but in a different language from those of the critics of the Bill. In Burke's mind were the starving millions of Hindustan: in theirs was the quotation of East India stock. On one side the Bill was a great good to many millions: on the other it was a violent injustice to a few hundreds. The battle had to be fought on the lower plane.

The tragedy is that Fox's credit was unequal to such a heavy draft. The very magnitude of the reform excited incredulity, and pointed attention to the incidental revolution it would effect in Fox's own fortunes. The very excellence of his intentions towards a people he had never seen aroused suspicions, and sharpened criticism of the *coup* he was accomplishing under such a specious cloak. So that the higher the defence was aimed, the lower the attack struck. Fox might be credited with noble objects, and every man in Parliament knew that there was no more generous soul alive.

But when he was accused of a violent party manoeuvre, of dividing the Kingdom with Cæsar, of engineering a *coup d'état*, he had no weapons to rebut the charge. His reputation would carry him unscathed through a fight against the slave trade or against religious tests, for his courage and liberality were the admiration of mankind. But in a squabble over a contested election, in an accusation of manipulating a job, he had no reputation at all. He was like a duellist with both weapons. So long as the fight was maintained with swords, Fox's weapon was truer and brighter than any: but when it came down to daggers, his was broken at the hilt.

Fox had been in Parliament fifteen years. He had not only inherited his father's evil reputation, but improved on it. He had been foremost in the Wilkes affair, foremost in the Lowther affair, both of them acts of political violence. He had conducted the opposition to the American war with unexampled violence, both of language and tactics. His resignation from Shelburne's cabinet was an act of violence: his denial of the King's right to choose a Prime Minister was a pretension of violence: his coalition with North did violence to the whole structure of party politics. He was the most violent public man since Shaftesbury and his Brisk Boys. Worse than this, for all his violent acts, he had contrived noble excuses. The persecution of Wilkes had been a noble defence of Parliamentary privilege: the persecution of Portland had been a noble rescue of the independence of the judges. With these high-flying arguments, he had repeatedly talked Parliament off its feet, into committing grave injustices. He was the supreme artist at doing a wicked thing for a specious motive. Parliament had been fooled too often by his perverse arguments: the loftier was his peroration, the more suspicious was their scrutiny. How could they know that he was not still the old Fox of 1770, when for the last year his course had been so crooked? The coalition had ruined him: it had lost him Parliament's credence. Grattan once said that Fox's oratory was never the same after the coalition: "The mouth still spoke great things, but the swell of soul was no more."

The mud stuck. The popular outcry drowned the panegyrics. Fox was caricatured as Carlo Khan, the Great Mogul, riding into Leadenhall Street on an elephant. He was his father's son after all, exulted his enemies; he was still the Black Boy, the British Alcibiades, at thirty-four. He was going one better than Lord Holland's proscription of 1762. He was aiming at supreme power. It was a damning imputation, and there was nothing in his record or in his character to neutralise its sting.

Above all, asked the opposition, why was the measure pushed forward with so much haste? Fox had forgone his shooting to prepare it; he had summoned Parliament early, and introduced it within the first week of the session. Within a month it had passed all its stages, and been sent to Lords. It was being hustled through like an indemnity bill. Yet the Indian question was a hardy annual. To the political mind a measure which had already brooked no delay for fifteen years might continue to brook no delay for a few more months. Their suspicions were confirmed by what happened in the Lords.

When the Bill was nearly through the Commons, the King sent it to Thurlow for his opinion on it. That opinion was crushing: the Bill was "a plan to take more than half the royal power, and by that means disable the King for the rest of his reign." The King then sent for his sagacious adviser Temple, and entrusted him with the following note: "His Majesty allows Earl Temple to say, that whoever voted for the India Bill was not only not his friend, but would be considered by him as an enemy; and if these words were not strong enough, Earl Temple might use whatever words he might deem stronger, or more to the purpose." Nothing stronger or more to the purpose, was required. The Lords stampeded. On December the 17th, the Bill was thrown out by 19 votes. The Lord President himself voted against it: the Duke of Richmond voted against it. The Prince of Wales failed at the crucial moment, and stayed away. Next day, peremptory messages were sent to Fox and North ordering them to surrender the seals through their under-secretaries, "as a personal interview on this occasion would be disagreeable." Fox's messenger found him at Brooks's, forgetting his sorrows. North's messenger found him in bed, imperturbable as ever, and demanded that he *must* see Lord North. "In that case," said his Lordship, "he must see Lady North as well, for I positively refuse to rise."

Fox's reactions were unfortunate. When one piece of violence failed, he became more violent still. The coalition had failed, and he knew he was ruined: his anger now led him into the most appalling series of mistakes any politician has ever committed. He was not the man to take a betrayal lying down: "I will never again be at the head of a string of Janissaries, who are always ready to strangle or despatch me on the least signal." He now prepared for a struggle between Lords and Commons. He forgot that a majority of King's friends in the Lords was a far less unnatural and heterogeneous body than a majority blended of his own and North's friends in the Commons. His following in the Commons was still intact. "We are so strong, that nobody can undertake, without madness, and if they do, I think we shall destroy them almost as soon as they are formed." But his strength was artificial. "Depend upon it," wrote Gibbon, "Billy's painted galley must soon sink under Charles' black collier." So it would have turned out, if size were the only criterion; but Fox could not trust his crew.

On December the 19th it was announced in Parliament, amid loud laughter, that Pitt had accepted to form an administration. A mince-pie administration, the Foxites labelled it. Wagers were freely laid whether it would last a week or ten days. Fox gave it till January the 12th, when he would first divide against it.

3. *Pitt Turns the Tables, 1783-1784*

The King had got his way in one respect. "The Pitts and the Grenvilles and other men of character and abilities" had come to his relief. But the difficulties ahead were frightful. The new Secretary of State, Lord Temple, who represented the Grenville connection, resigned on the 22nd, having been appointed on the 19th. The Foxites shook with laughter over this initial disaster. "This boyish prank," said one of them, "is already over." After Temple had gone, Pitt's right-hand man was no other than Richmond, a circumstance peculiarly unpalatable to Fox. There was also Thurlow. The rest were a cabinet of nondescripts, Pitt being the only cabinet minister in the Commons. The King did what he could to help: the fountain of honour, dry under the coalition, began to play once more: but it needed more than peerages to induce politicians to join a mince-pie administration—it needed courage of the first order.

To all these difficulties in scraping together a cabinet, Pitt added the greatest difficulty of all, by excluding Shelburne. It was a most audacious step. But Pitt was determined that this was to be *his* administration. Shelburne was old enough to be his father, and any cabinet in which Shelburne sat was Shelburne's cabinet, as the Rockingham episode had proved. Pitt was often reproached in later years with being a dictatorial Prime Minister: he would reply that any man who had started his official life under Shelburne had expiated that failing in advance. Moreover, he wanted his administration to be a complete breakaway from the party system, which had been contorted out of shape by the extraordinary events of the last two years. If Shelburne came in, the administration would be labelled as belonging to the Chathamite Whigs. This was not what Pitt wanted at all: he wanted a party of all the honest men who disapproved, or were willing to desert, the coalition. So he kept out Shelburne, and made him Marquis of Lansdowne instead.

Shelburne's exclusion was also meant as a loophole for Fox. It was clearly intimated to Fox that he might yet save his consistency: that if he would disown North and all North's followers, Pitt would be ready to reconstitute the Whig party in conjunction with him. Fox refused. Fox's subsequent career was the outcome of that refusal.

There followed three of the most exciting months in the history of Parliament. The perfection of Pitt's tactics during these months is a standing marvel; but no less extraordinary is Fox's increasing violence, which led him from blunder to blunder until the final catastrophe.

When a minister is appointed against the sense of a majority of the House of Commons, the majority's line of action is clear as day. They must base their claim to govern on the wishes of the people: they must demand an appeal to the people. There is nothing else they can constitutionally do. They can, of course, make the work of government impossible, by refusing supply and rejecting the annual Mutiny Bill: but these are violent methods, likely to make even a minority government popular. An appeal to the country, on the other hand, though entirely the prerogative of the King to grant, is what any party leader who is sure of his popularity is entitled to demand. The minister who has been arbitrarily appointed will dread a dissolution. What good intentions he may have had he will have been powerless to convert into actions. While his opponent can pose as the victim of despotism, he can only plead subservience to the King's wish. On the other hand, if he can postpone a dissolution, he has time to try his hand at an arrangement of parties and places which will enable him creditably to carry on.

Exactly the same situation arose in 1834. Melbourne, with a majority in the House, was virtually dismissed. Peel was sent for, much against his will; but, being a true Tory, obeyed and accepted to undertake the government, and with it the responsibility for Melbourne's dismissal. He carried on for four months, until the Whigs finally got their own way, and brought about a dissolution. As a result of an appeal to the country, the Whig government, which had previously been dying a natural and unlamented death, procured a fresh lease of life for six years; such was the unpopularity of the King's action, and the general misunderstanding of Peel's statesmanlike behaviour.

Fox took the exact opposite course to that which common sense and public spirit demanded. January the 12th arrived, and he unfolded his scheme to an astonished House. He was going to prevent a dissolution by every means in his power: he declared that the crown did not possess the prerogative of dissolving Parliament in the middle of a session—a theory never heard of before or since: he appealed to the House in this way to "preserve the beauty of the constitution." He moved two sledge-hammer resolutions. One declared that in case of a dissolution before the supplies had been voted, it would be a high crime and misdemeanour to issue any public monies from the exchequer: this meant that the executive would come to a dead stop if Parliament were dissolved before Fox came back into power. Another postponed the second reading of the Mutiny Bill until February the 23rd: this gave Pitt six weeks in which to resign before the army would be automatically released from discipline. These resolutions were carried by 39 votes.

Fox imagined that these methods would be entirely efficacious. Pitt would be out-voted consistently in the next few weeks, until, faced with a breakdown of government on February the 23rd, the King would recall Fox to power, and the authority of a Commons majority would be gloriously vindicated. He was to be sadly disillusioned. Fox's truculent methods played into Pitt's hands. Why, Pitt could ask, was his opponent so anxious to avoid a dissolution? The whole country could find an answer. Fox dared not go to the country on the India Bill, on the peace treaty he had first denounced and then signed, on the Prince's allowance. He dared not go to the country hand in hand with North and Sandwich and Loughborough. He could never explain why he had deserted Shelburne in the midst of the peace negotiations. His position was gone. Four years ago in Westminster Hall he had spoken in favour of annual elections, as giving the people a close control over Parliament. The Parliament was now four years old: its whole structure and balance of parties had been perverted and twisted out of shape to serve Fox's ambition: a coalition had been formed which misrepresented the people's will, in a way of which the people showed their detestation at every opportunity: the Parliament had three years to run, and Fox was moving heaven and earth to ensure that it should last to the bitter end, in order that his oligarchy might be established. The very country associations that Fox helped to found were now petitioning for a dissolution. Another great Yorkshire meeting was summoned, and came out strongly in favour of Pitt. And when Fox, again in Westminster Hall, on the fourth anniversary of the meeting at which he had been chosen candidate, had the audacity to ridicule their petitions, he was shouted down. A cartoon of the event shows him labelled with Cromwell's Ambition, Catiline's Abilities, and Machiavel's Politics. That was the pass to which the Man of the People had come in four years.

Fox was not defying the King; he was defying the people. The prerogative of dissolution, which he was forbidding, and even denying, the King's right to exert, is a prerogative whose exercise is always a concession to the people. It was the people Fox dreaded. He pretended to regard Pitt as a mere backstairs minister, a court puppet: but if he had believed it for a moment, he would have been the foremost to demand a dissolution. In fact, he placed his grotesque constitutional theories as a bulwark between himself and the retribution he knew was waiting for him. A House of Commons, he argued, was elected for seven years. For seven years its members were at liberty to play battledore and shuttlecock with their loyalties, their principles, and their constituents' rights, without accounting for their conduct to the people. For seven years the day of reckoning might be postponed. That was the only argument on which it was possible to defend the tactics of a man who had declared, four years before, for annual Parliaments. Rousseau observed that the people of England were free only at election times: if Fox had had his way, that celebrated folly would have been almost true. He and North were in the position of two partners who, having won the first rubber with marked cards, refuse to let their opponents send for a new pack.

Pitt's cunning during these three months is something above praise. One of his masterstrokes was an India Bill of his own, drafted in collaboration with the East India company. It was sufficiently like Fox's Bill to look like an efficient reform, but it entirely avoided the transference of patronage. Fox had to oppose it: but by opposing it he was made publicly to appear to confess that the patronage had been the feature of his own Bill on which he set most store. It was duly rejected, and the moral was left to the public to draw. But it is worth noticing that a few years later Pitt did appropriate a large measure of India patronage, and that it proved a sufficiently valuable electoral weapon to corrupt the whole of Scotland for eighteen years.

All through February Pitt sat tight. A shower of resolutions descended on his head: resolutions against improper use of the King's name, for the removal of ministers, for an efficient administration, against the continuance of present ministers in their offices, and, above all, resolutions against a dissolution. But the majorities by which they were carried showed that the unnatural alliance of Fox and North was not proof against the dread of facing the constituencies. The coalition had no binding principle in itself: it was based on mutual friendships and mutual dislikes: it was unfitted to stand a combined siege from the King, the Lords, the people, and Pitt's mounting minority. The garrison began to trickle away. On February the 2nd, Fox had a majority of 19; on the 18th of 12; on the 20th of 21 votes. By the end of February, he was allowing the House to pass snippets of supply, by way of giving Pitt more time to resign. Then came the fateful day when the Mutiny Bill was to be passed or to be thrown out. This was the desperate remedy, the final sanction that the House can use to turn out a minority government. Fox shirked the issue: he postponed consideration of the Bill until March the 9th: then, he suggested, the House might pass a Bill for a month or six weeks. On March the 1st, he beat Pitt by 12 votes: on the 5th by 9. On the 8th, he made a supreme effort: he moved what was called a Representation, a pompous document which stated at great length the full case against a ministry which did not enjoy the confidence of a majority of the House of Commons. It was an imposing argument, and the whole House knew that if it were sound it would have been vindicated at the expense of the Mutiny Bill a fortnight earlier. The hypothesis on which the argument rested was blown to pieces by the division taken upon it. It was carried by 191 votes to 190. A ministry which was only one vote short of enjoying the confidence of the House need worry little about the constitution, even if it did not know that it enjoyed universal confidence out of doors. It was impossible for Fox to refuse supply, or to reject the Mutiny Bill by one vote. It was impossible for him to accuse the Crown or the Lords of frustrating the will of the people, when the opinions of the people's elected representatives were divided in the proportions of 190 to 191. He had tried hard to pretend that public opinion did not exist, so long as an election was avoidable; but now public opinion had made itself felt, like a chilling wind from the river, within the walls of the chamber where he fancied himself supreme.

With this vote disappeared Fox's last resource. He had brandished his parliamentary majority as a title to omnipotence, and his majority had crumbled in his hands. The time had come for him to face the electorate, whom he had tried to cheat out of their rights more openly than any man since Charles the Second. He knew what was in store for him. He let the Mutiny Bill pass: as for the high crime and misdemeanour of issuing public monies without a vote of supply, Pitt could snap his fingers at that, so certain was he of an indemnity from the next Parliament. On March the 25th, Parliament was dissolved.

Pitt had one final card up his sleeve. The Clerkship of the Pells, that mysterious Irish sinecure, which Fox had sold in 1775, fell vacant during the first days that Pitt was clinging to office. By this time the emoluments of the post had risen to £3,000 a year. It was providential. Pitt had less than £300 a year of his own: he had little prospect of remaining in power much beyond the New Year; and if he fell then, he fell for good. The King, the cabinet, even his enemies felicitated him on the happy coincidence by which his political independence was assured just when his political future was most in doubt. But Pitt refused it: he gave it away, and he gave it away on a particular condition. Barré, it will be remembered, had been given a life-pension of £3,000 in compensation for his shabby treatment by the Rockingham party. Pitt now made Barré Clerk of the Pells in return for a surrender of the pension. He not only passed over his own admitted claims: he not only rewarded a deserving public servant: he saved the public £3,000 a year. In Parliament, such an action at a time when he needed every vote he could buy was regarded as akin to madness: in the country, it is said to have had more influence on the election results than any other single argument. It was the best foretaste he could give of his financial methods.

Pitt came before the electorate as a man of twenty-four, the son of England's greatest Prime Minister; who had opposed the American war; who had twice moved for Parliamentary reform; who had given concrete proof of economical reform; who had joined Shelburne when Fox had deserted him; who had "forbidden the banns" of the hated coalition; who had frustrated the India Bill; who had maintained himself for three months by skill and courage against the bluster of a hubristic majority. Fox came before the electorate as a man of thirty-five, the son of England's wealthiest time-server; who had started life as an outrageous re-actionary; who had thrown up his first government within three months out of disappointed ambition; who had allied himself to a man he had sworn to impeach; who had signed a treaty he had described as worse than any war; who had sold Parliamentary reform for North's support; who had paid only lip-service to economic reform; who had attempted to set up a permanent oligarchy founded on Indian patronage; who had used an ill-gotten majority of one House to flout both the other branches of the legislature, and to deprive the electorate of their right to be consulted; whose private affairs were a national scandal, and whose poverty was imputable entirely to his dominating vice.

Pitt came back with a working majority of over two hundred. A hundred and sixty of the supporters of the coalition were unseated, many of them in constituencies for which they had paid the full market price. Fox's Martyrs, they were dubbed. The mince-pie administration settled down to seventeen years of uninterrupted power.

CHAPTER FOURTEEN

1. *Political Causes of Fox's Downfall*

Less than half of Fox's political career was now concluded by the calamities of 1784: but there is material in those sixteen years to form a provisional verdict on his merits and his failings. Between 1784 and his death he will meet with triumphs and disasters: but he will never again rise to the pinnacle he reached in March, 1782, nor sink below the disgrace that overwhelmed him in March, 1784. The wheel has come full circle. Fox has lived already through the whole gamut of political fame. No public man has stood higher than Fox in the month when he stopped the American war, arrested the progress of personal government, and came into office with dazzling hopes of Parliamentary and economic reform. None has been more repudiated, execrated and lampooned than Fox in two years, Fox the frustrated Catiline, whose props had broken one by one.

He is a character compounded of extremes. Give him a great cause to fight, and he will fight it like a Bayard. Cross his path in cabinet, and he will revenge himself with the misdirected cunning of Dryden's Achitophel. The paradox extends beyond his public life. His friends thought him a saint: to the public he was the embodiment of voluptuous egotism. He saw himself as a man of retiring nature, called from his books and friends to the defence of expiring liberty: yet he never failed to create the impression, and to colour the imputation, of an insatiable and reckless lust for power.

"Fox had three passions," said a contemporary; "women, play, and politics. Yet he never formed a creditable connection with a woman; he squandered all his means at the gaming table; and, except for eleven months, he was invariably in opposition." The remark is profoundly lacking in insight, but up to 1784 it is true. He was yet to form a creditable connection with a woman, if not with a creditable woman. His means, if not recouped, ceased to be squandered. He ultimately regained office. But at thirty-five he seemed to have failed as completely as a man can fail. Fortune had lavished on him nine-tenths of all she has to give; yet he was landed, before he was middle-aged, in outer darkness. He was still what he had been at eight years old: "Fox's son Charles, with twice his parts, and half his sagacity." He had learnt nothing; he had shown that he could achieve anything.

The facile theory of Fox's failure is to say that he carried his gambling habits into public life. He played pitch and toss with his own and his party's prospects: the India Bill was a game of double or quits. Up to a point this is true. He was the most reckless of public men, and each time he lost he doubled the stake. His resignation having failed, he increased his throw to a coalition and an India Bill. He lost the India Bill, and proceeded to put everything on the same square as the coalition. It was certainly a rake's progress, but the parallel is far-fetched. What it does not explain is why all his wrong moves were in the same direction. Why did he, a Whig, a successful party leader, the unchallenged master of the platform, always move away from constitutional methods, away from the two-party system, away from the expressed wishes of the people? Why was he impatient of the slow working of the constitutional machinery, which was working all the time in his favour?

The answer is on the surface: Fox was a Stuart. He was not Charles James for nothing. With the thick desirous lips and heavy eyebrows of Charles the Second he had inherited the fatalism, the lack of judgment, the recklessness, the intemperance, the consistent bad luck, the unreliability, the unteachableness of a Stuart. Above all, he had inherited the Stuart negligence and incomprehension of law. Fox fought the Hanoverians as the Stuarts had fought their Parliaments—with the first weapons that came to hand, good or bad, wise or unwise, legal or illegal. He had no conception of the legal mentality; he thought in particular instances; he was incorrigibly opportunist, saying what he didn't mean, and doing what in anyone else he would condemn. No man alluded more often to the beauties of our glorious constitution: no man had less intention of abiding by it when it conflicted with his immediate whim. Take three instances within two years. In May, 1782, he opposed a motion to expunge from the journals the record of Luttrell's election thirteen years before: he declared (most courageously) that he still adhered to his old view of that matter. In July, 1782, he declared that the cabinet had the right to elect a

Prime Minister to succeed Rockingham. In January, 1784, he declared that the King was not entitled to dissolve Parliament in the middle of a session. In all these cases he was inventing constitutional law as he went along, to suit his own purposes. As far as the constitution was concerned, he was an habitual criminal. He had no use for such restraints: he failed to understand their generalised application. It was Charles the Second to the life.

So much for his hereditary failings. But they are not the core of Fox's character. Fox's real genius is something that cannot be put down to heredity, unless, like Burke, we trace it back to Henry of Navarre. It was his own contribution to his destiny: it was a contribution to the history of the century, and to the development of the national character. The central thing about Fox was not his ability nor his fearlessness, but his largeness of heart. There were abler men. Chatham was more brilliant, Pitt was more competent, Burke was more profound. But Fox was alone in his generosity, his nobility, his absolute lack of pettiness or deception. Burke, who knew him for thirty years, from his youth up, declared that "he was of the most artless, candid, open, and benevolent disposition, disinterested in the extreme, of a temper mild and placable, even to a fault, without one drop of gall in his whole constitution." One who knew him intimately in later life gave it as his opinion that "Charles Fox was not only the most extraordinary man I have ever seen, but also the best man." And Gibbon himself paid the ungrudging tribute of a small man: "Perhaps no human being was ever more exempt from the taint of malevolence, vanity, or falsehood." When a man's contemporaries consistently use superlatives about him, it is in vain that the biographer attempts to avoid them.

Such were the abilities, and such was the character, that were nullified by Fox's faults of judgment and his ineradicable love of violent courses. Of all unexpected people, George the Third's aunt has summed up the contrast best. "That Fox," said the Princess Emily, "that Fox may be a rogue, I know nothing of that: all I know is that he is a great man, and this country is ruined unless such a great man governs it, so I wish him success with all my heart." But in England a great man goes for nothing if he is a rogue, and an extremist is only tolerated if he is consistent. If Fox had been born in the previous century, he would have scaled the heights of power: he was born to beat arbitrary monarchs at their own game. In the second half of the eighteenth century Fox spoke and thought and acted like one of the great, turbulent Whigs of 1680. Like them, he stuck at nothing to gain his ends. They took money from France: Fox did nothing more scrupulous when he joined forces with North. He spoke in the very language of the old Whigs; he harped eternally on the revolution of 1688; he menaced impeachment and hinted at scaffolds. His means, like theirs, were constantly disgracing his ends. His principles were consistent to a fault: in action he was a scandalous opportunist. In opposition inflexible, in office a weathercock; in theory a Cicero, in practice a Catiline; he united all that makes a statesman with all that can undo a politician.

The rise of middle-class opinion began with the Wilkes agitation, and found its first voice at the elections of 1784. It was courted by Pitt, and unobserved by Fox. To Pitt, and his young friends at Goosetree's, public opinion was the only deity worth worshipping. To Fox, and his boisterous "comrogues" at Brooks's, politics were still a family affair, gentlemanly though acrimonious. Public opinion to them meant no more than a good audience in Westminster Hall. Petitions and resolutions from outside were serviceable enough in their way; but the real battle went on inside the charmed circle, where Whig and Tory struggled away and changed sides and coalesced and seceded, as their fathers had done before them, as if the electorate never existed. Fox in this respect had never altered from the young puppy who defended Wilkes' exclusion. "The business of the people," he had said then, "is to choose us. It is ours to maintain the independency of Parliament." On that principle he meant in 1771 to send the Lord Mayor to prison, and in 1784 to prevent an appeal to the country. The actions were alike, the arguments were alike. How was the public to know that he had undergone a change of heart? In that respect he was exactly the same man: he was still Lord Holland's son, carefully educated to be the most negligent member of a negligent set. His moral reputation was bad, and militated against him with the Dissenters: but his political reputation was worse, and ruined him with the whole body of middle-class opinion. He took as little care to improve the one as the other. In Fox, said the Duchess of Devonshire, "fear of seeming to yield what he thinks right to the bias of public opinion is superior to everything." That could never have been said of Pitt.

Pitt was born to show Fox up. They represented the Idle and the Industrious Apprentice, the eighteenth century *versus* the nineteenth. The country was as tired of Brooks's as it was of Buckingham House: Pitt was the negation of both. He was the symbol of a new era in politics. The old aristocratic parties, the old family cabinets, the pensions and sinecures, the nepotism, the log-rolling, the wire-pulling, were to be swept away. The Whigs were every bit as effete as the Tories; the country had no more use for a Portland than for a North. They would prefer to see "a kingdom trusted to a schoolboy's care" than a kingdom eternally wrangled for and bled white by the great families of the peak of Derbyshire and the reprobates of St. James's Street. All the political dynasties and clubs, the coalitions without principles, and quarrels without causes, were bewildering and nauseating to the middle classes. Pitt put a stop to these perpetual evolutions of shifty and unstable figures on the political stage. His was neither a Whig nor a Tory government: least of all was it a coalition. His colleagues might be young and little known: but they were a breakaway from all that had gone before. He gave the country eight years at least of good and straightforward government. If Fox had been his Foreign Minister, it would have been excellent government. Fox's exclusion from the new system is a major tragedy of English history. He had his last chance of joining it in January, 1784, and he rejected it. He clung to the old system, which had lost him everything he had: "his ease, his security, his interest, his power, even his darling popularity."

2. *Personal Causes of Fox's Downfall*

It was not his upbringing that made Fox so tenacious of the outworn system that was symbolised by Brooks's: it was the binding strength of innumerable friendships. He is not the only man who has been ruined by friendships: but no man has lost more on that account. If providence had meant to be kind to Fox, she would never had endowed him with his astounding charm.

Charm is a quality as accidental as good looks. Fox might have been every bit as noble a character, every bit as brilliant an intellect, without attracting a single friend: he might have been a monster without having a friend the less. But malignant fortune had thrust upon him a personal fascination which eclipsed all his other gifts. There had been charming men before Fox, but his friends could find no precedent with which to compare Fox's charm: there have been charming men since Fox, but Fox's charm remains a legend, a quality inseparable from his name. As a boy he had enslaved his family; and age seemed only to increase the delight of his companionship and the magic of his smile. In middle life he drew young men to him, from the Prince of Wales downwards, like moths to a candle. His charm had landed him, at thrity-five, with a collection of friends who might have ruined the most promising career.

In the attempt to arrive at an impartial narrative of his conduct, Fox's charm has been intentionally passed over. But its influence as a factor in his tragedy is unquestionable. It was perhaps the greatest of his handicaps. It put him above other men, and beyond their advice. A man like Fitzpatrick fell at once: a man like Pitt, while acknowledging that Fox was a "magician", held himself aloof from the incense-burning circle. So Fox became the head and centre of a devoted and wholly uncritical clique. He would make any sacrifice to his friends short of taking their advice: they would take any liberty with him short of offering it. This cult had disastrous consequences. Whatever Fox might decide was applauded to the echo by the select band of Townshends, Grenvilles and Cavendishes. They wrote to each other in terms of awe about their leader. When they applaud his kindness, his intelligence, or his simplicity of character, their superlatives ring true: but when they refer to his judgment or his wisdom, it is clear that the critical faculties of men of the world were not proof against charm, when charm was concentrated in such unparalleled strength.

When he wanted discussion or advice, which was seldom, he preferred to exchange his thoughts with women. This also was a misfortune. It is a woman who is his most incisive critic on the matter of his friends, and of all women, she who was most disposed to love him, and had known him longest. "Poor dear Charles," writes Sarah Lennox, "is so surrounded with flatterers that tempt him to think *he alone* can overset the whole fabric, that it's in vain to talk." Again, "those wretches who surround Charles quite undo him." But when all was said and done, she, like everybody else, forgave him. "I have overcome my anger upon the reflection that Charles has good qualities enough to atone for a thousand faults." He must have been irresistible.

11

CHAPTER FIFTEEN

1. *The Westminster Election, 1784*

The catastrophic election of 1784 was only redeemed by Fox's personal victory at Westminster. In the provinces his name stank: Anglicans shuddered at his public principles, Nonconformists at his private principles. But in Westminster it was different: when the "black animal" mounted the hustings in Covent Garden Piazza, and launched forth into one of his nervous and intemperate harangues, "blowing, and sweltering, and scratching his black behind," why, there was no resisting him. In other constituencies the issue was fought on Fox's politics: in Westminster, on Fox's personality. As Johnson said: "I am for the King against Fox; but I am for Fox against Pitt. The King is my master; but I do not know Pitt; and Fox is my friend."

It was an Homeric contest. Two ministerial candidates opposed Fox, of whom one, Admiral Lord Hood, was a certainty. The contest lay between Fox and one Sir Cecil Wray for the second seat. The poll was open for more than six weeks, an average of about four hundred voters polling every day. During the first fortnight, when the poll was heaviest, things went very badly for Fox. Wray got more than three hundred ahead of him, and he was gloomily considering whether to give up, when an unexpected auxiliary stepped into the arena. The Duchess of Devonshire began to canvass for him. Fox's colours were buff and blue, the colours of Washington's uniform, which he had defiantly worn in the House throughout the American war. Georgiana dressed herself from head to foot in buff and blue; she produced a hat covered with foxes' tails, and flung herself into the struggle with an abandon which charmed even more than it shocked the electorate. Where arguments failed she descended to entreaties: where entreaties failed she resorted to osculation. From Hounslow to Temple Bar, from eight in the morning till nightfall, the most beautiful woman in England was to be seen flying to and fro in an open carriage, bringing butchers and navvies to the poll. "Were I God Almighty," said one astounded labourer, "I should make her the Queen of Heaven." "I could light my pipe at her eyes," said another.

> "Arrayed in matchless beauty, Devon's fair
> In Fox's favour takes a zealous part;
> But oh! where'er the pilferer comes, beware!
> She supplicates a vote, but steals a heart."

From the moment of Georgina's intervention the tide turned. The ministers had no weapons to retaliate: Lady Salisbury, pressed into Wray's service, proved a miserable failure. The contest grew daily more furious. Stink-bombs flew: blood was shed: dying men were brought to vote with palsied hands: bookmakers established a ring around the hustings. At the rate of about twenty votes a day, Fox stole a march on Wray. Finally, in mid-May, the poll closed, having been opened on the 1st of April. The figures were: Hood, 6694; Fox, 6233; Wray, 5998.

A majority of 235 votes for the former Man of the People in the most popular constituency in England was the only consolation the Foxites could extract from the election results, and they made the most of it. A gigantic procession traversed the constituency; it was headed by a fleur-de-lys of ostrich plumes and a banner inscribed "Sacred to Female Patriotism": on the box of Fox's coach sat two symbols of the coalition, George North and William Adam: the rear was brought up by the carriages of the Duchesses of Portland and Devonshire, drawn by three pairs each. This cavalcade wended its way, with much window-smashing, from Covent Garden to Devonshire House, at the gates of which the Prince of Wales awaited it on a specially erected platform, from which Fox thanked the loyal six thousand. Next day there was a garden party at Carlton House, held at the same time as, and in full view of, the royal procession down the Mall for the opening of Parliament. Both sexes wore buff and blue: even Lord North appeared in the colours of Washington's volunteers. The Prince's dinner party was prolonged "in defiance of usage, and almost of human nature," far into the next morning. The Prince, in buff and blue, waited on the female patriots in person. "True blue and Mrs. Crewe," was the toast of the evening. "True blue and all of you," responded Mrs. Crewe. The Foxites were still a very happy family.

A very different celebration some week before had ended less happily. Pitt had been given the freedom of the City of London, the stronghold of true Whig principles. There had followed a city dinner, presided over by that emblem of municipal worth, John Wilkes. On his return, Pitt was preceded by a mob that grew larger and more enthusiastic at every step. This triumph turned from Pall Mall into St. James's Street just as its forerunners were trying to force the occupants of Brooks's to illuminate their windows in its honour. A council of war was held within the club, and resistance decided upon. An ambush was hastily arranged; a sally was made by the club servants from the ground floor; while their attack was covered by a shower of missiles from the upper windows. "Fox and popular government!" shouted the one party, as they demolished the Prime Minister's carriage. "Pitt and the Constitution!" roared the other, as they smashed the window-panes of the Whig citadel. In the mêlée, Pitt contrived to take shelter behind the opposing ramparts of White's: but he left an ugly scene behind him.

The blame for this extraordinary affair was immediately fastened on Fox. Brooks's was by this time devoted exclusively to his interests: it existed to hear Fox talk, and talk he did from the rising of the House of Commons until the rising of the sun, walking up and down the length of the Subscription Room, "with a train at his heels." A Foxite who was not a member of Brooks's was nobody, as can be seen from the extraordinary trouble Fox took to get Sheridan elected: on the other hand, a member who was not a Foxite did well to stay away, as this very incident showed, for Pitt lived and died a member of Brooks's. It was hardly surprising, therefore, that Fox was accused of having set on the chair-men to attack Pitt. But in point of fact, on this particular night he had not been in the club at all, as he was at pains to tell the world. He had not only an alibi—"I was in bed"—but a witness—"with Mrs. Armistead, who is ready to substantiate the fact on oath."

2. Mrs. Armistead

Mrs. Armistead's origins were wrapped in obscurity: as for Mr. Armistead, he is generally supposed to have been a figure of speech. She had been for many years the most prominent woman of the town: the Duke of Dorset, Lord Derby, and the Prince of Wales are among her ascertained lovers. "She lived in splendour, kept two sets of horses for her carriages, a proportionable establishment of servants; her table was the constant resort of all the young men of fashion in the kingdom; yet no one ever heard of any person being ruined by his attachment to her, which is more than can be said of any other woman who has been fashionable for many years." She had had the sense and taste to buy or lease a little house at Chertsey, St. Anne's Hill, exquisitely situated on a little incline, with the Thames not far behind it and the Surrey hills in front— a house and a view whose charm and elegance a dozen Stowes or Chatsworths could not afford. Thither she took her new lover, Fox, at the end of 1783.

She was just the woman for Fox. It is impossible to imagine him married to a woman of his own class. He had so little to offer. He was worse than poor, none too faithful, free in his speech and a bad listener: worse than all, he had a mind impervious to social distinctions. He would never have done for a débutante. But Mrs. Armistead's character had been tried in as many fires as Fox's own. She was extremely beautiful; she had been very poor; her charm and wit had endeared her to the most fastidious men of her day; she had made herself rich without ceasing to be extravagant; and when she met Fox she had no more worlds to conquer. With looks above envy, and a reputation beneath contempt, she was at peace with the world. She knew more men, and knew them better, than any woman of her day, and her final choice was Fox.

Fox was more wearied than disheartened by his continual failures in the great world. After his first three months in office he had spent six months recruiting in the arms of Mrs. Robinson. After his second term of nine months, he came to rest on the experienced bosom of Mrs. Armistead. From her only death was to part him.

3. *The Westminster Scrutiny, 1784-1785*

Although Fox had won such a famous victory at Westminster, he was not allowed to take his seat. A petition was lodged against him, and accepted with the connivance of the government. A scrutiny was ordered. In those days election appeals and scrutinies were the rule rather than the exception, and a scrutiny meant re-examination not of the votes but of the *bona fides* of the voters. In Malmesbury, with its thirteen voters, or in Midhurst, which apparently had none, this was all very well: but in Westminster, with several thousand, it was a farce. Fortunately, the news arrived that Fox had also been elected by the voters of Orkney and Shetland, who had taken a detached view of the India Bill controversy; and Fox was able to appear in Parliament to state his case. It was a strong case, indeed. The scrutiny could not be expected to take less than three years, or to cost less than £40,000, of which half would fall on the Treasury and half on Fox: and at the end of it all there was no serious prospect that he would be unseated.

It was fine oratorical material for Fox. "To the honourable gentleman over against me (Pitt) let me offer a little advice. Let him well weigh the consequences of what he is about, and look to the future effect of it upon the nation at large. Let him take care that when they see all the powers of his administration employed to overwhelm an individual, men's eyes may not open sooner than they would if he conducted himself within some bounds of decent discretion, and not thus openly violate the sacred principles of the constitution. . . . Though he may exert all the influence of his situation to harass and persecute, he shall find that we are incapable of unbecoming submissions. There is a principle of resistance in mankind that will not brook such injuries; and a good cause and a good heart will animate men to struggle in proportion to the size of their wrongs and the grossness of their oppressors." Nobody ever doubted that the member for Kirkwall Burghs had a good heart: now, for the first time in two years, he had a good cause as well. He reduced Pitt to a very lame reply. The scrutiny went on. After eight months, one-eighth of the list had been checked, at a cost of £10,000 to each party, with the result that Fox had lost eighteen invalid votes more than Wray had lost.

There were a number of debates on the matter, until in March,

1785, Pitt's own followers could tolerate the proceeding no longer. The Prime Minister was outvoted handsomely, and Fox came in for Westminster next day: he subsequently got heavy damages from the returning officer.

As a matter of political morality, the scrutiny was bad: as a tactical blunder, worse. Yet Pitt was as far from being a knave as from being a fool. His is an unattractive nature, and has suffered particularly from the lifelong contrast with Fox: but it is not repellent. He had from December to March given a display of Parliamentary skill that has never been approached: how did he come in May to lend his name to a proceeding that in England had no chance of success? Pitt loved power. He hated to share a responsibility with anyone: he could not tolerate advice or criticism. In his heart of hearts he found an arbitrary use of power more gratifying than judicious restraint. He was just twenty-five; he had swept the country; he had turned the tables on his only rival, as it seemed, for good. He was always cold and remorseless: there was a high-handed strain about him. The later treason trials, the events of 1798, the methods by which he forced through the Union with Ireland; all these show that he was not so strong a man as to be above the use of coercion. He had not the genius of being able to give way. He had little love of justice for its own sake. When he struck, he struck hard. In this instance he struck below the belt.

CHAPTER SIXTEEN

1. *Foreign Policy versus Finance, 1785-1787*

If it had not been for the Westminster scrutiny, Fox would have had uncommonly little to do in the new Parliament. There was little to oppose, and few to oppose it: and Fox was already beginning to find in his home and his mistress an attraction stronger than Westminster, Brooks's and Newmarket combined. For the first time in his life he begins to complain of the trouble and fatigue of public life: he is always straining to be back at St. Anne's Hill, where he has discovered a whole new continent of pleasures—the library, the garden, the beloved Thames. He was precocious even in decline. An Alcibiades at Eton, he became a Horace at thirty-five.

The few years after 1784 afforded poor hunting for a troublesome politician. Party was forgotten in Pitt's overwhelming triumph: a Whig ruled, and the Tories backed him. Foreign politics were neglected after the treaty had been signed. It was a time for economic recovery, the least spectacular sort of politics. Pitt could give the country exactly what it needed—sound finance and tranquillity. Pitt had studied the finance of government at the feet of two original thinkers: Adam Smith and Lord Shelburne. He had joined these pioneers in a firm determination to ease the flow of foreign trade as far as was compatible with maintaining the revenue. His mind was fascinated by the simple automatism of finance. He ushered into the world with great pride a scheme for a sinking fund by which a million a year should be set aside at compound interest to redeem the national debt in so many hundred years. If the budget showed a million deficit on the year, two millions were to be borrowed, one for the deficit, the other for the sinking fund. That was how Pitt's mind worked.

To Fox's thinking, all this was abracadabra: as indeed much of it was. Fox, somebody said, regarded finance as an invention of Pitt's. He openly admitted that he despised political economy as a science. His education had not been one of which Adam Smith would have approved: he had no love for anything associated with Shelburne. As Dr. Price, Shelburne's intimate friend and the principal protagonist of the sinking fund, proclaimed from his dissenting pulpit, could the nation expect a man who had been so little of an economist in his own affairs to be an economist in the affairs of the nation? Fox had no use for Dr. Price; neither for his political friends, nor for his religious sect, nor for the simple chastity of his financial methods. Fox was rather like Disraeli's Lord Roehampton: "He is the man. He does not care a rush whether the revenue increase or declines. He is thinking of real politics; foreign affairs; maintaining our power in Europe."

Pitt's finance came into contact with Fox's "real politics" over a Commercial Treaty with France in 1787. It was a sound treaty in its way, a piece of work after the heart of Peel or Gladstone. But Fox would have none of it, and for two reasons. In the first place, he had found that free trade was unpopular with the mercantile classes: its benefits were widespread and dimly felt, while its hardships fell on compact and vocal interests: by opposing an Irish Commercial Treaty in 1785, he had secured a sudden popularity in Manchester and Liverpool. In the second place, he would have no amicable relations of any sort with France. The house of Bourbon was his bogey; it was to be shunned and dreaded, our relations with it must be as bad as possible. This was a Whig inheritance from William the Third: as a policy, it had been sanctified by the victories of Chatham over the French: as a prejudice, it had been born afresh in Fox's mind by the perfidy of France in 1778. He had then declared boldly for attacking France, as our natural enemy: he had been more reluctant to make peace with France than Shelburne had been, and had come within an ace of provoking a renewal of the war: and a study of the Foreign Office files of 1777-1778 had only deepened his feeling that France was most dangerous when most friendly.

This virulent anti-Bourbon feeling was often justified, but it missed its mark in the French Commercial Treaty. He attacked it as though it were another Treaty of Dover. "France is the natural political enemy of Great Britain. Her overweening pride and boundless ambition make her so; her invariable and ardent desire to hold the sway of Europe. . . . Past experience shows that whenever France sees this country weak, and thinks her incapable of resisting, she seizes the opportunity and aims at effecting her long-desired destruction." He added a further argument that is useful for future reference. "One reason to distrust France is the amiable character of the French king, a monarch celebrated for his love of justice, for his desire to serve his country, and his wish to aggrandise her name." These arguments were misdirected. *Timeo Danaos et dona ferentes* is all very well: but the French offerings in this instance consisted principally of claret, an import we might take from our worst enemy without weakening ourselves, or fortifying him.

Fox made himself a little ridiculous by his furious opposition to this treaty; but, in general, his pronouncements on foreign politics carried great weight. It was a sphere of politics conceded to him. He was the advocate of the Northern Powers: his stock stood high at St. Petersburg and Berlin: contrary to the rest of English opinion, he thought the partition of Poland a less sinister act than France's intervention in the American War. He believed in a forward foreign policy, and the continual support of a balance of power. "This country should always attend to foreign affairs, and mix in them." To this end, he declared that England must be strongly armed. He said that it was "necessary, open, and manly for the government to come to the lower orders of the people, those who were labouring under the heaviest burdens and say, 'Severely taxed as we know you are, you must nevertheless contribute something towards the expense of keeping political power upon a balance in Europe'." This was no ordinary line for an opposition leader to take. But Fox was sincere in his foreign politics. He did not conveniently forget in opposition the grim and expensive necessities that had been impressed on him in office, when he had his finger on the pulse of national affairs. When France was getting the upper hand in Holland, and Prussia in return invaded that country at the direct instigation of the British Ambassador, Fox overwhelmed the government with congratulations. He was always ready to support a supplementary vote for the navy. He had no facile, vote-catching illusions about the cliffs of Dover.

2. Warren Hastings, 1786-1795

In the prevailing political torpor, Burke's uneasy spirit was roaming around for an injustice to redress or an institution to defend. He finally pitched on Warren Hastings, who came home from his thirteen years' Governorship of Bengal in 1785. Burke had been preparing his subject for some years previously: he had undertaken an inquiry that would have been prodigious on the part of a government department: he knew by this time as much about India as he had previously known about America. He persuaded the party that Hastings must be impeached. The next thing was to persuade the House of Commons.

Hastings' guilt will not be canvassed here. The full story belongs to the life of Burke. It was Burke who undertook the labour: it was Sheridan who walked off with the laurels: but Fox lent them the support of his eloquence, and not a little hard work. There were three charges to divide between them, and each charge had to be opened twice—once before the House of Commons before the impeachment could be decided upon, and again before the Lords when the trial began in form. It was a feast of oratory. Burke opened the charge on the extirpation of the Rohillas in June, 1786: it was defeated. A fortnight later Fox opened the charge on the desecration of Benares: to the astonishment of the prosecutors themselves, it was carried. What had happened in the interval was a sudden change of opinion on the part of Pitt. His motives were twofold. Firstly, Hastings was in great favour with the King, who wished to appoint him to the Indian Board of Control: Pitt saw no way so efficacious to prevent this as to let him be put on trial. Secondly, the opposition were evidently in earnest, and the trial would be long: Pitt would far prefer to have the greatest orators of the day kept busy attacking Hastings in Westminster Hall than attacking himself in St. Stephen's Chapel. It has been suggested that Pitt was acting in good faith, and actually was convinced that the second charge was valid. But this defence falls to the ground at once, since Pitt cannot possibly have acted in good faith in voting against the first charge. The function of the Commons in deciding for or against an impeachment is precisely the same as the function of a grand jury. The case for the prosecution only is heard, and on that it is decided whether there is or is not a case worth trying: the defence is reserved for the trial before the Lords. Burke's speech to the Commons on the Rohilla charge is extant: no man in possession of his faculties would have listened to that speech, and sincerely believed that there was no true bill. Pitt certainly voted in bad faith against the first charge: there is no reason why he should not do the same on the second charge, except the explanation of subtle (and not unjustifiable) policy.

The third charge, relating to the despoilment of the Begums of Oude, was entrusted to Sheridan, who brought it before the House in February, 1787, in a speech of nearly six hours' duration, which was universally agreed at the time to constitute the final consummation of English eloquence, and has certainly not been rivalled since. The actual trial began a year later. Pitt's stratagem was abundantly justified. The opposition turned their heaviest guns on to Hastings, and very heavy they proved to be. To read the volumes of speeches at the Hastings trial is to realise that the spoken word is a lost art. That art never had a more perfect chance to display itself. Burke's profundity of thought, Fox's lucid argument, Sheridan's wit and imagery; all were necessary, and all different. If the exponents were a matchless team, the case for the prosecution was a matchless occasion for oratory. The wrongs that Cicero avenged on Verres were petty larceny beside the wrongs of which Hastings was either the instigator or the scapegoat. He was acquitted; and history has been kind to him: but Burke's purpose was achieved when once the trial was instituted. The East would never submit to the same sort of rule again, when once they knew, what they had never guessed, that there was some public morality in the people of the West.

Pitt's purpose was achieved many times over. The trial lasted till 1795. Long before that the Foxites were tired to death of the whole thing. They wished, they said, that Hastings would fly the country, with Burke at his heels. But for several sessions profound peace reigned in the Commons, while all London flocked to witness this judicial siege of Troy in Westminster Hall.

3. Mrs. Fitzherbert, 1787

In 1787 Fox again burnt his fingers badly by his intimate connection with the Prince of Wales. Three years before, just at the time the coalition was breaking down, the Prince had fallen in love with a woman six years his senior. Mrs. Fitzherbert was a beautiful widow, a Catholic, and a woman of irreproachably difficult virtue. She was gravely embarrassed by his importunity: finally, when the Prince stabbed himself, and declared that he would die unless she promised to marry him, she was forced to go abroad to avoid him. The Prince was inconsolable. At first he intended to follow her, and the King was reduced to enlisting Fox's help in dissuading him. He bombarded her with letters of enormous length. He came constantly in a state of distraction to St. Anne's Hill, where he would roll on the floor and pull his hair out and bellow with grief before the sympathetic eyes of Mrs. Armistead. He declared that he would sell everything, sign away the crown, and run off with his beloved to America.

Fox did what he could to cool this hopeless passion. But late in 1785 he heard with consternation that Mrs. Fitzherbert, whether she had given way to his insistence, or thought that it was over, had returned to England. He wrote a long, sensible, and persuasive letter to the Prince, pointing out the imperative arguments against marriage with a Catholic, which would either be morganatic, in which case the Prince would regret it, or else an imposition, which was hardly right by the woman. "A mock marriage, for it can be no other, is neither honourable for any of the parties, nor, with respect to your Royal Highness, even safe. This appears so clear to me, that, if I were Mrs. Fitzherbert's father or brother I would advise her by no means to agree to it, but to prefer any other species of connection with you to one leading to so much misery and mischief." The Prince's reply was prompt and explicit: "Make yourself easy, my dear friend; believe me the world will now soon be convinced that there not only is not, but never was, any ground for these reports which of late have been so malevolently circulated." Ten days after he wrote those words, the Prince was secretly married. Mrs. Fitzherbert had fallen for him but "any other species of connection" she had resisted to the last.

There for a year the matter remained. Mrs. Fitzherbert was satisfied that she had been well and truly married. The public was satisfied that the two were living in sin, though there were some scandalmongers so malicious as to insinuate that it was wedlock. The legal position was simple, but curious. By the Act of Settlement the Prince by marrying a Catholic had cut himself out of the succession: but by the Royal Marriage Act of 1772, passed through no fault of Fox's, he was not married at all. It was a mock marriage, as Mrs. Fitzherbert found to her cost: but, in spite of its invalidity, the effect of its publication upon public opinion would have threatened the Prince's prospects of the crown.

In 1787 the House was debating the evergreen topic of the Prince of Wales' debts, when a back-bench member gave voice to the suspicion that the Prince had married his paramour. This called up Fox, who denied the report "*in toto*, in point of fact, as well as law. The fact not only never could have happened legally, but never did happen in any way whatsoever, and had from the beginning been a base and malicious falsehood." He added that "he had direct authority for what he said." And, being Fox, he further added that the rumour was miserable, wanton, base, malignant, low, gross, malicious and scandalous, only fit to impose on the lower orders in the streets. Whether he went on the Prince's letter, or had challenged him about it since then, is not known. At all event, the House was satisfied with this downright assurance on the part of an intimate friend that the liaison was totally illicit, and proceeded to vote the Prince £160,000. But one member was not satisfied: Pitt turned to his neighbour on the Treasury bench, and quoted the words of Othello: "Villain, be sure thou prove my love a whore."

Next day there was the devil to pay. First the Prince broke the news to Mrs. Fitzherbert: "Only conceive, Maria, what Fox did yesterday; he went down to the House, and denied that you and I were man and wife. Did you ever hear of such a thing?" She was wounded to the quick: the Prince in great distress sent for Sheridan and begged him to say something in the House which would remove Fox's imputation that Maria was a concubine, without making a clean breast of the marriage. But such a task was beyond even Sheridan's ingenuity: he went down and murmured a few compliments about the Prince's taste in women, which were taken by the House for mere Sheridanic sycophancy. Then Fox, still blissfully ignorant, went to Brooks's, where a member accosted him with a stunning piece of information. "I see by the

papers, Mr. Fox, you have denied the fact of marriage of the
Prince with Mrs. Fitzherbert. You have been misinformed. I was
present at that marriage." Fox was caught in the ugliest dilemma
imaginable. Either he must let his name stand as the sanction of a
lie: or he must recant, at the risk of another Gordon Riot and the
departure of the Prince, on whom he staked his political hopes,
to Hanover. He decided to say nothing about it; for which he
cannot easily be blamed: but the rest of his party continued less
discreetly to take refuge in the legal quibble, and to deny loudly
that a ceremony had taken place at all, which in the eyes of one
party had legitimated her whole conduct.

Mrs. Fitzherbert relished Fox's public reflections on her status
so little that she never spoke to him again: the Prince on his side
never summoned the courage to confess to her that the fault was
entirely his. It would be natural to suppose that Fox broke off
relations with the Prince immediately and for good. Poor judge
as he was of human nature, he can never have credited the Prince
with a particle of character or good feeling. He must have known
from the start that the Prince, even as a private individual, was a
discreditable acquaintance: now, for the second time, it was made
clear to him that their intimacy was dangerous on public grounds.
Yet this incident was far from ending their relations. For about a
year, it is true, Fox avoided the Prince, who rather forlornly
pursued him to country houses where he was supposed to be
staying. But they were on terms again before very long. Fox was
so convinced that the Whig party would never get into power on
its merits, without the Prince's help, that he conquered his dislike
for that untruthful character. The next year, they were working
together as usual—Fox and the Prince against Pitt and the people.

From this episode also dates the increased ascendancy of Sheridan over the Prince. Poor Sheridan is a figure so brilliant and so
tragic, so capable of enjoyment and so consistently denied it, that
to criticise him posthumously is almost to associate oneself with
the regiment of prigs and pedants who cheated and frustrated him
alive. Public life was a much harder struggle for him than for Fox
—a struggle against his own poverty, and against the exclusiveness
and respectability of others: yet he achieved great triumphs in a
sphere to which he was born. In the end the orthodox Foxites
were too strong for him. They ousted him from public life, and
hounded him to a miserable death: as soon as he was gone, they

set about blackening his name in order to clear Fox of the injustices he had done him. Sheridan only attached himself to the Prince because he needed any foothold he could get: and in all their relations he was sensible, courteous and scrupulously honest. He got from the Prince that confidence and condescension that Fox inflexibly refused him. He acted as a liaison officer between the two. It was not a very reputable position for a politician, still less for a man of genius. But he fulfilled it honourably, and it was his only resource. It was largely the fault of Fox's intolerance that he could find no other object for his ambition. Sheridan regarded himself as second in command of the Whig party: but Fox thought him disqualified both by his lack of social position and by his lack of moral stamina. He used to speak to Sheridan, it was noticed, "as if he were talking to a swindler." Possibly Fox was right. Sheridan had less stamina than a politician ought to have, but it would be difficult to prove that he had less stamina than Fox.

CHAPTER SEVENTEEN

1. *The Regency Crisis, 1788-1789*

In 1788, having cleared several thousand pounds at the New-market April meeting, Fox took Mrs. Armistead abroad. Their first stopping place was Geneva, where Fox had sent a deaf and dumb natural son to school: from there they went on to Lausanne, where their arrival caused a great flutter in Gibbon's breast. He has recorded the episode to perfection: he gives one of those really vivid pictures of Fox which become so rare after Horace Walpole's Journal ceases. "He seemed to feel and even to envy the happiness of my situation, while I admired the powers of a superior man, as they are blended in his attractive character with the softness and simplicity of a child. Perhaps no human being was ever more perfectly exempt from the taint of malevolence, vanity, or false-hood. . . . Our conversation never flagged a moment; and he seemed thoroughly pleased with the place and with the company. We had little politics, though he gave me in a few words such a character of Pitt, as one great man should give another, his rival; much of books, from my own, on which he flattered me very pleasantly, to Homer and the Arabian Nights; much about the country, my garden (which he understands far better than I do), and upon the whole I think he envies me, and would do so were he minister. . . . The people gaze on him as on a prodigy, but he shows little inclination to converse with them. The wit and beauty of his companion are not sufficient to excuse the scandalous impropriety of showing her to all Europe, and you will not easily conceive how he has lost himself in the public opinion, which was already more favourable to his rival. Will Fox never know the importance of character?" Here are all the essential features of Fox's middle period. Four years of opposition has made him an expert gardener; he is quite the Cincinnatus; but he still captures the imagination of foreigners. All his defeats have not lessened his absolute refusal to conciliate public opinion. He resents being looked on as a prodigy: he flaunts his reputation in front of those who think his morals to be their concern. In this he was unflinching to the day of his death: his morals, like his politics, were there to be taken or left. He never adapted or concealed them.

On this tour it suited Fox's purpose to be under a cloud. They had come to look at Italian pictures, and they were able to look at them in peace, cold-shouldered by the English colony where-ever they went. Fox is said to have looked at only one English newspaper in several weeks, and then only at the Newmarket column. But he was not beyond the reach of gossip. His nephew, Lord Holland, was very seriously ill: and one silly Englishman, hearing a rumour that he was dead, went so far as to address Fox as "My Lord." Fox's holiday was ruined. He was sincerely devoted to his nephew: and he was sincerely devoted to remaining in the House of Commons. Holland's birth in 1773 had not been exactly opportune; his death in 1788 would have been more intolerable still.

While Fox was in Bologna, wondering what to believe about his nephew's health, and on the point of leaving for Rome, a despatch reached him from the Duke of Portland, which roused him to extraordinary activity. Leaving Mrs. Armistead behind him, he travelled night and day without leaving his chaise, and covered the thousand miles to London in nine days, arriving on November the 24th.

The news which spurred him to such indecent haste was that of the King's illness, which in the course of October had begun to affect his wits, betraying itself by various unseasonable pranks and catcalls. It was only too true: but some very rash consequences had been deduced from it. The opposition had leapt to the con-clusion that the King was raving mad; that the Prince of Wales was going to rule in his place; and that they would all be in power in a few weeks. These were three very impertinent *non sequiturs*.

Parliament met a week after Fox's arrival, and he attended, haggard with dysentery as a result of his journey. Pitt had decided to act on the assumption that the madness might prove temporary. He played for time. He moved for a committee to search for pre-cedents. Fox's course was obvious: he must at all costs second the motion, oil the wheels of the committee, and so hasten the Prince's rise to power. That the Prince was the most natural candidate for the Regency nobody could deny, and no committee could dis-prove. If, as Fox untruthfully asserted, there were no precedents to be found, the whole thing was unanswerable—unless it was pitched too high.

Instead of this, Fox rose in a passion, to make the most foolish speech of his life. The proposed committee, he said, was a farce and a subterfuge. No precedents existed. The Prince was Regent already, and only his own exemplary moderation had restrained him from seizing the kingly power, in defiance of the machinations of his father's ministers. The House of Commons had no right to interfere in the matter: it was an impertinence on their part even to debate it. The Prince's succession was automatic: "it so belonged of right, during what he would call the civil death of the King, that it could not be more completely or legally his by the ordinary and natural demise of the Crown."

The House of Commons sat thunderstruck as this torrent of High Tory doctrine poured from the lips of Fox. Not Strafford lecturing them on the divine right of kings, not Queen Elizabeth putting the Commons in their place, had stretched the prerogative of the Crown further, or more belittled the privileges of Parliament: if Seymour had addressed the 1688 Convention in such haughty terms, he would have been shouted down. Pitt was exultant. As Fox fell deeper and deeper into his own trap, Pitt was seen to slap his thigh with delight, and exclaimed to his neighbour: "I'll un-Whig the gentleman for the rest of his life." As it happened Pitt was exceptionally well prepared for this emergency, for at the age of thirteen (only sixteen years before) he had written a tragedy in blank verse entitled "Laurentius, King of Clarinium," in which a loyal minister defeats the intrigues of a dastardly conspirator in the matter of a regency.

These tactics now came into play. During the ensuing debates Pitt amused himself by parodying the typical old-fashioned, full-blooded Whig speech. The glorious revolution of 1688—the great deliverer—the bill of rights—the beauty of the constitution—the need for checks and balances—all the dreary old tags were maliciously paraded in front of the party whose oratorical staple they had alway been: one after another the grand Whig doctrines were deftly hammered in, each one a nail in the coffin of Fox's consistency. Pitt had not overstated: he could and did un-Whig Fox for the rest of his life by this exquisite exposure.

This was not the limit of Fox's folly. The committee reported in a few days, and Pitt introduced a series of resolutions to make the Prince of Wales Regent subject to four restrictions. He was to have no power to create peers; he could make no life appointments;

he could not touch the King's property; and not he, but the Queen was to have custody of the King. These were unobjectionable restrictions, except on the assumption that the Prince wished to acquire a political influence that would outlive his father's recovery. That assumption Fox openly made. If Fox had not opposed the resolutions, the Prince would have been in power before the end of January. All Pitt's playing for time could not protract an unopposed bill beyond that. Actually, Fox fought the resolutions tooth and nail at every stage. He loudly and ignorantly denied the possibility of the King's recovery. He claimed unrestricted power for the Prince, and argued that it belonged to him of right. It did not require great political skill to pulverise these arguments. Why was Fox so anxious for the Prince to have full powers? Because he assumed that the Prince would call him to power at once, and he wished to create peers and life appointments and pensions sufficient to support a minority government. Fox was proposing to do precisely the thing for which, five years previously, he had execrated Pitt. He was proposing to form a government at the behest of the sovereign, in opposition to the sense of the House of Commons. But with one important difference—that while in 1783 the King, in appointing Pitt, had done what nine-tenths of the nation wished, in 1788 the Prince, in appointing Fox, would be doing what not one-tenth of the nation wished, and fewer still could approve. Fox's majority in 1783 had been an ill-gotten, accidental, temporary majority, representing nobody: Pitt's majority in 1788 was compact, powerful, and deservedly popular out of doors. The Prince was detested by the nation: if Fox were going to act as his Prime Minister he would have the Queen, the Lords, the Commons and the public solidly against him. He would never dare dissolve Parliament: he could only rule by the fullest possible use of the royal prerogative: he would need every peerage, every job, every pension he could lay hands on to keep a ministry together. That was why he opposed the restrictions. By opposing them he lost valuable time; and he, pleaded guilty to contemplating an exercise of royal prerogative and an outlay of public money beside which the corruption and coercion of North's *régime* would appear as blameless as a distribution of Maundy Pence.

The demeanour of the two parties in this crisis presents a painful contrast. Pitt was pessimistic. He expected to be out of office as soon as the Regency Bill passed—in opposition and badly in debt. The merchants of London voted him £100,000 in recognition of his masterly financial measures: he waved it aside. He took chambers in Lincoln's Inn: he proposed to seek a living at the Bar.

At Brooks's all was optimism and revelry. The Prince of Wales entertained the young gentlemen after dinner with mimicry of his father's ravings. Burke burnt the midnight oil over a pile of books on lunacy, and nauseated the House (until their groans stopped him) with a disgusting account of the antics a royal maniac might be expected to display. Sheridan horrified public opinion by warning the House not to provoke the Prince into asserting his right: Burke went one better by declaring that the King had been hurled from his throne by the decree of the Almighty. Fox wrote letters all round, allotting peerages and posts: this for Lord Sandwich, that for young Mr. Grey, the other for young Mr. Townshend or young Mr. Grenville—and, is it to be believed, the Pay Office once more, and nothing but the Pay Office, for Burke. His subordinates busily counted their chickens, and distributed hypothetical sinecures to their relations. The Lord-Lieutenant-to-be went so far as to strike a medal with his own crest on one side and the Regent's effigy on the other.

Some few Tories joined in this disgraceful death-dance, of whom the most illustrious was the Lord Chancellor Thurlow, who of all of them was most deeply indebted to the King. Thurlow was a most dangerous and treacherous man to have in a cabinet: he had hampered Fox's first cabinet in 1782 so much that in his second cabinet Fox had no Lord Chancellor at all rather than have Thurlow. Moreover, the Woolsack was already in pledge to Loughborough. But Fox realised that any cabinet he could form under the Prince would be miserably short of talents: he could not pick and choose: he threw over Loughborough: he connived at Thurlow's odious intrigue with the saving remark that it was "a bitter pill to swallow." An even bitterer pill, if possible, was the fact that Lansdowne—the Jesuit, the Malagrida, the prince of intrigue and past master of duplicity—although he had no longer any love for Pitt, stood disdainfully aloof from the attempt to dislodge Pitt by these indefensible methods.

Fox was saved from the worst of this squalid display by his bad health. He went off to Bath to recruit his strength for the arduous responsibilities which were soon to be his. But he was ready to return at a moment's notice. "I think it certain," he writes, "that in about a fortnight we shall come in. The King himself (notwithstanding the reports which you may possibly hear) is certainly worse, and perfectly mad." February came, and he was still quite undaunted: "If you could let me know by the return of the post on what day the Regency is likely to commence, I should be obliged to you."

While Fox was at Bath, Parliament was discussing a series of medical reports. Dr. Warren, who denied the possibility of recovery, was extolled by the Whigs as an Æsculapius of medical skill: Dr. Willis, who said that recovery was imminent, was denounced as a mercenary quack. But it gradually became clear that Willis was right: and on February the 19th, the King's return to sanity was announced in Parliament.

For all the indignities he had ever suffered from the Whigs, the King was amply repaid by the scene of panic which greeted his clearing senses. Such an eating of words, such a scuttle of rats, had never been seen or heard. Thurlow moved the Lords to shouts of laughter by expressing the hope that when he forgot the King, his God might forget him. The Prince of Wales was closeted with the Whig leaders, composing a long and eloquent memorandum in exculpation of his conduct. Fox was diplomatically detained at Bath, although there was now no immediate danger of his being overworked. London was illuminated for several nights, and the Whig houses were lit up for the same excellent reasons as the Tory houses had been lit up during the Keppel riots. All the London clubs gave magnificent balls in celebration: Brooks's very loyally gave a promenade concert at the Haymarket. It must have been a singularly rueful entertainment.

The whole Regency crisis was over in three months, but its importance is very great. Fox was caught red-handed in yet another attempt to govern unconstitutionally. In 1784 he had denied and encroached upon the rights of the Crown, the Lords and the people; in 1788 he had denied the rights of the House of Commons; it was truly said that there was now no branch of the constitution left for him to attack. All the old Adam in him had taken control at the first whisper of a return to power. His flatterers had persuaded him once more that he alone could overset the whole fabric. He had finally proved himself incorrigible. The lapse of five years had led some people to wonder whether the

India Bill had really been as revolutionary a measure as it had been made out. Fox's conduct on the Regency crisis set their doubts at rest. He was not merely as black as he had been painted, but blacker by far. This time he had attempted a thing which not even success could have justified. Cromwell's Ambition, Catiline's Abilities, Machiavel's Politics—they were fastened on him now like bells on a cat. His Whig principles would never again be very formidable, as long as Parliament remembered how they all had been flung overboard in a single debate, so soon as they had ceased to serve his purposes. Pitt had always maintained that his was a Whig government, by lineal descent from Chatham and Shelburne: it was an incalculable benefit to Pitt when Fox suddenly made him a compliment of his Whiggism, and exhibited him to all England as the defender of the privileges of Parliament.

The Regency crisis had a greater publicity than any of the events of these quiet years. Every man in England was a keen partisan either for or against the Hanoverians: there was no luke-warmness on the question of the royal family. Even those who most disliked the King were found to pity him while he was mad: while the Prince had no sympathisers at all. It was within the capacity of the smallest mind to compare the government formed by Pitt in December 1783, with the government proposed to be formed by Fox in 1788. The latter was to be summoned by a detested Prince, to depend for its existence on patronage and corruption, and to govern in flat defiance of public opinion. The former had come to the rescue of the King at his time of humilia-tion, had broken the power of an unprincipled and truculent oligarchy, and had been ratified a thousand times over by its triumph at the polls. Yet for forming that government, Pitt had been accused by Fox of giving a death-blow to the constitution.

Since then, Pitt had exerted his utmost strength to carry a reform of Parliament; he had failed; his own and Fox's ducal supporters overpowered him. He had drastically reduced corrup-tion. He had the King well under control: he derived his strength from the undiminished support of the people. The King's influence, thanks to Pitt, was never so low as at the moment when Fox proposed to come in on the Regent's influence. It was not difficult for the people to see who was their true friend.

2. The Otchakoff Affair, 1791-1792

To do justice to Fox's abilities, it is essential to do justice to the enormity of his mistakes. A man who could live down such a disgrace as the Regency crisis involved was no ordinary mortal. To slur over such a catastrophic exposure, is to under-estimate those qualities in Fox which enabled him to remain in political life, and even to play a valuable part, after an incident which might have exiled any other man. Bolingbroke had been ostracised for less.

Fox henceforward had no popular following worth mentioning outside the range of his impregnable personal popularity in Westminster. The reforming associations disowned him: the dissenters were as much horrified by his conduct as the established church. Yet at the general election of 1790, he was top of the poll at Westminster. There would be nothing extraordinary in that if he were the saint he has sometimes been represented; being the sinner he was, it is a proof of amazing powers. He was greatly helped on this occasion by the conduct of the defeated candidate. The Reverend John Horne had already played a part in Fox's story, by writing a libel on behalf of Mr. Tooke. He had dropped the prefix of Reverend by now, and assumed the suffix of Tooke. Horne Tooke stood for Westminster as a representative of the reformers against their lost leader. He was very comfortably beaten, but lodged a petition against the result. This was a proceeding too reminiscent of the scrutiny to be popular: the petition was found to be vexatious and frivolous; Fox once again benefited greatly from the ungenerosity of his enemies.

The real cause of his rehabilitation was that his criticism of foreign policy was indispensable. Pitt had no suitable candidates for the Foreign Office among his whole party: he was as feeble in diplomacy as he was invulnerable in finance. Since Fox could not join the ministry as Foreign Secretary, his advice as leader of the opposition was the next best thing. That was Fox's niche: so long as he stuck to that, he could perform a public service. On one occasion the aspect of foreign affairs became so threatening that he was very nearly given office, rather as a mutinous pilot might be released from his irons to take the helm in an emergency.

The crisis arose in this way. Fox's policy was based on loathing of the Bourbons, and firm reliance on the Northern Powers. He saw in the Family Compact between France and Spain the one great menace to this country's safety. Whether they were weak or strong, well or ill governed, so long as those two Powers were united, he maintained that we could never live long at peace with them. He had already shown his indiscriminate hostility to France by opposing the Commercial Treaty. Two years later, there was a naval "incident" in the Pacific between British and Spanish ships. Pitt adopted an intransigent line, and obtained a crushing concession: Fox declared that he had acted if anything too leniently. It was very different when the interests of Russian and Prussia were involved.

A war between Russia and Turkey broke out in 1788, during the first months of which the Russians seized a fortress called Otchakoff in the Black Sea. Pitt, as Disraeli would have done, bridles at this serious threat to the predominance of the Porte. Fox was as pleased by it as Gladstone would have been. Pitt demanded its restitution, and, encouraged by the success of his high-handed action against Spain, came to Parliament for an augmentation of the navy "to add weight to his representations." Fox would have none of it. The humiliation of Spain he had considered cheaply bought with a naval vote of three millions: but he would not vote a penny to help Turkey against Russia, in spite of his strong prejudice in favour of a powerful navy. Pitt carried his motion, but the debate was no sooner over than an extraordinary revolution of opinion took place. The whole country, from Pitt downwards, realised overnight that Fox was right, and that Pitt's proposal was one of those cardinal mistakes of foreign politics—a threat which could not be enforced. The country was in no mood for a Crimean war. The very fact that we could safely despise Spain, and dared not provoke Russia, showed that Fox's policy, however opposed to a correct balance of power, at least relied on the strongest supports.

The blow to Pitt's prestige was sudden and heavy. He was humiliated in cabinet; he lost his Foreign Secretary; he had contradictory messages sent to St. Petersburg in rapid succession; his ambassador was insulted by Catherine. He was perfectly right to climb down, but it cost him dear. All that Pitt lost, Fox gained. He was within an ace of coming into office. Pitt acknowledged that he would have been turned out if the opposition had been led by anyone else.

Otchakoff drew from Fox one speech which exhibits his debating style at its very summit. "If it was so important to recover Otchakoff, it is not recovered, and ministers ought to be censured. If unimportant, they ought never to have demanded it. If so unimportant, they ought to be censured for arming; but if so important as they have stated it, they ought to be censured for disarming without having gained it. Either way, therefore, the argument comes to the same point: for whether Otchakoff be, as they told us last year, the key to Constantinople, or, as they must tell us now, of no comparative importance, their conduct is equally to be condemned for disarming, and pusillanimously yielding up the object in the first instance; for committing the dignity of their sovereign, and hazarding the peace of their country, in the second. But they tell us: 'It is unfair to involve us in this dilemma; there was a middle course to be adopted. Otchakoff was certainly of much importance; but this importance was to be determined by circumstances.' Sir, we are become nice indeed in our political arithmetic. In this calculating age we ascertain to a scruple what an object is really worth. Thus it seems that Otchakoff was worth an armament, but not worth a war; it was worth a threat, but not worth carrying that threat into execution. Sir, I can conceive nothing so degrading and dishonourable as an argument such as this. To hold out a menace, without ever seriously meaning to enforce it, constitutes in common language the true description of a bully: applied to the transactions of a nation, the disgrace is deeper, and the consequences fatal to its honour. . . . I cannot conceive any case, in which a great nation, having committed itself by a menace, can withdraw that menace without disgrace, The converse of the proposition I can easily conceive—that there may be a case, not fit to be asked at all, but which being asked for, and with a menace, it is fit to insist upon. This undoubtedly goes to make a nation, like an individual, cautious of committing itself, because there is no ground so tender as that of honour. How do ministers think on this subject? Otchakoff was everything by itself, but when they added to Otchakoff the honour of England, it became nothing. Otchakoff, by itself, threatened the balance of Europe. Otchakoff and honour weighed nothing in the scale. Honour is, in their political arithmetic, a minus quantity, to be subtracted from the value of Otchakoff." It is a pity Palmerston was not there to listen.

It needs no more than that quotation to explain how Fox contrived to be formidable long after he had ceased to be reputable. A blow like that, backed with so much intellectual muscle, guided to its aim with such clear vision and common sense, might lay the strongest minister on the ground. Fox was only prevented from turning this moral triumph into a political triumph by a piece of uncommonly bad luck. He was known to be hand in glove with the Russian ambassador in London, and some exception was taken to that. But he also had an intimate friend, Adair, visiting St. Petersburg. He had lent Adair a cypher code which he had formerly used with Burgoyne in Canada, and in this way they corresponded. Moreover, Catherine chose to emphasise her insults to Pitt's emissary by treating Adair with every possible distinction, as the emissary of Fox, whom she had always fervently admired. This was an unusual situation for the leader of the opposition. The public were so deeply mistrustful of Fox already that they quickly leapt to the conclusion that he was acting in an unconstitutional way, in having his private ambassador at a foreign court. The charge was ill-founded, but it serves to show how readily a suspicion against Fox could gain a hold. Well might Pitt say that any other leader of opposition could have turned him out in 1791.

The Otchakoff crisis passed over, but it paved the way to a proposal for a coalition in 1792, which will be dealt with in its proper place. Fox on that occasion declared outright that he loved coalitions. The King—with great generosity, it must be conceded—said that he was not so wedded to Mr. Pitt as not to be able to give his confidence to Mr. Fox. Pitt's domination had become irksome: the King began to remember the Leicester House rule, always to keep in touch with opposition. Fox's supremacy in foreign affairs was acknowledged, and a government of wonderful balance and ability might have been constituted. We shall see how the proposal came to grief. Fox had been already fishing in more troubled waters.

CHAPTER EIGHTEEN

1. *First Dispute with Burke, 1790*

On the 14th of July, 1789, the Bastille fell to a Paris mob. Fox took a decisive line about the coming revolution from the very first. To Fitzpatrick, who was leaving for Paris, he wrote: "How much the greatest event it is that ever happened in the world! and how much the best! If you go without my seeing you, pray say something civil for me to the Duke of Orleans, whose conduct seems to have been perfect: and tell him and Lauzun, that all my prepossessions against French connections for this country will be at an end, and indeed most part of my European system of politics will be altered, if this revolution has the consequences that I expect." Nothing could be more explicit than that. The Revolution, of which this was the first milestone, is approved both on internal and external grounds. It is a turning-point in foreign affairs. The Bourbons will no longer be formidable if they are unable to control their own subjects in their own capital. It was not France, it was the French dynasty, that Fox detested. He did not detest them as oppressors of their country. We have seen that he approved "the amiable character of the French king, a monarch celebrated for his love of justice, for his desire to serve his country." He detested them as rivals to the power of England, and disturbers of the balance of power in Europe. No Englishman had more friends among the French aristocracy than Fox. He had no desire to see their heads roll. The primary reason why he approved the fall of the Bastille in 1789, when he had disapproved of the fall of Newgate prison in 1780, was that it was a sign of internal weakness in a foreign Power that he regarded as England's inevitable enemy. If France were to expel the Bourbons, if the Family Compact were to be disrupted, all his prepossessions against French connections were at an end. The idea that the French revolution was a great blow struck for human liberty was an afterthought.

The first years of the French revolution were not wildly exciting to any school of thought. The intellectuals were in command, and the months were spent in bandying ready-made constitutions and codes of laws, one more childish than another. "Bliss was it in that dawn to be alive," to one disgruntled undergraduate on a French walking-tour; but few sober observers could feel much enthusiasm about the proceedings of the Constituent Assembly. And there was one man in whom they aroused the deepest mistrust.

Burke had been an infrequent visitor to France. He had been repelled by the tone of the intellectual circles in Paris. Their flashy atheism, their blithe generalisations about government, revolted his believing and painstaking mind. He had read Rousseau, whom Fox admitted he had found unreadable. He had often expressed his intense dislike of modern French thought, "the philosophy of vanity," with its smart disparagement of all the continuity of institutions that he held dearest. When the intellectuals began to have their own way with the French constitution, in 1789 and 1790, he watched their innovations with an alert and mistrustful eye. He was not content with Fox's light-hearted approbation: he studied, sifted, tested the new constitution, and finally rejected it.

Fox's opinion had been given as early as July, 1789; Burke did not show any sign of opinion either way until September. In that month he wrote that the French people, "along with their political servitude, have thrown off the yoke of laws and morals." That was incontestably true: it shows also that Burke was alive to the provocation that had caused the upheaval. In October his criticism was a little more explicit: he wrote to a French friend to say that he would rejoice over the revolution as loudly as any man, so soon as he learnt that life, property, the use of industry or faculties, and the freedom of speech were secured by the law to every Frenchman. Till then, he said, "I must delay my congratulations on your acquisition of liberty. You may have made a revolution, but not a reformation. You may have subverted monarchy, but not recovered freedom." This was still cautious and non-committal: his first sign of positive disapproval was reserved until the next year. In February, 1790, he wrote: "I hate tyranny, at least I think so; but I hate it most of all where most are concerned in it. The tyranny of a multitude is but a multiplied tyranny. In the forty years of my observation, as much injustice and tyranny has been practised in a few months by a French democracy as by all the arbitrary monarchs of despotism. This democracy begins very ill; and I feel no security that what has been rapacious and bloody in its commencement, in its final settlement will be mild and protecting." Here he has shown his hand at last. Burke treated the advent of the French revolution exactly as he had treated the American war. He judged it by the Tory test, looking to its effects and actual probabilities: he judged it by the Whig test, looking to its causes, its professions, and the theoretical issues that it raised. He collected a vast mass of information, he wrote to scores of eye-witnesses, he scoured literature to find the roots of the movement, he compared and considered its professed objectives. In all its aspects, in its means and its ends, in its principles and in its practices, in its genesis, its growth, and its probable development, Burke made himself master of the French question, as of the Indian, the Irish, and the American questions. He used the same industry, he applied the same tests: and after eight months of sleepless investigation he pronounced that its principles were cant, and its practices savagery: while Fox had decided in a few days, after looking at a few newspapers, that it was the best and greatest event that ever happened in the world.

Between the relative value of their opinions there can be no comparison. Fox's was a generous and jovial exaggeration, biased by his views of foreign policy. Burke's was a studied and ponderous under-statement, irrefutable unless we are prepared to say that Burke set too high a value on laws and morals. Burke, who had not yet completed his fifteen years' toil on behalf of the masses of India, can scarcely be accused of indifference to the interests of a suffering population, indeed, he admits the "political servitude" of France. But he refused to be fooled by the first imposture that called itself liberty. In his view the basis of liberty was law, and the basis of law, morality. To go from servitude to anarchy was to fall out of the frying-pan into the fire. The Bourbons had chastised their people with whips: but the time came when the Jacobins flayed them with scorpions. That was the consummation Burke foretold, from his knowledge that the revolution was directed by worthless men, and based upon a worthless philosophy. It had no roots except in personal interest: it could have no end except in anarchy. Burke's views evolved gradually and cautiously, as one by one his prophecies came true. Fox's views, gaily scribbled down on paper in the heat of the moment, remained unaltered throughout the whole series of metamorphoses. From Mirabeau to Napoleon, through every gradation of government that France endured, Fox remained deaf to the cries of justice and mercy, infatuated by his original idea that liberty had come at last. Burke became the leader of English thought: the stream of opinion left Fox behind.

The first open divergence between Fox and Burke occurred in February, 1790. The army estimates were under debate, and Fox went out of his way to advertise his views on France. "The new form which the government of France is likely to asume will, I am persuaded, render her a better neighbour, and less disposed to hostility, than when she was subject to the intrigues and cabals of ambitious and interested statesmen." That was safe ground. He had held up the excellence of the French king as an additional reason to fear France: he might logically point to the badness of the Assembly's measures as a reason not to fear her any longer. But this he did not do: instead, he harped on his admiration for the conduct of the French soldiers in heading the riots and shooting at their officers. "If there ever can be a period when I shall be less jealous of an increase in the army, from any danger to be apprehended to the constitution, the present is that precise period. The example of a neighbouring nation has proved that former imputations on armies are unfounded calumnies: and it is now universally known, throughout all Europe, that a man, by becoming a soldier, does not cease to be a citizen." It was an odd angle from which to approach the army estimates, to contend that the army might safely be increased, because it had just been set the example of a successful mutiny: while it might equally safely be diminished, because that very mutiny had fatally weakened our most dangerous rival.

Such a slovenly confusion of reasonings on a matter of so much public importance was not likely to go long unpunished while Burke was about: four days later, Burke found his opportunity to reply. He agreed with Fox that France was no longer to be dreaded: "She was to be considered as expunged out of the system of Europe." But he differed violently from Fox's contradictory argument that the example of her troops should be held up for emulation to ours. "I am sorry that my right honourable friend has dropped even a word expressive of exultation on that circumstance: or that he seems of opinion that the objection to standing armies is at all lessened by it. I attribute this opinion of Mr. Fox entirely to his known zeal for the best of all causes, liberty." He went on to heap the most eloquent encomiums on Fox; and to explain with painful deference that he thought that Fox had been for the moment misled as to the effects on liberty of the French revolution. The new French army, he pointed out, was efficient for any purpose but that of national defence: it was a weapon of popular tyranny, and had won its spurs in action against its own officers. He drew a masterly contrast between the French revolution and the English revolution of 1688, and exploded the idea that liberty could conceivably be gained by the efforts of such men as the new French rulers had proved to be.

Burke's speech was as carefully argued and conciliatory as Fox's had been confused, dogmatic and provocative. The effect of such mature opinions, and such a mass of information, brought to bear upon a question about which other men had scarcely begun to think, was overwhelming. Fox's glib little epigram about the soldier and the citizen evaporated before Burke had said a few sentences. The contrast between the far-fetched optimism of the first and the solemn, solid warning of the second was a mortifying blow to Fox's usual superiority in debate. He felt called upon to make some sort of explanation: but it was not a great success. He said that he rose with a concern of mind almost impossible to describe, at the hard necessity of replying to "one of the wisest and most brilliant flights of oratory ever delivered in that House." "Such is my sense of the judgment of my right honourable friend, such my knowledge of his principles, such the value which I set upon them, and such the estimation in which I hold his friendship, that if I were to put all the political information which I have learnt from books, all which I have gained from science, and all which any knowledge of the world and its affairs has taught me, into one scale, and the improvement which I have derived from my right honourable friend's instruction and conversation were placed in the other, I should be at a loss to decide to which to give the preference." He was not to be outdone in compliments: but in argument he collapsed. Did his former declaration, he asked, warrant the idea that he was a friend to democracy? He was averse to all extremes, and a friend only to mixed government like our own. He should never lend himself to any scheme to introduce any dangerous innovation in our constitution. He imputed

Burke's warmth to a laudable anxiety, lest any man should be rash enough to render what had passed in France an object of imitation in this country.

Burke regarded this halting rejoinder as a recantation. He was on his feet at once, overjoyed to think that the misunderstanding was over. "I can, without the least flattery or exaggeration, assure my right honourable friend, that the separation of a limb from my body could scarcely give me more pain than the circumstance of differing from him, violently and publicly, in opinion. I am exceedingly glad, however, that I delivered myself so plainly in my former speech, since what I have said has drawn from my right honourable friend an explanation not more satisfactory to my mind, than I am persuaded it is to the House, and all who heard it."

Fox took no pains to remove the impression that he had recanted, though the opportunity was to hand. Sheridan followed Burke's speech with a defence of the revolution: Burke retorted that henceforth Sheridan and he were separated in politics: Fox sat by without saying a word to indicate that he agreed with Sheridan. He allowed the House to remain under the impression that his defeat in debate had convinced him that he was wrong. He had been ignominiously unhorsed, in lists that he considered as his own: the spectators realised, and thought that Fox realised, that the fault was in the mount and not in the rider. Possibly he did realise it, for the time being: but Fox was not a man to be easily persuaded, even when he was silenced. So long as he had about him a troupe of young friends who regarded his every word as an oracle, it needed more than the wisest and most brilliant flight of oratory to put him in the wrong.

2. Rupture with Burke, 1791

The first brush between Fox and Burke was in February, 1790. It was followed by a long period of calm. The autumn saw the publication of Burke's *Reflections on the French Revolution*, the effect of which was stupendous. It sold 32,000 copies in a year, a circulation unheard of at that time. It fixed once and for all the opinions of the thinking public. "One would think," said Windham, "that the author of such a work would be called to the government of his country by the combined voice of every man in it." Fox took a different view: he described it as a libel on all free governments. The *Reflections* made it necessary for Fox to nail his colours to the mast.

He was not over-scrupulous in his attention to the rules of debate, or in his choice of an occasion on which to give vent to his views. In April, 1791, there was a full-dress debate about Otchakoff. Fox wound up the discussion with a long speech about Otchakoff, to the end of which he suddenly appended a few remarks about France, of which the most notable was to the effect that the new French constitution was "the most stupendous and glorious edifice of liberty which had been erected on the foundation of human integrity in any time or country." The effect of these words on Burke may be imagined. He had come to listen to a discussion about Otchakoff, perhaps of all places on the map the least closely connected with the new constitution of France. At the end of a long day of relevant and informed debate, for no reason at all this fatuous rhapsody about France was dragged in by the heels. However little forewarned, Burke was always fore-armed. His memory was full of facts and figures; "his flow of mind," in Johnson's words, "was perpetual"; he was ready, even at a moment's notice, to overturn Fox's edifice of liberty, along with its foundation of integrity, with one blast of his trumpet. He was on his feet at once, his face glowing with anger. But the House was not prepared for an hour or two of Burke. Fox's speech had wound up the debate, and it was three o'clock in the morning. Loud cries of "Question!" drowned his opening sentence. He sat down, and went home bursting with suppressed indignation. Fox had trailed his cloak; but he can hardly have expected such an onrush as awaited him.

He had six days to wait, six days during which Burke's anger simmered and boiled. On the sixth day, there was to be a debate on the Quebec Bill, which was to settle a new constitution for Canada. The new French constitution was clearly a pertinent, and even a necessary, topic for comparison in any discussion of the future of a French-speaking province. Fox recognised that the matter would inevitably be raised: apprehensive of a personal quarrel, he went round to Burke's house, and found him preparing a studied reply from a mass of reports, pamphlets and books sent over from Paris. They went down to the House together, arguing the matter out in a tolerably friendly way, only to find that the debate had been postponed for another fortnight. For another fortnight Burke had to nurse his grievances. If it had not been for that, the personal rupture might have been avoided: for Fox's visit had been an acknowledgment that the Quebec Bill was a legitimate occasion for the discussion of their differences.

The tragedy was that Fox receded from that acknowledgment. The fortnight's lapse soured him as well as Burke: when the Quebec Bill was re-committed in the first week of May, he had come to the decision to put a gag on Burke's long-cherished reply. Burke opened the debate. He illustrated the relevance of his remarks by pointing out that, on the new French principles, the House had no right to legislate for Canada at all. But no sooner had he begun to open his indictment against the French principles than he was repeatedly called to order by the Foxites. After eight of these pestilent interruptions, a member finally moved that dissertations on the French constitution were out of order on the Quebec Bill. That motion Fox seconded. He did not explain how dissertations on the French constitution came to be in order on the Otchakoff debate: he contented himself with heavy sarcasm. His right honourable friend might with equal appositeness abuse the government of the Gentoos, or the law of Confucius, as the new French government. At this point Pitt intervened, and asked that Burke should be heard, since it was only Fox's henchmen who had tried to smother him, and the rest of the House were anxious to hear him out. But Fox persisted, and made a long speech in the most unfortunate vein. He declared, what was not true, that "when he had on a former occasion mentioned France, he had mentioned the revolution only, and not the constitution." Were he to differ from his right honourable friend on the constitution of Athens or of Rome, was it necessary that the difference should be discussed in that House? From this he went on, even more unhappily, to taunt Burke with superficial inconsistencies, smartly adapting phrases from his American speeches. He was sorry to find that his right honourable friend had learnt "the method of drawing up an indictment against a whole people." Such inquisition into a man's past utterances are the most unfair of all forms of argument: and by the time Fox had finished his long (and most disorderly) speech, Burke was at boiling-point. "Mr. Fox," he said, "has ripped up the whole course and tenor of my public and private life, with a considerable degree of asperity. The right honourable gentleman, after having fatigued me with skirmishes of order, which were wonderfully managed by the light infantry of opposition, then brings down upon me the whole strength and heavy artillery of his own judgment, eloquence, and abilities to overwhelm me at once. In carrying on the attack against me, the right honourable gentleman has been supported by a corps of well-disciplined troops, expert in their manoeuvres and obedient to the word of their commander." At this point he was called to order for the ninth time; but he proceeded: "I have differed from Mr. Fox in former instances: but no one difference of opinion has ever before for a single moment interrupted our friendship. It certainly is indiscreet at my time of life to provoke enemies, or to give my friends occasion to desert me; yet if my firm and steady adherence to the British constitution places me in such a dilemma, I will risk all; and as public duty and public prudence teach me, with my last breath exclaim, 'Fly from the French constitution!' " At this, Fox leant across, and whispered audibly: "There is no loss of friendship." "Yes, there is," said Burke. "I know the price of my conduct. I have done my duty at the price of my friend. Our friendship is at an end."

Fox rose to speak with the tears falling down his cheeks. He had not been prepared for this. For some minutes he stood there unable to speak. The House sat dead silent as he struggled to overcome his sobbing. He began with a moving reference to their friendship of a quarter of a century, and the many differences of opinion that it had survived. "Nothing but the ignominious terms which my right honourable friend has heaped on me——" Burke: "I do not recollect any." Fox: "My right honourable friend does not recollect the epithets: they are out of his mind: then they are completely and forever out of mine. I cannot cherish a recollection so painful; and from this moment they are obliterated and forgotten." That was a generous flash of the real Fox; but it was short-lived. He was too cunning a debater to be able to resist the temptation of making a few smart points by garbling Burke's classic speeches on other matters. What had begun as a sincere attempt at reconciliation, ended in acrimony. It was a very poor olive branch, and Burke rejected it. "Under the mask of kindness a new attack has been made upon my character and conduct in the most hostile manner, and my very jests brought up in judgment against me. I did not think the careless expression and playful triflings of my unguarded hours would have been recorded, mustered up in the form of accusations, and not only have a serious meaning imposed upon them, which they were never intended to bear, but one totally inconsistent with any fair and candid interpretation. Could my most inveterate enemy have acted more unkindly towards me? The event of this night's debate, in which I have been interrupted without being suffered to explain, in which I have been accused without being heard in my defence, makes me at a loss to understand what is either party or friendship. . . . Yet if the good be to many, I willingly take the evil to myself." Fox made no reply: the motion was withdrawn: the House returned to the discussion of the Quebec Bill.

3. *Burke and Fox*

It is obvious that between April the 21st, when he discussed with Burke the heads of his speech, and May the 6th, when he tried every Parliamentary dodge to prevent him from delivering it, Fox had been got at by someone who was indifferent whether they quarrelled or not. The fact is, that the last few years had brought into the House a number of young men of the sort Fox liked to live with most, and Burke did not like at all. Burke had never cared much for Sheridan, but the bevy of Greys and Grenvilles and Cokes and Lambtons who now dogged Fox's footsteps, and hung on his words, were even less to his taste. They made no attempt to disguise their feeling that Burke, who had been famous before they were born, was not their equal socially, while Fox was the acknowledged leader of their circle of society. At the time of the Regency crisis, when offices were being confidently parcelled out, Burke was disgusted to find that he was still destined for nothing better than the Paymastership, which he had held twice already. His priceless services to the party were held of less value than the social qualifications of young men who were born in the purple of the great Whig families, and could drink, race and gamble to the standards of their leader. With all his wisdom in the affairs of nations, Burke was a child in party affairs. For seventeen years he had followed Rockingham without doubting for a moment that he was the best leader the Whigs could have: for another nine years he had followed Fox blindly through all the blunders of the resignation, the coalition, the India Bill, and the Regency. His mind was set on statesmanlike ends: he had no eye for the political means. He was too innocent to realise what a bungler his leader was, and sorrowfully attributed to the influence of the crown the setbacks which were due to the recklessness of Fox. During the short periods when he had been in office, and in an office ludicrously inadequate to his deserts, he had displayed the contrast between the lofty statesmanship which led him to surrender £25,000 a year to the public, and the clumsy misjudgment which led him to reinstate a pilfering clerk.

"Of all the politicians of talents I ever knew," said Walpole, "Burke has the least political art." It is a mistake to regard him as a politician at all. In the pursuance of duty, he

"born for the universe, narrowed his mind,
And to party gave up what was meant for mankind:
Though fraught with all learning, yet straining his throat
To persuade Tommy Townshend to lend him a vote."

He took part in politics, just as Shakespeare acted, and Bach gave lessons on the organ. But he was not a man of action. He was utilised and imposed upon at every step. He must long since have realised that Pitt represented the true Whig principles, and that the Foxites were merely pursuing a personal quarrel to the detriment of the public interest. Yet he still clung to his friend's cause. But there was an end even to Burke's patience. When he found at the age of fifty-nine that all his toil and all his inspired eloquence had won him no more than the Pay Office, and that the chance even of that miserable prize was snatched from him by the ineptitude of his leader, his allegiance might well be shaken.

It needed more than disappointment to sever Burke from Fox:

but the first difference of opinion gave him the opportunity of breaking off this impossible loyalty. He was not picking a quarrel; he was passionately sincere: to anyone who praised the French revolution, he refused even to speak. He had originally won Fox over to the Whig party. He had deferred to his leadership without question. If Fox chose to throw up Whig principles, and become a Jacobin, it was not for his old teacher to follow him into that labyrinth of fallacies. His readiness to part from Fox was caused by discontent at being repeatedly passed over: but the grounds of the separation were firm and solid. Burke remained a Whig. He said farewell to Fox, only when Fox started chasing the fantasies of Rousseau, and condoning the outrages of Robespierre. "The French Revolution," he said, "has not merely shaken all the thrones of Europe, but has shaken my friend Fox's heart and understanding out of their right places."

It had been a great partnership. Their talents were largely complementary. Burke's solid industry and power of thought needed the augmentation of Fox's quick argument and intuition: they were both passionately devoted to liberty and justice: the only thing they lacked between them was practical judgment. Separated from each other, neither was the same man. Burke missed Fox's quick revulsion from exaggerated ideas of patriotism and national prestige. From horror of the French revolution, he was led on to clamour for a war with France long before that war was necessary, and to extend its objectives beyond any that a war could achieve. Fox's criticism, given in friendship, would have ridiculed the undertaking of a premature war for an unspecified and hopeless end. Fox, on the other hand, missed Burke's reverence for the achievements of the past. He became an innovator on principle, an indiscriminate admirer of anything and everything that was either new or French. A sham consistency, which he had often evinced before, led him on to change his politics as often as the French changed theirs. Burke might have shown him, across a dinner table, what he could not persuade him of across the House, that not everything that is bloody constitutes a reformation, and that the most painful transition can still be a transition from bad to worse.

Burke lived till 1797. He lived to see Fox deserted by almost the whole of the Whig party. He lived to see the war, for which he had clamoured, become inevitable. During these years he wrote much of his finest work. Some of it was directed to exposing Fox's conduct: some of it was written in the attempt to turn a war of defence into a counter-revolutionary war. Most of it is unbalanced, both in sense and expression. It has sometimes been said by those who "love the martyrdom of fame," that his mind was deranged towards the end of his life. This is only true if it was madness to believe that civilisation was coming to an end, and to regret it. Many people have feared the same thing on slighter grounds. But that he retained his love of true liberty and real reform is shown by his hearty support of Kosciusko's revolution, a genuine struggle for liberty, at this very time, in Poland. The loss of his only son went far to upset his mind: even then his fear for the world was stronger than his personal sorrow. "I begin to think that God took what was dearest to me to Himself in a good time." It is no wonder that he would have no relations with those whom he thought to be abetting the downfall of all he had ever stood for: but he always did justice to the rare quality of Fox's nature. "To be sure," he would say, "he is a man made to be loved." When he was dying, Fox sent a note to ask if he could see him. Like some old Roman, Burke refused.

Fox was rather more outspoken about his lost friend. "After all," he observed, "Burke was a damned wrong-headed fellow, through his whole life jealous and obstinate." As one after another Burke's most gloomy predictions about the French Revolution came true, he was forced to take a wider view. "It is difficult to say whether he is mad or inspired; whether one or the other, everyone must agree that he is a prophet." Burke's death moved him profoundly, but he was quite incapable of understanding the refusal of his request for a last interview. "I have always found that every Irishman has a piece of potato in his head," he is reported to have said. A rather graceless epitaph on the man from whom he had learnt his politics; but ever since his rupture with Burke, he had put Burke's politics firmly behind him. As soon as that guiding hand was removed, Fox was emancipated from Whig principles. He soared above Burke's rigid practical criticism into the thinner air of Jacobinism, of political pure reason. The abstraction of liberty attracted him more than reality. He forgave in the travesty what he condemned in the established system. From 1791 onwards, the speculative rights of men interested him more than their actual wrongs. Liberty, whatever crimes were committed in her name, became his deity.

"Liberty," says Halifax, "is the mistress of mankind, she hath powerful charms which do so dazzle us, that we find beauties in her which perhaps are not there, as we do in other mistresses." But Burke loved liberty too well for even that amount of self-deception. He knew that liberty, like happiness, is most perfect when least remarked. As most misery is caused by the pursuit of an abstract happiness, distinct from the occupations that make men happy, so most tyranny springs from the struggle for an abstract liberty, distinct from the laws and institutions that make men free. It was not old age that taught him these reflections: his hatred of Jacobinism was not a manifestation of senility. The French Revolution might have found him in his prime: he would still have put it to the test of the same intellectual honesty.

CHAPTER NINETEEN

1. *Proposal for Coalition, 1792*

The backwash of the Otchakoff affair lasted into 1792, and indeed the great speech already quoted was delivered in March of that year. The government sustained the full shock of that blow, before they began to be strengthened by a national revulsion against France in the autumn of the year. The blow was so great that at one time it was generally considered necessary that Fox should join the government as Foreign Minister. Various negotiations to that end occupied the month of June. Pitt had just got rid of Thurlow, whom he had been trying to dispense with ever since his treachery at the Regency crisis. The Woolsack was vacant, and Loughborough had his eye on it. It was Loughborough who instigated the proposal of a coalition. The King was willing, having been downtrodden by Pitt for eight years now. Fox was willing. "It is so damned right a thing," he said, "it *must* be done." "I *love* coalitions," he confessed, with his usual impenitence. "As a party man, I think it is a good thing for my party to come into office, were it only for a month." Pitt pointed out that on the questions of parliamentary reform, religious disabilities, and abolition of the slave trade, they were of one mind.

Burke, at a party meeting, spoke for an hour against Fox, declaring that he was tainted with French politics and principles, and that he had deserted his old friends and preferred a new set in the party. Fox did nothing to disarm this accusation. He behaved throughout these negotiations with "a peevishness and obstinacy very unlike him." He gave himself away by asking too much. He insisted, as a *sine qua non* of coalition, that Pitt should resign the Premiership to a neutral third person. In making this impossible demand, he was acting in flat opposition to the advice of the older and more influential half of his party. It was quite clear by whom he was encouraged to ask for more than he could possibly hope to get. He confessed that he had friends in the Commons for whom something must be done in any coalition that might be formed:

and everyone knew who those friends were. The confidence he denied to Portland, Elliot, and Fitzwilliam, was freely given to Grey, Lambton, Coke and Erskine. These clever young men were the new generation of flatterers, whose task it was to persuade Fox that "he alone can overset the whole fabric." He lived in their company, shared their amusements, and entertained them at St. Anne's Hill. They were charming, clever, and devoted; they were irreverent about the senior members of the party. With their jokes and their applause ringing in his ears, Fox once again made a grand mistake, and wrecked the suggested coalition.

Burke's primary object of making Fox recant was frustrated: but his secondary object of ejecting French sympathisers from the Whig party was well begun. Loughborough soon joined the government as Lord Chancellor. The others hesitated for a few months. They were disgusted by the lack of confidence and respect with which they had been treated, but there was yet no open breach. "They are secretly galled," said Burke. "They agree with me to a tittle; but they dare not speak out for fear of hurting Fox." In this uneasy condition the Whig party remained for six months, with Fox only listening to the left wing, and the right wing hanging on only out of personal attachment to Fox. Burke's *Appeal from the New to the Old Whigs*, unanswerable as it was, did not yet overcome that loyalty.

2. Fox's Opinions Develop, 1792

At about this period Fox began to correspond with his nephew Lord Holland, who was just leaving Oxford to go on his travels. From these unreserved letters can be traced the process by which Fox's mind became hardened to the excesses of the revolution. Having in the first instance embraced a fallacy, he was slowly led on from ignoring its first ill-effects, to conniving at, and finally apologising for slaughters and barbarisms which, if they had not been committed in the name of the French revolution, would have roused him to a white heat of anger. So there emerges the curious phenomenon of a man, whose humanity and liberalism were his outstanding characterisitics, championing a system whose inhumanity and illiberalism are a low-water-mark in the history of civilised nations.

The sack of the Tuileries, the slaughter of the Swiss guards, and the imprisonment of the King in August, 1792, provoked a note of regret: "It seems as if the Jacobins had determined to do something as revolting to the feelings of mankind as the Duke of Brunswick's proclamation; but, though it must be owned they have done their utmost for this purpose, yet, with respect to mine, they have not succeeded." But second thoughts were more indulgent: "I do not think near so ill of the business of the 10th of August as I did upon first hearing it." He finds the National Assembly very French: "There is a want of dignity and propriety in everything they do. When the enemy is at their doors, to be amusing themselves with funerals and inscriptions, and demolitions of statues, and creations of honorary citizens, is quite intolerable; and to talk so pompously of dying for liberty and their country, before one single gallant action has been performed by any part of their army, is worse than ridiculous. And yet, with all their faults and all their nonsense, I do interest myself for their success in the greatest degree." As he wrote these words, the Commune, going rather beyond a want of propriety and dignity, had just initiated a massacre of fourteen hundred prisoners in four days. This might have upset the strongest stomach, but Fox was by this time inured. He admits there is not a "shadow of excuse for this horrid massacre, not even the possibility of extenuating it in the smallest degree." But he still looks beyond the crime to the imaginary principle, and regrets it chiefly because it harms that principle. "I really consider the horrors of that day and night as the most heart-breaking event that ever happened to those who, like me, are fundamentally and unalterably attached to the true cause." What was this but extenuation of the very crime he had declared admitted of no extenuation—to disapprove a murder, not from pity for the victim, but because it was likely to hurt the reputation of the murderer, and to cast discredit on the ideals which had led him to commit his crime? And this, although everything the French revolution had done in three years, or was yet to do, was harmful to the true cause of liberty. Fox had forgotten the lesson Burke taught him twenty years back—to judge a tree by its fruits. All the fruits of the French revolution were poisonous, and he should have known from that, that it sprang from a poisonous root. Instead, he took its origins on trust, on the strength of those fine words, which all its deeds belied.

Wonderfully inept is his comment on the victory of the French over their invaders at Valmy. "No! No public event, not excepting Saratoga and Yorktown, ever happened that gave me so much delight." The very framing of such a comparison might have awakened some lingering sense of values. That a man who had admired Washington should rejoice in the victories of Dumouriez was enough to point the contrast. The leaders of the American revolution were solid men, of almost legendary virtues, cautious to a fault: their work has endured a hundred and fifty years. The French revolution produced no single leader who was not detestable; while it destroyed much that was bad, it substituted nothing that was not worse; and nothing that it created outlasted the decade.

Speaking of political syllogisms, Burke has said that "the majors make a pompous figure in the battle, but the victory of truth depends upon the little minor of circumstances." That was what Fox forgot. In theory, the French revolution was a liberation: in fact, it was the vilest of all tyrannies. Fox lost touch with the truth, and sank into this sea-green hypocrisy, because he ignored the "minor of circumstances." When he gushed over the good intentions of men who were wholly bad he could not expect to carry with him the opinion of those who had admired the American rebels for their character even more than for their cause. The ordinary English citizen, when he read in one column of his newspaper, that the French had dragged a community of nuns from a hospital where they were nursing and scourged them naked through the streets, and in the next column that the French (according to Mr. Fox) had at last established a system of complete, perfect, and universal toleration, might be forgiven for supposing, what many of them did suppose, that Mr. Fox was being paid to say such things.

3. *Popular Panic Spreads, 1792*

So far the dispute had raged between Fox and Burke: Pitt had ignored the French revolution entirely. It was his interest to do so. Though he could not foresee what a bad war minister he became, he knew what a good peace minister he had been. In eight years, revenue and trade had grown fat under his nourishment: debt and taxation had dwindled. Pitt's lot was cast in a good time. He had seized power at the lowest point of England's fortunes: he was still immensely powerful at home: another eight years and England would be able to look back upon an almost miraculous recovery. All he wanted was peace, and no man ever tried harder to keep it. He was not to be frightened out of his course by any disturbances in France. He went ahead with his liberal policies, accepting a great measure of Fox's to reform the law of libel, removing Catholic disabilities, and trying to abolish the slave trade. Till late in 1792, he had no more intention of invading France than of invading the moon.

In February, 1792, Pitt introduced estimates which reduced the navy by one man in nine, and dispensed with foreign mercenaries. This drastic disarmament he defended by remarking that "unquestionably there never was a time in the history of this country when from the situation of Europe we might more reasonably expect fifteen years of peace than at the present moment." Yet within a year of that statement he was at war. Events moved confusedly during 1792. Some historians point to a sympathetic revolutionary movement in England as the main cause of the sudden change: some blame it upon a reactionary wave of feeling. The truth lies somewhere between.

In 1792 there happened to be an uncommonly bad harvest, and a bad harvest during the early stages of the industrial revolution was a disaster so cruel as to strain the bonds of the strongest society. Unemployment and discontent were widespread. The inflammable material lay about, and there were some assiduous individuals ready enough to light it. By far the most successful incendiary was Thomas Paine, whose *Rights of Man* had a large circulation, and spread among its readers a fanciful enthusiasm for the new institutions and methods in France. A number of societies were formed in various hard-hit industrial towns, under pedantic names, whose members greeted each other as Citizen So-and-So, and sent childish messages to the National Assembly, to be rewarded with even more childish replies. There was very little harm in all this, but a great deal of ostentation. It was a middle-class, and for the most part a nonconformist, movement. Dissenters at that time were bad citizens: under the operation of repressive laws, they necessarily put their sect above their civil allegiance. Their grievances took the form of sympathy with Jacobinism. The sort of discontent which finds an outlet in the adoption of outlandish costumes and modes of address is a bourgeois discontent, but it can make a great noise. The greetings exchanged between the clubs and the Jacobins, the riots in the larger towns, the proclaimed French sympathies of the Dissenters, and the popularity of the *Rights of Man*, all combined to produce a violent reaction.

The anti-revolutionary movement was incomparably stronger than what was called the Corresponding movement. Though supported by the gentry, it enlisted the vast mass of the common people, who hated the French at all times, and hated them most of all now they had run amok. As early as 1791, Priestley, the dissenting leader, the friend of Shelburne, and the apologist of the revolution, had had his house sacked by an anti-French mob at Birmingham. In many places it was unsafe for a Dissenter to show his face in public. Thomas Paine was substituted for Guy Fawkes on the fifth of November. These things were not done by government instigation: they were not done by panic-stricken gentlefolk: they were done by mobs. "It required," says Burke, "the most active and vigilant attention of government to prevent the people from falling everywhere upon the French federations, with perhaps as much eagerness and violence as at Birmingham. They were not thus protected, from any approbation of their proceedings, but from a just dread of the consequences of suffering the populace to be led by their own precipitate impulses."

This popular feeling, which was held in check in 1791, grew past all control in 1792. It enlisted the propertied classes, by now throroughly frightened. It finally overthrew the pacific determination of Pitt himself.

The first sign that appeared of any yielding to the popular clamour was the issue in May of a proclamation against seditious writings, to which the approval of Portland, Fox's nominal leader, had been obtained. This was aimed particularly at Paine, who fled to France, where he was first made a French citizen and then sent to prison. The events of August the 10th and September the 2nd fanned the counter-revolutionary flame. Not the least alarming portent was the formation of a society called the Friends of the People, of which Grey was the leading spirit: Fox was acutely embarrassed by this action on his friend's part: and although he refused to join the association, it did untold harm both to him personally and to the cause of Parliamentary reform, by trumpeting its demands loudest at the precise moment when the British public was least inclined to venture on a reform of any sort.

By the autumn of 1792, the government's position had become difficult, but their intentions were still unshaken. In November, both Pitt and his Foreign Secretary still spoke as if there were not yet the remotest possibility of war. After that events moved precipitately. On November the 19th the Convention issued a decree by which they pledged the assistance of the French nation to any other nation still struggling to regain its liberty. This might seem to be mere vapouring, but with the success of the French arms before their eyes, and signs all round them of a conspiracy with France, whose importance they had no means of gauging, the ministry took the wiser course of preparing for the worst. On December the 1st, the French decree was answered by a proclamation drawing attention to widespread evidences of insurrection concerted with foreign powers, and calling out the militia. That the government exaggerated the danger of internal trouble is unquestionable. But they had no way of assessing it: there was a doubt about it: some were genuinely scared, others were sceptical: they would have been wrong to gamble on the chances of an optimistic calculation.

The December proclamation was the Rubicon of the Whigs. Fox was furious at it. "None of our friends have sanctioned this most detestable measure, and I hope none will." He was soon undeceived. On the 11th he dined with Portland, Devonshire, Fitzwilliam, Malmesbury, and Tom Grenville. He was in an "acrimonious and opinionative" mood. He "treated the alarms as totally groundless," and said that "the whole was a trick, and as such he should oppose it." He found himself in a minority of one: not a single one of those devoted friends and experienced public men could bring themselves to agree that the Proclamation was a false alarm. Perhaps Fox in his innermost heart agreed with them too, for the next day, when Malmesbury tried to dissuade him from opposing the address, he "declared with an oath that there was no address at this moment Pitt could frame, he would not propose an amendment to, and divide the House upon." This, says Malmesbury, was putting an end to all discussion. As always, he was allowing personal links and personal hatreds to take precedence of public interests.

Parliament met on the 13th and debated the Proclamation. Fox had an easy task in the debate. Where, he demanded, were all these insurrections? He had heard of nothing except riots directed against those who were suspected of Jacobin sympathies. Of those there were plenty, but they did not demand the calling out of the militia. As for the French decree, he agreed it was an insult, but it was an empty threat, not aimed at this country. The ministry had a difficult task to reply to this. The actual evidences of insubordination were few enough, though suspicion of it was universal. Pitt, moreover, knew exactly the circumstances in which the French decree had been issued, and how little it was worth. That is the whole tragedy of Pitt's situation. The question was not, how much anger of invasion or insurrection there really was, but how much danger the public thought there was. The situation had passed beyond Pitt's control. He was not a dictator. He might still avert war, but he could no longer resist the clamour for expensive and alarmist measures of defence. Fox himself had demanded the calling out of the militia in 1777 on far less ostensible evidence of the aggressive intentions of France.

To demand concrete proof of the national peril was no more than a debating point. It was an attempt to untie a knot which needed cutting. Fox divided 50 on the address; and an experienced observer counted 25 even of these who were voting against their sentiments: Fox knew from that moment that his party was smashed in two. Nor did his speech carry any more conviction outside the House. "He uttered everything his worst enemy could wish," says Gibbon. "Every man in the street asked, Is he mad?" The Whig party had come to the parting of the ways. A week later there was a meeting of the leaders of the party at Lord Malmesbury's, which Fox did not attend. At this meeting Burke spoke again at great length. He said that "Fox's abettors had seduced his principles, and made him believe that a government like ours was not a proper one for great talents to display themselves in; that by working on his ambition, which, carried to excess, becomes wickedness, they had made him from these reasons approve and praise the French revolution." These were harsh phrases in which to address an assembly of Fox's oldest and most intimate friends: but there was no answer that any of them could make. It was clear that Fox was now lending his ear exclusively to the young Friends of the People group: but the idea of a separation from Fox appalled even the oldest of the party. Portland sat silent for two solid hours, "benumbed and paralysed," when his friends urged him to make the separation at once rather than later. Fitzwilliam left London "from distress of mind relative to Mr. Fox."

After all, war was not yet declared: They would leave him a loophole as long as they could. When war actually began, he might recover some of the spirit he had shown in 1778.

4. France Declares War, 1793

December, 1792, and January, 1793, were crowded months for both Fox and Pitt, whose severest critics have never pretended that either of them left anything undone to prevent the catastrophe. Pitt went so far as an heroic attempt to stop the existing war between France and the Austro-Prussian league by the intermediacy of Russia. That failing, he had to work with such tools as the French gave him. Chauvelin, the French agent, a lying, conceited fool, half envoy and half spy, bears the lion's share of responsibility for the war. His seditious intrigues with the Corresponding societies gave colour to the ministry's worst fears. His insufferable bearing alienated everyone he met. He left England before he need, and suppressed a letter appointing his successor. With the possible exception of his colleague in America, he was the worst ambassador on record. But there were two intelligent Frenchmen at that time in London, in touch with both Fox and Pitt, namely, Maret and Talleyrand. Acting for Danton's minority in France, they tried to calm the fears of the majority in England: and acting for Fox's minority in England, they tried to moderate the recklessness of the majority in France, and in particular to secure the withdrawal of the November decree.

Against these forces working for peace were ranged unescapable facts. The opening of the Scheldt, which we were engaged to keep closed by treaty, was a legal pretext. The overrunning of the Netherlands by a triumphant French army was a menace of which it needed no treaty obligations to remind us. The fate of the Netherlands is a question about which England has never been indifferent. She has fought to save them from falling a prey to one country after another: she could hardly stand while they were swallowed up by what Burke called the Cannibal Republic.

Lastly, there was the decree of November the 19th, offering assistance to all nations struggling to regain their liberty—in which category, by the standards of Rousseau, England was included. Fox took the line that this announcement was not to be taken seriously, that it was no more than a phrase, like so many other pronouncements of the Convention. This was true. At this very time, Poland was genuinely struggling to rid itself of a genuine tyranny. Kosciusko went to Paris to claim help from the French under the terms of their splendid promise. He was sent away with contemptuous refusal, as soon as it was found that he had come without the necessary bribes. Of course, the November decree was an empty threat: of course, the promises that the Convention sent to societies in Birmingham and Edinburgh were empty threats. But no nation can treat with a government which makes such menaces, even in bad faith. England could never live in peace with such neighbours, wielding such power, professing such principles, and openly proclaiming their intention of spreading to other countries the disease which had seized their own. It is a position difficult to conceive, because, thanks to our efforts, it lasted but a few years. France, the Netherlands, and all too likely Ireland, permanently threatening not only our shores with their armaments, but our civil liberties with their propaganda, afforded a prospect which roused Britain to the realisation that war was the only protection. The Prime Minister was still unmoved: the ghost of a possibility of peace nerved him to resist the cries for war. Fox was unmoved for another reason. He cared not who held the Netherlands so long as it was not the Bourbons: his system of European politics was altered: the revolution had had the consequences he expected.

The final scene came quickly. On January the 21st, Louis XVI was guillotined. London went into mourning: no Frenchman was safe in the streets: Fox himself was nearly set upon. On the 23rd, Chauvelin was ordered to leave the country. He went, and arrived in Paris screaming for war. He had his way. On February the 1st, the Convention declared war on England and Holland.

5. *Fox and His Party, 1793-1797*

Coleridge, writing in 1823, astutely traces the impotence of the Whig party to its causes thirty years back. It originated, he said, "in the fatal error that Fox committed, in persisting after the first three years of the French revolution, when every shadow of freedom in France had vanished, in eulogising the men and measures of that shallow-hearted people. So he went on gradually, further and further departing from all the principles of English policy and wisdom, till at length he became the panegyrist, through thick and thin, of a military frenzy, under the influence of which the very name of liberty was detested." Though the transition from believing in fools to believing in knaves, and finally to believing in Napoleon, was as Coleridge says a gradual process, the retribution it brought upon his party was sudden and dreadful. From the moment war broke out, Fox was lucky if he could command forty votes.

The Prince of Wales deserted him. Portland, the leader of the party; Carlisle and Fitzwilliam, his early travelling companions; Devonshire, though his Duchess was faithful, and Spencer: these were the most notable deserters in the Lords. In the Commons, Windham, that brilliant man who was enthralled and almost hypnotised by Burke, was the most notable deserter. Sir Gilbert Elliot, who became distinguished as Lord Minto, and Tom Grenville, Fox's representative in Paris in 1782, were two others who were badly missed. They carried with them about sixty or seventy others, all the less volatile members of the party.

Those who were faithful to Fox were faithful to him for personal not political reasons. They would have followed him if he had gone to France, to claim French citizenship. "There are but forty of them," said Thurlow, "but every man of them would be hanged for Fox." They certainly would not have been hanged for Robespierre, or Danton, or even for Napoleon. Without Fox, the opposition to the French war would have been non-existent. Throughout his career, there were always a few who preferred his smile and his talk to anything else that public life could offer. In the deserted rooms at Brooks's, or in the exquisite peace of St. Anne's Hill, Fox's company seemed better worth having than offices or peerages or a tenable cause.

In the Lords, those who kept aloft the Jacobin flag were the

Duke of Bedford and Lord Lauderdale, and by what sort of methods they defended it can be ascertained from the scathing pages of Burke's *Letter to a Noble Lord*. In the Commons, Fox saw to it that more decency was observed.

Sheridan was at first his right-hand man, and welcomed the opportunity to distinguish himself in debate against such an over-whelming majority. But Sheridan was out of place in Fox's "hackney-coach-full." He was too nearly Fox's intellectual equal to endure the complete subservience demanded of him: the rural calm of St. Anne's Hill was a far cry from the roaring eighties and the Pharo bank: and his financial position forbade an impossible loyalty. He cast longing eyes towards Carlton House, where the Prince was joking and drinking with new friends; there was his real allegiance. He trimmed. He wrote a jingo play, which greatly disgusted Fox. Finally, when Fox seceded from Parliament, Sheridan stayed behind, half-supporting the ministry. Fox and Sheridan always seemed to bring out the worst side in each other. So long as Fox drank and gambled, Sheridan would rather drink and gamble with him than with anyone else. But he could never bring himself to burn as much incense as the others, or to join in the chorus of indiscriminate adulation. And with Fox the Cincinnatus, Fox the elder statesman, he had nothing in common. The real link between them was his wife. Fox worshipped Eliza-beth Sheridan. It was he who persuaded her not to divorce Sheridan, in spite of more than ordinary provocation. When she died they drifted apart, and towards the end their relations were embittered.

Fox's rank and file were a distinguished company. There was Whitbread, the enlightened brewer; Grey, the Reform Bill Prime Minister; Francis, the reputed Junius; Coke of Norfolk; Lambton, the Byron of politics, who produced the Durham Report; and Erskine, that inspired egotist who could wind a jury round his little finger. These men, most of them under forty, put up a brave fight in Parliament, and had their reward in sitting at Fox's feet while he read Virgil aloud to his mistress, or in helping him to build the greenhouse in his beloved Surrey garden. He was extremely happy with them, and snapped his fingers at the seceders. "I think they have all behaved very ill to me, and for the most of them who owe much more to me than I do to them, I feel nothing but contempt, and do not trouble myself about them."

There had been one direction in which Fox confidently looked for support in opposing the war, and met with disappointment. The dissenters, whose ancient grudge against the government under which they lived took the form of partiality for an atheist anarchy, proved a broken reed. They had always opposed Fox, in spite of his attempts to get their disabilities removed: in 1790 Dr. Price had denounced him in a political sermon. Now when he made a bid for their favour, he found that their support was as feeble as their opposition had been noisy. But his attempt at reconciliation led to his being joined by one most unexpected ally: no other than Shelburne, under his new title of Lansdowne. Lansdowne had taken his view of the French revolution from his dissenter friends, Price and Priestley. Price had died of grief: Priestley, finding Birmingham too hot to hold him, had fled to America: Lansdowne, fortified by his grudge against the ungrateful Pitt, was staunch. He found himself acting once more with Fox, whose personal antipathy to him had disrupted the party system. They had, too, a personal link. Fitzpatrick hated his brother-in-law as much as ever, but Fitzpatrick had gone to the war. Caroline Fox, who had Lansdowne for her maternal and Fox for her paternal uncle, was a young lady after Lansdowne's heart, a blue-stocking to the tips of her toes, learned, serious and advanced. She was almost an adopted daughter at Bowood and Lansdowne House, where Jeremy Bentham, another inmate of that strange coterie, lost his pedantic heart to her. Caroline provided the necessary link between Fox and Lansdowne. Fox dined once more at Lansdowne House, on which he had kept an eye from Perdita's windows. They co-operated in both Houses of Parliament, as Lansdowne returned four members to the Commons. "I never can have a good opinion of him, and still less a great one," said Fox. However, "the events of these last years make one less nice about one's associates." A fine comment from the past, and future, associate of the Prince of Wales.

CHAPTER TWENTY

1. *Objects of the War, 1793-1797*

When war began, the whole undertaking of opposition was changed. They had failed in one thing: they must begin to attempt another quite different. Their quibbles and questions and little barriers of sophistry had been carried away by a tide of passion. They had tried to sweep away the ocean with a broom, but now it was upon them. We were fighting not for the Scheldt, but for civilisation. Paris was not far away, and it was not in human nature to stand by unmoved while such a city and civilisation fell a sacrifice to Caliban. There had been "bad sleepers" in European diplomacy before, but never before had an European nation slipped backwards into barbarism in a few years. Nor had any nation ever declared its resolve to spread its own rabies as fast and as far as the infection could be carried. Illogically and without proper reflection, the British decided to stamp out the disease before it spread. The question was no longer Whether, but How, and in that question the opposition had a say.

To Burke the war was a holy crusade. Assisted from above by the thunderbolts of his eloquence, the armies of England were to march on Paris, leaving a settled royalist countryside in their wake, and finally restore the monarchy, the church, and the laws intact. It was a chivalrous dream, but never more than a dream. The Allies with whom we had to fight had very different ends in view. They had their eyes on Provence, on Burgundy, on Alsace-Lorraine, and on Flanders. They were kings, fighting for territory: we were a nation, fighting for nationalism's sake.

Between these conflicting aims Pitt oscillated unhappily. One day he would declare for a counter-revolution. "No argument could lead him to believe that a numerous and enlightened people willingly submitted to the most severe and sanguinary despotism that ever stained the page of history. It was impossible to put an end to this furious tyranny without destroying the present government of France." Next day he would send a squadron to secure a sugar-island. Either way Fox had him at a disadvantage. Were we fighting to restore the Bourbons?—it was a visionary task, beyond the resources of a dozen Englands. Were we fighting for Martinique?—much thanks we should have from the restored dynasty, for parcelling out their dominions beforehand. Pitt never succeeded in making up his mind. The rapacious motives of Austria and Prussia were unconcealed. They wanted to make their crusade pay, either in portions of France or in British subsidies. If France looked unpromising, they always had Poland or Bavaria as an *arrière-pensée*. Prussia welcomed our intervention mainly as a chance to suppress Kosciusko with armies paid for by England to be used against France. As a member of such a confederacy, it seemed hard that England alone should fight for altruistic motives. Pitt invented the theory that England should secure herself tit-bits in the West Indies and elsewhere, as a reimbursement for the outlay of the principal campaign. On such a programme it was impossible that we could ever win.

Pitt was as incapable in the execution as in the conception of his campaigns. He made Windham his Secretary for War in 1794, and allowed him to indulge an enthusiasm for far-flung expeditions to remote and unhealthy islands in almost every part of the world except the proper theatre of war. He gave important commands to his brother, Chatham, and to the Duke of York, between whom it would be difficult to award the prize of incompetence. He never once made Paris his goal: he never once assembled a force superior in numbers to the revolutionary forces it was likely to encounter. His father had conquered America in Germany. Pitt tried to conquer France everywhere except on French soil, and with every means except "the big-battalions." During these years of constant defeat, the navy was our only salvation. It is almost entirely due to Pitt and Windham that England could never achieve on land what she achieved at sea. North and Germaine hardly did their country greater dis-service.

Fox's main preoccupation was to hold the door open for peace. His motions were mainly directed to making sure that negotiation should not be conditional on a change of government in France. Things might improve without a counter-revolution; France might cool in her frenzy, and England in her revulsion. Fox was determined that no punctilio should stand in the way of peace. He had a strong case. It was easy to ridicule a "war of opinions," to demand precisely what sanctions we meant to exact for the restoration of the rule of law in France. It was easier still for him to point to our wasted subsidies, our treacherous and disgraceful allies, the uniform failure of our futile little expeditions. But one pitfall he did avoid. Although he failed to face the peril in which England stood, he did not suggest half-hearted defence. When the contest was engaged, he demanded that we should fight it out in proper fashion. Even before the war began, when he condemned the calling out of the militia as a measure of panic, he still said explicitly that he would vote with all his heart for an extra 25,000 seamen, or for 40,000 were they asked for. "The neglect of building a single ship that could possibly be built was a neglect highly criminal." The navy, which had always been the favourite child of the Tory party because it could never be used against English liberties, was Fox's favourite because it could never be used to impose a restoration in Paris. In this he showed a spark of the old spirit with which he had turned from denouncing the American war, to denouncing the false security of peace with France. This alone should have refuted the calumny, widely believed of him during the war, that he was reckoning on a French invasion to set him once more in power. Despite the loss of all his judgment and all his credit, he kept his patriotism to that extent unsullied.

2. Repressive Laws, 1793-1797

A great field for the activity of the opposition lay at home. The governing classes were thoroughly frightened of internal disaffection caused by French ideas. The bench of judges and the bench of bishops collectively lost their heads. Pitt himself, however calm, was extremely alive to what danger there was, and even believed himself to be in constant danger of assassination. A feverish demand sprang up, all over the country and from every class, for legislation to suppress the fancied conspiracy. So unanimous was the agitation that impartial spectators wondered where was the minority of whom the nation was so mortally afraid.

Pitt certainly did not pooh-pooh this agitation: it suited his purposes admirably: but that he exaggerated the danger there is no evidence. He was sincerely afraid, and all the more afraid because he had to go by guesswork in estimating the extent of the danger. A riot here, an outbreak of incendiarism there, somewhere else a correspondence with France intercepted, were all he had to go upon. The common people imagined danger all round them, and broke out into violence on the slightest suspicion. Pitt did the least he could, and passed coercive laws. It is said by one observer that Fox played into Pitt's hands, by exaggerating the membership of the French clubs in England. At all events, Fox and his friends were alone in opposing the repressive laws. On the testimony of the actual leaders of the subterranean movement, these laws were immensely popular, and the demand for them irresistible. The humblest agricultural labourer slept sounder, when he knew that the prison doors had closed on his dissenting neighbour, who had been supplied with a French dagger to stab him in the name of liberty, fraternity, and equality.

The legislature played a smaller part in this coercive *régime* than the judiciary. Habeas Corpus was suspended: a Treasonable Practices Act and a Seditious Meetings Act were passed: the press was regulated and taxed. Free speech was no very agonising deprivation in the days of Thomas Paine. The injustices committed by the anti-French mobs were appalling: they sprang from blind fear: the only way to pacify those fears was to tighten up the laws. Pitt did the least he could.

The same cannot be said for the judges. The suspension of Habeas Corpus was a weapon in their hands, with which they laid about them in terrible earnest. Particularly was this the case in Scotland where a revolutionary club was discovered among men of education and position. Its members were sentenced to from seven to fourteen years transportation. "God help the people who have such judges," said Fox: but in this case there was little the opposition could do. Pitt refused to interfere: public opinion endorsed his action. The Foxites' protests were based especially on the fact that these men were educated lawyers: but an overwhelming majority of the Commons felt that in men of such position the offence was all the more serious—as serious, in fact, as the penalty.

In England the judges were never inspired with quite the same enthusiasm, and in any case their ardour was soon checked by a resounding failure to convict Horne Tooke, who was prosecuted along with several others on a charge of constructive high treason. He was defended by Erskine, who had defended Keppel. Erskine's advocacy and Tooke's irrepressible wit proved too much for an English jury. They subpoenaed Pitt, Richmond, Sheridan, and

Fox, to prove that they too had advocated the reform of Parliament. They successfully defied the prosecution to show that anything more than a reform of parliament had been advocated by the London Corresponding Society. Fox was magnificent: he heaped coals of fire upon the little man who had opposed him, and petitioned against him, and finally had to pay him damages, at Westminster in 1790. A little later, he supported Tooke's claim to sit for another constituency, in spite of his clerical disability. Tooke had not expected such treatment: he was taken aback. "God Almighty made that man," he exclaimed, "to show his omnipotence." Yet Fox detested Tooke above all other men.

In 1780 when we were at war with America, France and Spain, a reform movement had swept the country, culminating in Dunning's triumphant motion against the influence of the Crown. In 1795, to organise in favour of reform was an indictable offence, and any prominent reformer, or even a prominent dissenter, was in danger of being mobbed in the streets. Yet Pitt was a far more liberal man than North: and the English temper for freedom had not evaporated in fifteen years. The change lay in the entirely different danger which faced us. In 1780, we were menaced with fleets and armies of invasion: in 1795, with what Pitt called the liquid fire of Jacobinism. In 1780, the Channel was full of enemy sail: in 1795, the air was full of enemy ideas. England faced the danger: Fox did not. Once again he failed to judge the tree by its fruits. Pitt's coercion was a success. Whether the danger had been great or small, nobody knew, and nobody knows yet: the great thing is that it passed away. The risk of mutiny and disaffection was too great a price to pay for the right of Englishmen to pass resolutions and to read the works of Thomas Paine. Internal security was bought ridiculously cheap. One crack-brained spy, whose guilt was patent, had to be executed. That was the only blood shed in England in several years, when hundreds a week were being executed in France for no crime at all. Those who rend the air with lamentations over Pitt's bloodless precautions against Jacobinism, are the very people who pass over with averted glance the carnage with which Jacobinism, in its native home, was enforced.

"For forms of government let fools contest:
Whate'er is best administered is best."

Fox declared in a heated moment that Pitt had set up "a system of cruelty and oppression worse than any devised by the See of Rome, or the Spanish Inquisition, or any other tyrant, spiritual or temporal." But he and his followers disproved their words by their actions. Not one of them succumbed to the temptation to leave his native shores, during the whole duration of this dreadful state of affairs. Not one of them availed himself of the stupendous and glorious edifice of liberty, erected on the foundations of human integrity, just across the Channel. Though six of them were millionaires, they continued to enjoy both their revenues and their civil liberties in peace at home: and the example of Thomas Paine, who only escaped the guillotine by a lucky chance, did not encourage them to make the great denial.

Pitt could afford to ignore such sort of opposition: but his true vindication waited till he was in his grave. In 1830, Grey, the leader of the Friends of the People, was Prime Minister: Holland, the repository of Foxite tradition, and Lambton were in the Cabinet. England was at peace: Jacobinism, thanks to Pitt, was dead. A few farmhands in the western counties burnt some haystacks to draw attention to the fact that they were starving. And how did the political disciples of Fox respond to that challenge? They hanged seven, imprisoned four hundred, and transported four hundred and fifty-seven. Surely, when those poor victims got to heaven, Pitt was released from purgatory without a stain upon his name.

3. Fox as a Pacifist, 1793-1797

Fox's pacifism is his principal claim to fame. Apart from his early enthusiasm for fighting the Bourbons, it was consistent. It was a complete departure from Whig policy. To a true Whig, like Windham or Burke, France had been the natural enemy under Louis Quatorze, was the natural enemy under Louis Seize, and remained the natural enemy under Danton, under Robespierre, under Napoleon. To Fox, once the Family Compact with Spain was broken by the Revolution, France was like any other country. From 1789, his pacifism knew no exceptions. He was never tired of repeating the maxim of Cicero: "I prefer the most unjust peace to the most just war." On a premise so comprehensive, a noble policy can be built. It is impossible to cavil at a pacifism that makes no exceptions at all: the weakness in Fox's position was that he only adopted it at the moment when our inevitable enemy became more formidable than ever before.

On the arguments Fox held out against war in 1793, it is clear that he would have done the same in 1914. The parallel is extraordinary. In each case, there was a *casus belli* in a treaty obligation. In each case, the treaty obligation was an insignificant consideration beside the national feeling that Europe was being engrossed by a state with whom it would be impossible ever to live at peace. In each case, the policy of this country was guided by a Prime Minister pacifist in every fibre, who stolidly refused to identify himself with the national feeling until he was absolutely certain that it was not hysteria, but the genuine recoil of civilisation from the encroachment of bestiality. All this left Fox unmoved.

Even mistakes can be noble, and Fox's "fear of seeming to yield what he thinks right to the bias of public opinion" was carried to sublimity. That one man is right, and a nation wrong, has often been maintained by the one man: but to act in 1793 on principles, on which only a few dared act in 1914, is greatness of a kind. He was not afraid to be ahead of his own time, not even to be ahead of ours. A pamphlet of his, in which he puts his case before his constituents, is quite superb in its indifference to the real issue, in its tenacious argument on ths small points of law. "My proposal was rejected by a great majority," he says simply: "I defer with all due respect to their opinion, but retain my own."

The fear of misrepresentation scarcely entered his head. His love for England was so obvious—it breathed in every word he said or wrote—that it was inconceivable to him that the cheap taunts against his patriotism could be believed. Pacifism is a development of patriotism. You must see the fine points in your own country before you can see the fine points in civilisation: you cannot love war *and* England. When the Tory press laughed at Fox for wishing well to every country but his own, the accusations fell dead, infinitely wide of the mark. It was because he loved England too well that he overrated her immunity, and put an exaggerated value on her freedom of speech and thought. He could not rouse himself to the danger that threatened institutions he thought immovable, so deeply rooted in the minds of a phlegmatic race. In a brilliant simile, he accused Burke of loving the constitution as Regan and Goneril loved their father, with extravagant protestations of devotion: for himself, he said with Cordelia, I love it as I ought. That Burke carried his trepidation too far cannot be denied: Fox carried his confidence to the opposite extreme. Yet it was a confidence born of unshakeable faith in the excellence of English institutions and in the sound determination of the English people to preserve them.

Four years of hopeless opposition made no impression whatever on Fox's views: he never entertained a suspicion that he was wrong. But his dejection grew upon him. It was a very different form of low spirits from Burke's. Burke, as he saw the world crashing round his head, the government blundering, and all his worst predictions fulfilled with mythological accuracy, was stirred to a sort of religious frenzy. Goading on the government, raising subscription for the refugees, and collecting material for his comminations, he worked harder now than ever in his arduous life. Fox was driven in the opposite direction. "Oh," he would sigh,

> "Oh for a lodge in some vast wilderness,
>   Some boundless contiguity of shade,
>   Where rumour of oppression and deceit,
>   Of unsuccessful or successful war,
>   Might never reach me more! My ear is pained,
>   My soul is sick with every day's report
>   Of wrong and outrage with which earth is filled."

By 1797, a state of affairs had been reached which killed Burke, and drove Fox despairing into private life. The war was heading for disaster. Austria had made a separate peace at Leoben: Prussia had made a separate peace at Basle, and had marched off with an army paid for by Pitt, to suppress Kosciusko in Poland. The navy, at Portsmouth, at Sheerness, and on the high seas, was in a state of mutiny. Ireland was in a blaze, and inviting the French to land. The harvest had failed. The Bank had suspended payment.

Pitt had sent two successive missions to France to treat for peace, though he confessed he had to "stifle every feeling of pride to the utmost" to do so. His emissaries found that the people of France were longing for peace: but the Directory were not: all the Directory were longing for was bribes. Pitt felt he could put no confidence in a bought peace, though the sum mentioned was small enough, any more than in 1793 he could remain at peace on the strength of his conviction that the French threats were made in bad faith. With Pitt reduced to such an extremity, Fox very reasonably argued that there was nothing he could do. In the American war he had been the great opponent of secession from Parliament: but the analogy between this and the American war was a poor pretence. He was too disheartened even to exult in Pitt's discomfiture. For a time before seceding from Parliament he was held back by the memory of 1776 and Rockingham's feebleness. "I am so sure that secession is the measure a shabby fellow would take in our circumstances, that I think it can scarcely be right for us." Then he had stopped the war: now he could not. The secession had been a gesture of disgust: now it was a mere bowing before the storm. "In these bad times, here I am with Liz, enjoying the fine weather, the beauty, and, not its least beauty, the idleness of this place as much as if these horrors were not going on. When one has done all one can, as I think I have, to prevent mischief, one has a right I think to forget its existence." In May, 1797, he announced that he would attend Parliament no more.

CHAPTER TWENTY-ONE

St. Anne's Hill, 1797-1802

Fox's retreat into private life in 1797 was preceded by two happy events—a financial settlement and marriage.

In 1793 the Whig Club, by way of a set-off to the loss of half their membership, set on foot a subscription to pay Fox's debts. The response was altogether unexpected. Contributions poured in alike from Whig millionaires and from dissenting shopkeepers. A sum was raised which not only paid his debts, but fetched about three thousand a year. Indeed, there was some embarrassment at the prospect of being so well endowed: there was a question whether he would be altogether pleased. "How do you think he will take it?" a nervous subscriber asked a friend of Fox's. "Why, quarterly," was the reply; and quarterly he took it, with a most charming letter of acceptance. The trustees took what precautions they could against his using the annuity as a security for further debts, but there was no necessity. Mrs. Armistead had weaned him completely from the gaming-table; and with the death this same year of his partner, Foley, his devotion to Newmarket faded away.

Fox and Mrs. Armistead were married in September, 1795, after twelve years' irregularity. This step was probably taken with a view to another foreign tour, Mrs. Armistead having been hurt by the lack of civility on the part of the English they met abroad in 1788. But the tour did not materialise, for the very good reason that men of Fox's opinions were liable to be assaulted in foreign capitals. Until 1802, when they next travelled, they told nobody, not even Lord Holland. "Mrs. A." she had always been, and "Mrs. A." she remained. It is the best example of Fox's deliberate flouting of public opinion. He was determined that those who had slighted his mistress should not have the gratification of calling on his wife. He had his reward: it was a great moment when the collective virtue of England learnt that they had been man and wife for seven years.

Fox was more or less excluded from London society at a time when every house was full of French *émigrés*. He could have derived little pleasure from finding his brilliant Parisian hostesses of the seventies living on the charity of his political enemies: while to them every post brought news of another of their relatives dead at the hands of Fox's paragons of justice, integrity and toleration. There is record of his having met Talleyrand during his mission in 1793: but it was a disappointing occasion. The company was brilliant: but Fox had no attention to spare from his deaf and dumb son: and Talleyrand went away complaining bitterly that he had dined with the most eloquent man alive, and only seen him talk with his fingers. Talleyrand was furious at the cold contempt with which he was treated in London on this mission: Fox's social unpopularity must have been as great.

His faithful band of followers could provide between them enough hospitality to satisfy most tastes, and they visited each other in droves. At Woolbeding, Lord Robert Spencer's; at Southill with Whitbread; at Knowsley or at Woburn, the same parties assembled every year. Every September would find Fox shooting with more passionate enjoyment than ever. He shared a lodge of sorts with Spencer at Thetford: but Holkham was his great resource, though Coke was the only host of them all who would not receive Mrs. Armistead. Partridges, and partridges alone, could separate Fox from his "Lady of the Hill." At every other time of the year his one wish was to be back at his earthly paradise near Chertsey.

Cowper at Olney did not pursue a more tranquil routine than Fox at St. Anne's Hill. He rose very early: in summer he would begin the day with a canter and a bathe in the Thames, in winter with a short walk to his favourite beech tree. A part of the morning was given over to reading Italian or French with Mrs. Armistead, after which he would retire to his own studies of the classics, reading Homer and Virgil three books at a sitting. The dinner-hour varied between half-past two and four. A frugal collation, a few glasses of wine (often sent him free by an admiring vintner), coffee, and after that an evening's gardening, or a walk to Laleham, or if it was very fine an excursion by river to Maidenhead. After tea, there was reading aloud, usually of novels. Supper, consisting of fruit and pastry, came at ten, and at half-past ten they went to bed. Into this framework was fitted a good deal of letter-writing, a minimum of newspaper reading, some rather longer walks, some agricultural activities, and a certain amount of sheer idleness. One visitor found him on the grass teaching the birds to think he was dead: others marvelled at his industry: but, idle or busy, he could always find time for an interminable flow of talk, with a total stranger in the lane, with a nearby farmer, or with a guest. There were few guests, the Duke of Bedford the only one who came frequently. Fox was too uxorious to be a very willing host, and both of them firmly resisted the smallest infringement of regularity. When Fanny Burney's *Camilla* arrived, and Fox in his impatience began to read it aloud at dinner instead of tea, Mrs. Armistead confiscated the book.

Fox's letters to Lord Holland are a revelation of what intellectual resources a public man can bring to private life. They are written to a very stereotyped model, and repeat themselves a lot, but they are never dull for a moment. He starts off with an account of the decay of politics, exaggeratedly gloomy and bitter. "What a rogue Pitt is! It is quite unpleasant that a man with such parts should be totally devoid of all right feelings." He proves to his own satisfaction that the public is mad, that the House of Commons has lost all its power, and that what he calls "Mr. Hume's Euthanasia," in other words, arbitrary government is beginning. He laments equally our defeats and our victories. Sometimes his bitterness gets the better of his good sense, as when he speaks of a "desperate expedition, which I believe as well as hope has not the smallest chance of success." But his imprecations against England's conduct are balanced by the reflection that "France is worse." "What a pity that a people capable of such incredible energy should be governed by those of such unheard-of crimes and cruelties." But he always finds consolation from these horrors in his private happiness. "The Lady of the Hill is one continual source of happiness to me. I believe few men, indeed, ever were happier in that respect than I. I declare my affection for her increases every day. She is a comfort to me in every misfortune, and makes me enjoy doubly every pleasant circumstance of life; there is to me a charm and a delight in her society, which time does not in the least wear off, and for real goodness of heart, if she ever had an equal, she certainly never had a superior." Then he goes on to say what he is reading at the moment, and to explain just why it is the best thing he has ever read. The extent is perfectly astounding.

Homer, Virgil and Ariosto are read annually, if not oftener. Shakespeare, Euripides and Dryden come almost within this magic circle. "Freedom and rapidity" are his criteria of literary merit, and in these Ariosto, he says, vies with Homer. Neither length nor familiarity have any terrors for Fox. *Don Quixote*. *Boccaccio,* the *Faerie Queen, Paradise Lost*—these are mere bedside books. At the other end of the scale, he refuses to be disconcerted by obscurity, however profound. Lope de Vega interests him as much as Cervantes, and he is continually singing the praises of a pastoral writer of the name of Buonarotti. Literary disputes fascinate him; above all the question of whether the nightingale's note is merry or melancholy. For himself he is convinced that it is merry, and scours antiquity to prove his point, bringing Theocritus and Chaucer into the fray against Sophocles, on whose knowledge of bird-notes he pours out his scorn. In contemporary literature, he considers Burns one of the cleverest men who ever lived: as a boy he had seen the merits of Goldsmith, and before he died he was to acclaim Scott: best of all, he appreciates Crabbe, whom Burke had discovered.

Literature is by no means the main topic of his letters to Holland, for they always contain copious instructions about what to see and do in whatever part of the world he is in. If his nephew is in Spain, Fox writes in Spanish: if in Italy, in Italian. He is to visit so-and-so; not to miss this or that view. He is piloted round the picture galleries of Italy by a sort of remote control. Mrs. Armistead is wild about Correggio: but Fox's favourite is Domenichino, and his St. Jerome the finest picture in the world, Hardly a painter who is not discussed with loving detail, and with a memory (for the days before reproduction) quite astonishing. And then he returns to the theme of how happy he is, almost apologising for such unbounded felicity. "I could not name any time of my life when I was happier than I am now, but I do not believe I should be so, if I had acted otherwise than I have done."

So catholic were his tastes, that it is easier, and almost a relief, to catalogue a few dislikes. He had no ear for music, unless sung by his wife. He thought political economy a nonsensical science, though he read Adam Smith. Metaphysics he found the least agreeable of his studies. His enjoyment of Virgil was marred by his hatred of Æneas: "Dido," he says, "has us all to herself." He found Rousseau too "extravagant" to be readable: he was not impressed by Gibbon's style. Alas, he passed no recorded verdict on Boswell.

It is a picture of what Bacon calls a full man. Never bored, never boring, he has turned from a life of feverish dissipation and publicity to one of sedate rustic seclusion, with just the same active, absorbing mind and the same entire lack of introspection. Love in a cottage at fifty came as naturally to his appetite for life as Newmarket, Parliament, and the faro table, with no time for bed, at twenty-five.

"'How various his employments whom the world calls idle' is my motto," he wrote. One of these employments was a work of history. He decided to write a *Reign of James the Second*, not thinking apparently that Burnet was enough of a Whig, and inspired by intense antipathy to Hume. This marvel of tendentious history never came to very much. He started to read up the period, and before he knew where he was, he was planning a new edition of Dryden, with notes by C. J. Fox. "I fell into it, upon my honour, with real diligent views in regard to history, but soon forgot the object." That in turn fell through, and he returned to history. Lord Holland in Spain got copies of the original papers of Ronquillo which were of first-rate importance: and on his own later visit to Paris, he had access to Barillon's reports. It was therefore a work of research of some importance. Two years after his death, what there is of it was published: an agreeable, rather underrated, work, marred by all the prose weaknesses of an orator and all the pre-conceived opinions of a Whig: in all, a slim quarto, far removed from the pile of tomes of "Fox's History," which, in the engravings, extend from his reclining elbow to the floor. From the great-great-nephew of Monmouth, it is an unworthy production.

That Fox's scholarship was real and not dilettantist is proved by a curious correspondence on abstruse classical points between him and Gilbert Wakefield, who dedicated to him his edition of Lucretius. Shortly after the correspondence had begun, Wakefield was sent to prison for two years for writing a seditious pamphlet. Fox wrote twice as frequently after that. One day, Wakefield heard that Fox was in bed with a smashed wrist, his gun having burst in his hand. He wrote in bitter reproach that a Liberal statesman should not amuse himself "indignis homine docto voluptatibus." But Fox could cap Cicero with Cicero. "Si quem

228

nihil delectaret nisi quod cum laude et dignitate conjunctum foret, huic homini ego fortasse, et pauci, deos propitios, plerique iratos putarent." And Wakefield, like the gods, found it impossible to be angry with such a man: for it is all too seldom that a Whig is not a prig.

Finally, he was something of a poet himself. On the 24th of January, 1799, he presented his wife at breakfast with the following lines:

Of years I have now half a century passed,
And none of the fifty so blessed as the last.
How it happens my troubles thus daily should cease,
And my happiness thus with my years should increase,
This defiance of Nature's more general laws
You alone can explain, who alone are the cause.

CHAPTER TWENTY-TWO

1. *Peace Proposals, 1800*

B etween 1797 and 1800, Fox's name came before the public only once, and then in a connection most favourable to himself.

The Whig Club, or what remained of it, made a practice of celebrating Fox's birthday with a great public dinner at the Crown and Anchor. On his forty-ninth birthday, the Duke of Norfolk was presiding over an assembly of two thousand people, when he exceeded the bounds of discretion by giving as a toast: "Our Sovereign, the People." The premier duke was not one of the brightest ornaments of the party, and was notoriously never very sure of himself after dinner: but the affair created a considerable scandal. Norfolk recanted in the newspapers and apologised to the King: but it was thought necessary to make an example of him. He was deprived of the Lord Lieutenancy of Yorkshire, which carried with it the command of the Yorkshire militia. His disgrace created no surprise: humbler men were in prison for uttering milder sentiments: the militia could hardly be left in charge of a Jacobin. Public opinion was not at all sorry for the faintly ridiculous tipsy jockey of Norfolk.

Fox took a stronger view. To him it was another of the accumulating symptoms of arbitrary government. It was a return to the methods of 1762. At the next dinner of the Whig Club he finished a long speech about the revolution of 1688 by giving the toast: "Our Sovereign, the People." The public liked him for this: his friends were angry: Pitt was perplexed. Prosecution was out of the question, as the jury would be drawn from his adoring constituents. At first it was decided to treat the matter as a breach of privilege, but the penalty was a foolish one. As Pitt said: "We might send him to the Tower for the remainder of the session, which, though doing little in fact, would assert the authority of the House. The chief objections are that *weak and moderate* men might call it severe and vindictive, and at the end of three weeks he might be led home in procession, and have the glory of breaking windows." Finally it was decided to strike him off the Privy Council.

Pitt was admittedly in a dilemma. Norfolk's punishment had not been excessive, and it was difficult to let Fox do with impunity what Norfolk couldn't. But the penalty took an invidious form: it was depriving him of something he had earned: it placed Fox, a giant whichever way he was regarded, beneath all the creeping politicians whose claim to be called Right Honourable none despised more than Pitt. Of all the penalties that could have been chosen, it had the least effect in mortifying Fox, and it created the most sympathy in his favour. Pitt should have let the challenge lie. Unfortunately, that was exactly his weak spot. He was a rigid man: he never had the strength to yield. It was the Westminster scrutiny over again.

Apart from this Fox was altogether out of the public eye. His secession had the effect of making the proceedings of the Commons eminently ridiculous. Sheridan and three or four others bore the whole burden of opposition. Pitt's splendid oratory fell dead upon an empty House. The Treasury bench pined for Fox, but no number of military disasters, no amount of repressive legislation, could draw him out. Only in 1800, the government, by exceeding all their previous blunders, provoked him to break his silence.

On Christmas Day of 1799, Bonaparte submitted to the British government a proposal to treat for peace, worded in a flowery but quite diplomatic style. The value of this overture is a questionable matter. Our government had already endured two nasty rebuffs from the First Consul's predecessors. It may have been that he was aiming at a military *coup* under the cloak of a truce. He was still an unknown factor. Perhaps the government were right to turn the proposition down: but they were certainly wrong to turn it down in the way they did. The Foreign Secretary, Lord Grenville, happened to be the leader of the war party within the cabinet. This was his chance to aggravate the feelings of France against England, and he took it. He wrote a reply which would have made Palmerston blush. He dwelt on the internal state of France, on the circumstances of Bonaparte's rise to power, on the virtues of hereditary monarchy; and intimated that it was beneath England's dignity to treat with a *régime* so recently established. Napoleon simply published the reply, to the delight of the French, and sent a most damaging answer. The war continued.

Fox was torn between his anger at the conduct of the government, and his determination, formed though not admitted, to put politics behind him for ever. His friends represented that this occasion was an exception to every rule, a deadly disadvantage for the government, and a popular issue. In the end they prevailed. "I have determined against inclination, common sense, and philosophy to attend upon the question of Bonaparte's letter." He dragged himself up to Holland House with infinite grumbling. "Iterum mergor civilibus undis," he groaned. When he arrived, it was to find that the debate had been postponed, and he must spend two nights in London instead of one. At that dreadful intimation, says Lord Holland, "he sat silent and overcome, as if the intelligence of some great calamity had reached his ears. I saw tears steal down his cheeks, so vexed was he at being detained from his garden, his books, and his cheerful life in the country." This was the man who had sat up all night drinking at Hockerel, on his way back from Newmarket, then washed his face and debated all next day.

He was changed, but he was not decayed. Three years had added greatly to his prestige: they had taken nothing from his powers. He never spoke better in his life. Pitt had been so unwise as to say that England must wait for experience before treating with the usurper. He got a terrible punishment from Fox.

"We must keep Bonaparte for some time longer at war, as a state of probation. Gracious God, sir, is war a state of probation? Is peace a rash system? Is it dangerous for nations to live in amity with each other? Is your vigilance, your policy, your common powers of observation, to be extinguished by putting an end to the horrors of war? Cannot this state of probation be as well undergone without adding to the catalogue of human sufferings? 'But we must *pause*.' What! must the bowels of Great Britain be torn out, her best blood spilt, her treasure wasted, that you may make an experiment? Put yourselves—oh, that you would put yourselves in the field of battle, and learn to judge of the horrors that you excite. In former wars, a man might at least have some feeling, some interest, that served to balance in his mind the impressions which a scene of carnage and of death must inflict. . . . But if a man were present now at a field of slaughter, and were to inquire for what they were fighting—'Fighting!' would be the answer; 'they are not fighting, they are *pausing*.' 'Why is that man expiring?

Why is that other writhing with agony? What means this implacable fury?' The answer must be: 'You are quite wrong, sir; you deceive yourself. They are not fighting. Do not disturb them; they are merely *pausing*. This man is not expiring with agony— that man is not dead—he is only *pausing*. Lord help you, sir, they are not angry with one another; they have now no cause of quarrel, but their country thinks there should be a *pause*. All that you see, sir, is nothing like fighting—there is no harm, cruelty, or blood-shed in it whatever; there is nothing more than a political *pause*. It is merely trying an experiment, to see whether Bonaparte will not behave himself better than heretofore; and in the meantime we have agreed to a *pause*, in pure friendship.' "

He was on firm ground again. In the division he only mustered sixty-four, not a spectacular opposition after seven years of un-successful war; but outside the House the effect was immense. The millions who had left him on the question of fighting the revolutionaries began to come back to him on the question of making peace with Napoleon. Merely by keeping his mouth shut for three years he had gone far to reinstate himself. His consistency weighed heavily in his favour: his contemptuous aloofness gave him some of the old prestige of an elder statesman. Like Chatham's gout, Fox's domesticity added weight to his utterances.

2. *The Peace of Amiens, 1802*

For the present, France was kept in a state of probation. Then suddenly, in February 1801, for no reason in any way connected with the war, Pitt resigned, the King went momentarily mad again, and the Speaker—a prince of incompetents—was made Prime Minister. Fox at first was incredulous: Addington, "the Doctor," was a Prime Minister of farce: when the appointment was confirmed, he was angry, and declared that it was all a juggle. Addington was known to be hand in glove with Pitt. Addington's administration was simply Pitt's under another name. The opposition were no better off than ever.

What happened was this. Pitt was pledged to grant Catholic Emancipation in Ireland, but the King refused. He could only resign, thinking his own position impregnable. But it was not. Loughborough, his Lord Chancellor, had decided on the sixth of those timely betrayals by which he kept himself almost permanently in office. An alternative government was ready, and Pitt was out. He was angry with Addington, who had always been his friend, but he made no attempt to prevent his majority from supporting him. The division-lists were the same, but Fox was wrong in thinking that the government was the same. It was far weaker, and proportionately more pacific. Indeed, Pitt may well have had this additional motive for acquiescing in Addington's promotion. A study of history. may have taught him that England always turns upon any government that makes a treaty, good or bad. Peace was becoming inevitable: he would hand the poisoned chalice to his friend. He would take a holiday after seventeen years, keep his party intact, and return when the King's mind should be composed and the odium of the treaty passed away. This may well have been his line of thought.

The extreme war-party in Pitt's cabinet, Windham and Grenville, did not join Addington. Napoleon was attracted by the spectacle of such an excessively feeble administration. The war had reached a deadlock. Nelson was omnipotent at sea, Napoleon on land. Through no fault of his own, Addington was able to make peace: he sustained his reputation by making the worst peace imaginable. This put Pitt in a nasty position, as Fox saw. "How Pitt will defend it, it is difficult to conceive; but it is universally believed he will; what indemnity or security he will find I know not, nor how he can deny that these, or better terms, were to be had long ago, and consequently that all the money and lives lost since that period at least have been squandered wantonly and wickedly. You will have observed of course that France does not give up one acre she possessed before the war or conquered during the course of it."

Clearly, the worst for Pitt, the better for Fox. If it was a bad peace, it merely proved that every word Fox had said was true. He could return to public life, in all the splendour of inflexible consistency, enhanced by years of awful silence and unusual restraint, and demolish Pitt and Addington together, not by opposing the peace, but by pointing to the authors of the humiliation. With the exception of Windham and Grenville, who wanted war for war's sake, even the most fervent supporters of the anti-Jacobin war were ready for peace with Napoleon. The object of the war was altered: Fox's pacifism, so wrong for the first six years of the war, was right in the last. Outside Parliament, his moral position was almost as strong as it had been in the closing stages of the American war. A general election was soon due. Pitt would be blamed for the war, Addington for the peace. Fox would have his reward.

This is not what happened. Fox took a very different line. He was too embittered to act moderately. As had happened so often before, he threw his chance away because he could not conceal his rage and impatience. The trend of his thoughts in the last few years had been towards the unfounded belief that liberty in England was already dead. He exaggerated Pitt's tendency to arbitrary government so much, that he came to think that "Mr. Hume's Euthanasia" had actually set in. Anything was better than that. "Since there is to be no political liberty in the world," he wrote, "I really believe Bonaparte is the fittest person to be master." Detestation of Pitt blinded him to the faults of Napoleon: he was fascinated by Napoleon's career, and taken in by his fine words. "The truth is, I am gone something further in hate to the English Government than perhaps you and the rest of my friends are, and certainly further than can with prudence be avowed. The triumph of the French Government over the English does in fact afford me a degree of pleasure which it is very difficult to disguise." It proved impossible to disguise: he was incapable of that much prudence. When the time came to attack Pitt, he attacked England: when the time came to praise himself, he praised Napoleon. At a meeting in Westminster he gave utterance to the worst of his sentiments. "The peace is glorious to France— glorious to the First Consul. Ought it not to be so? Ought not glory to be the reward of such a glorious struggle? France has set an example that will be highly useful to all the nations of the earth, and above all to Great Britain." This was a new variation of the demand for peace at any price. It was one thing to denounce in 1793 a war against opinions: it was another thing, in 1801, when the revolution had changed, in meticulous fulfilment of Burke's prophecies, into a gigantic scheme of aggrandisement, to maintain that the aggressive campaigns of the usurper were merely another embodiment of the humane aspirations of 1789--that every country lost to England was a country won to liberty. It was folly even to formulate such a paradox: to express it in public was political ruin. His friends were horrified by Fox's speech: Grey and Sheridan "scolded him till he almost cried" about it: the public was disgusted. If liberty meant Bonaparte, they thought, then give us Pitt.

Retribution came upon him from an unexpected source. Coleridge, an indomitable supporter to the pacifist cause throughout the war, was enraged to find his political leader lauding Napoleon. He rushed into print, with a letter of hysterical anger. "Did you utter one word of alarm at the atrocious ambition of the First Consul? One sentiment of pity or indignation at the iron despotism, under which this upstart Corsican has reduced forty millions of your fellow-creatures? Not a syllable! Not a breathing! You *exulted*, Sir, that the war had ended, as it ought to end, gloriously for France, ignominiously for Great Britain! For the spirit of a man and patriot you abandoned yourself to the low and womanish temper, which finds in a triumphant 'Did I not tell you so, now?' a pleasure that overpowered, and sunk into oblivion, all the dangers and all the disgrace of a whole nation, and that nation your country!" That came from an advanced liberal: it was true: it was what the public felt. Plenty of men had been ready to forgive Fox for swallowing Robespierre: nobody could forgive him for swallowing Napoleon. There had been a Jacobin party of sorts, there was no Bonapartist party at all. Opinions differed as to whether Danton was hostile, or Dumouriez a formidable opponent: but not a soul besides Fox did not fear Napoleon.

In this way it came about that the war he had denounced ended miserably, without the smallest improvement in his political prospects. All the credit which had accumulated with the increasing unpopularity of the war, all the repute of a vindicated tenacity, was lost to the man who had earned it. Addington, as the author of the peace, was doomed. But the laurels which should have gone to Fox went instead to Pitt. Fox had once again shown himself to be his own worst enemy.

3. Visit to Paris, 1802

Having advertised his admiration of Napoleon in the manner best calculated to disgust the nation, the worst thing Fox could do was to avail himself of the peace to visit Paris. That was his next move. The instant he had been re-elected for Westminster—his fifth and easiest victory—he set off with his wife, now for the first time acknowledged, and one John Bernard Trotter, a young Irish secretary who wrote a book about the trip. Trotter had in him some of the makings of a Boswell: his hero-worship was as great and his sententiousness puts Boswell in the shade. But he contents himself with an exuberance of adulatory remarks, and gives us little or no actual conversation of his deity. The result is a statue rather than a re-animation. Fox appears, bathed in glory and cumbered with haloes, a saint, a sage, a prodigy, but not a living creature. His strange blend of modesty and assertiveness, his childlike enthusiasm brought up by his prim and doctrinaire rigidity, his self-reliance and inattention, his alarming mental abstraction: these are hinted at rather than drawn. Fox was the least self-conscious of men, and he had a horror of being feted or made much of. Gibbon has recorded how he had little inclination to converse with the Swiss: in France, where his long championship of each successive stage of the revolution had won him universal fame, he suffered more than ever from the attentions of mayors and crowds and theatre audiences.

His brusque manner with admirers is the only thing about Fox that Trotter comes near criticising. It is a weakness in him that is remarked by most of his contemporaries. It led to positive accusations of rudeness and insolence. There are many examples. There was the occasion when he turned his back on Thomas Moore with a grunt, although he had been implored to be polite. There was the occasion when he refused to thank Horace Walpole for rising from a bed of sickness to vote for him at Westminster in 1784. The Duchess of Devonshire, most partial of critics, puts it among his outstanding traits. "Whilst I have long lamented, and often been provoked with his negligence, sometimes even to decent attention, I must say that this kind of carriage in a Man whose Idol was popularity is perhaps the greatest proof of the real greatness of his mind, and must give security of the sentiments he professes." This failing she classes as an example of his "contempt of necessary expedients." It is very true that his rudeness is a guarantee of his disinterestedness. The fact was, that he never concealed either his interest or his lack of interest in anything. He lived always as if he were living unobserved. If he wanted to talk about turnips, he would talk about them to the neighbouring farmer with such undisguised interest and concentration that he made a friend for life. If he did *not* want to talk about Irish melodies he would turn his back on Tom Moore, who had not forgotten the slight thirty years later. He turned to whatever interested him with as little apology as a dog turns to his dinner. He was incapable of adapting himself, afraid of seeming to ingratiate himself, and wholly unaware of the impression he made. This was where he was the precise opposite of Lansdowne, whose oozing courtesy and uniform attentiveness were carried to a point where they repelled more than they impressed. Lansdowne left men puzzled and suspicious: Fox left most men his slaves, but a few he turned away disappointed and resentful. The problem of Fox's life is not why he achieved so much, but why he did not achieve more. These failings are not set down in malice, but as clues to this problem. "Contempt of necessary expedients" is a large set-off to talents.

The ostensible object of the journey to Paris was to examine Barillon's papers in the French archives and James' memoirs in the Scotch College, for the *History of James the Second*, and to find out the real truth of those shameful transactions in which his ancestress de Kéroualle had been the intermediary. If he was to concentrate on this object, he needed all the rudeness he could muster. Even at Calais a municipal reception was with difficulty avoided. Their progress was circuitous, and the long, hot days by coach were spent in immense readings aloud. Cassel and *Joseph Andrews*; Lille, Antwerp, and the *Æneid*; Utrecht and *Tom Jones*; Amsterdam, Rotterdam, Brussels and *Orlando Furioso*; such was their progress, with public dinners and addresses to be waived aside wherever they halted. In Paris they took the Hotel Richelieu, and tried to divide the time between the Scotch College and the Quai D'Orsay. But there was too much else to be done. Paris grew on Fox: he was said to love it like a cat, who is fond of the house though the family be gone. There was the Louvre, to which Napoleon had considerately brought from Italy half Fox's favourite pictures. There were the theatres he knew so well, reigned over now by Mlle. Duchesnois, and all his old favourites, *Phèdre*, *Roxane*, *Andromache*, *Tancrède*; even the unwelcome ovations of the pit could not keep him away. There was Versailles and the Tuileries, where he found his own busts alongside Nelson's. They dined with Talleyrand, with whose wife Mrs. Fox had many interesting recollections to compare. They called on Sièyes, and Kosciusko called on them. Fox went shooting with Berthier, and stayed in the country with Lafayette. Mme. Cabarrus had them to dinner: Mme. Recamier lionised him more outrageously than anyone since Georgiana had dared to do. Paris teemed with interesting people: and the whole of it centred round the court of Bonaparte.

It was a vexed question whether Fox should pay his compliments to Napoleon or not. It suited Napoleon's book admirably that he should. For the moment a liberal, a man of peace, he could hardly find a better way of convincing the French nation of the purity of his pacifism than to be seen embracing Fox. This was all the more reason that Fox should refuse. An interview between them would be misrepresented not only in England to Fox's disadvantage, but in France to Napoleon's advantage. He was damaging himself: he was assisting Napoleon's imposture. But it was not in Fox's nature to refuse: so they met. Napoleon loaded Fox with compliments, and Fox was embarrassed: then he fired off some elaborate historical platitudes, and Fox's attention wandered. It was a very boring interview: but a week later they dined and talked foreign politics in serious. Napoleon criticised Windham, as well he might, and accused him of a plot against his life. "Premier Consul," said Fox, "ôtez-vous cela de votre tête." Napoleon was not used to such rebukes. "Il me combattait avec chaleur en son mauvais français," he said afterwards, but the impartial opinion was that Fox's French was considerably purer than Napoleon's.

He stayed three months in Paris, going everywhere and seeing everybody. His research work languished so much that Trotter was sent home. When he returned to London, he had achieved little and enjoyed himself much: he was a little disillusioned by Napoleon's passion for military display, but he was much damaged in public opinion by interviewing him at all.

CHAPTER TWENTY-THREE

1. *Renewal of the War, 1803*

Fox returned from Paris to find himself regarded on all sides as the "apologist of France" and the "agent of the First Consul." He did nothing to dispel the suspicion, either in public or in private. "Fox has given great surprise by his conversation," writes Creevey, " as he has given offence to his friends here. He talks publicly of liberty being *asleep* in France, but *dead* in England. He will be attacked in the House of Commons, and I think will find it difficult to justify himself. He has been damned imprudent." When Fox used this sort of language, he was perfectly sincere. His private letters show that he had really come to convince himself that "Bonaparte was the fittest person to be master." His sense of frustration, at the age of fifty-four, had got the better of his sense of proportion. "The only glimmering of hope which I see is from the Court, when that shall fall into other hands." It was a bad omen. He was looking to the Prince of Wales once more—"the worst anchoring ground in Europe," as Thurlow had said. He was embittered, and at such times there was no knowing where his mistakes would stop.

The Peace of Amiens was visibly breaking down. Addington was insistent where he should have yielded, and weak where he should have been firm. Napoleon declared that England clearly wanted war: "*J'en suis ravi,*" he confessed. Addington was possibly to blame about Malta: Napoleon was to blame about a dozen infractions of the treaty, as everybody saw but Fox. "With regard to the Consul, I am very obstinate in my opinion that he meant nothing insulting to England, either in the German or Swiss business." Even his closest friends, especially Grey, were amazed at his lack of perception, but Fox was immovable. "I am obstinate in my opinion that Bonaparte's wish is peace—nay, that he is afraid of war to the last degree." Grey expostulated with him on grounds which history has amply confirmed, but without effect. "The truth is, I do not feel half the indignation you all do." His opinion was supported by no attempts at reasoning: it was a flat assertion. "I am more convinced than ever that, if it is war, it is entirely the fault of ministers, and not of Bonaparte." He was not an extravagant admirer of Bonaparte, but he was such an extravagant hater of George the Third and his ministers, as to refuse to face any facts that stood to their credit.

He was not likely to make much headway towards popular favour in this direction. The British nation shared Fox's contempt for Addington, but they saw no sense in whitewashing Napoleon. Without wishing for war, they were not going to lie down under such provocations as the reoccupation of Switzerland by French troops. In March, 1803, occurred the scene between Napoleon and our ambassador. In May, the war was renewed. Pitt returned from his seclusion at Walmer Castle, and delivered a marvellous oration on the necessity for war. It fell to Fox to answer him, and the spirits of his followers sank with apprehension as he began to speak.

Actually he restrained himself uncommonly well. In his own opinion, it was the best speech he ever made. It certainly had to overcome great obstacles. Napoleon's countless provocations could not be extenuated: instead, he magnified Addington's obstinacy over the evacuation of Malta into the sole cause of the war. On the whole, there was less praise of Napoleon and less disparagement of England than was expected by those who knew his private thoughts. And there was a lot of commonsense embedded in it. Pitt had referred to Egypt as consecrated by English blood. "What seas should we ever quit," demanded Fox, "what territories should we ever surrender, if we were to retain all that had ever witnessed the triumphs of the British arms?" He complained that Pitt always spoke best when he was speaking in favour of a war. "The right honourable gentleman, when he appears before us in all the gorgeous attire of his eloquence, reminds me of a barbarous prince of Morocco, a Muley Molock, or a Muley Ishmael, who never puts on his gayest garments, or appeared in extraordinary pomp, but as a prelude to the murder of many of his subjects." Speaking on less strong grounds than in 1793, he skilfully pointed to the mistakes of that period. "I do sincerely hope, sir, that we shall hear nothing more of wars undertaken for religion, or of the blessings of social order; but I speak of that detestable hypocrisy which held forth these as the ostensible objects of the contest, while we were all along fighting for ends of a nature totally opposite."

The opponents of the war voted 67 strong. It might have been worse. The public never learnt how completely Fox had shed his allegiance, how deeply the iron had entered into his soul.

2. Coalition with Grenville, 1804

War in 1803 was historically unavoidable. War, with Addington at the head of affairs, was a gloomy prospect. The King liked Addington as a feeble and pliable servant: and a large majority of Pitt's old supporters were prepared to go on voting for Addington, as long as the King wished him to remain. It was borne in upon Pitt that the power he had so lightly surrendered was not going to be regained without a struggle. He had encouraged his followers to support the worthy Doctor as long as the peace lasted: the difficulty now was going to be to get them back.

In this way Addington was faced with three separate oppositions. There was Fox with 70 supporters. There was Pitt with 60 supporters. And there was what was called the "new opposition" with about 36 supporters. The genesis of this last group is of great importance.

The "new opposition," or the Grenvilles, to give them the family name, were those who had opposed the peace in 1802. Within Pitt's cabinet all during the war there had been two distinct parties: one group, the majority, were for making peace whenever possible; the other, led by Grenville and Windham, and taking their views from Burke, were against any peace on any terms whatever short of a restoration of the Bourbons. They had opposed Pitt's negotiations with the Directory: Grenville, by his insane despatch, had made peace impossible in 1800: and in 1802, when Fox and Pitt had supported the treaty, they had denounced it as an infamy and a stain on British honour. Grenville, the nucleus of this group, was a mediocrity, the slave of his brother Buckingham, the Earl Temple of 1783. Windham, on the other hand, was an accomplished man and fine a speaker, but his mind had become disordered by adopting, and even exaggerating, Burke's frenzied conception of a royalist war. It is more than a coincidence that these two men were as incompetent in their departments as they were dangerous in council. There have been few worse Foreign Ministers in our history than Grenville, and few worse War Ministers than Windham. These men, with their gang of extremists, were known as the Bloodhounds: they had done all they could to prevent a peace, and when it came, they were untiring in their efforts to bring about a renewal of the war. The unpopularity of this course was no deterrent to them, for they relied entirely on influence and solidarity. They were, in fact, representative of the worst type of Whig of fifty years before, and they had revived and exaggerated the old Whig creed of perpetual war with France.

It may seem paradoxical that the most fervent supporters of the war, long after the Tories had sickened of it, should be a group of Whigs, most of whom had only with difficulty brought themselves to separate from Fox at the actual outbreak of the original hostilities. But the party tradition died hard. To the Tories, the object of the war ceased when Napoleon became supreme. To the Whigs, France under any ruler was as much the natural enemy as she had been under the Roi Soleil. "It is the first half of Pitt's career," said Disraeli, "which I select as his title deed to be looked upon as a Tory Minister—hostility to borough-mongering, economy, French alliance, and commercial treaties. The latter half is pure Whiggism, close Parliaments, war with France, national debt and commercial restriction." The career of the Grenvilles gives point to that audacious generalisation.

Fox now found himself voting in the same lobby with the Grenville party. What is more, he found himself in actual agreement with them on the question of defence. Napoleon was at this time preparing his invasion of England. Addington fussed and flurried and did nothing. Windham produced a drastic defence scheme. Fox, who had always been sound on defence, and had actually enrolled himself in the Chertsey volunteers, supported Windham's scheme.

It was a pleasure to be able to agree with Windham once more after ten years' savage opposition. He had known Windham quite intimately, and, as he had said to Napoleon: "Il n'y pas sur la terre un être plus noble, plus humain, plus rempli d'honneur et de talents que M. Windham." Most of the Grenvilles were gentlemen, and had been Whigs. They could see a joke against Pitt. They were good fellows: Pitt was not. There was Tom Grenville, whom Fox had always liked; there was Fitzwilliam, his oldest friend. It was pleasant to have them calling on him again. Before he knew where he was Fox was drifting into another coalition. The Prince of Wales was all for it: he loathed Pitt, and wanted a reconciliation with Fox: there was no better way of dishing Pitt and making Fox a possible candidate for power than to induce him to co-operate with the extreme war party.

By January 1804, Fox is murmuring about "a systematic opposition for the purpose of destroying the Doctor's administration." For that they were bound to vote together. "Let us first get rid of the Doctor is my first principle of action." And then what? Separate again, Fox to move at intervals for peace, Windham to move for war on a wider front? Surely not. They had one great link. They both hated Pitt. To be sure, one party hated him because he was too fond of war, and the other because he was not fond enough. But the real link went deeper. Both the Foxites and the Grenvilles were aristocratic parties. Pitt's party was full of parvenus like Canning, Dundas and Wilberforce: Pitt himself was not one of themselves.

The Prince was active: Tom Grenville was active. Fox had a parley with Lord Grenville and liked him, as usual on personal grounds: "a very *direct* man," he said. It came as quite a surprise to Fox to find that the proposal was regarded with horror by his followers. Grey protested loudly, but as Grey could seldom be prevailed on to leave Northumberland, his warning carried little weight. "Our co-operation with the Grenvilles has no secret in it of any kind," said Fox. "I should have had no objection to a closer connection, but I found some friends so prejudiced on the subject that it was agreed, with the mutual consent of both parties, that we should make no engagement of any sort, but simply co-operate upon such measures as we were agreed upon." The prejudices of his friends aroused in him nothing but contempt. "Whether some of them may not be so *alarmed* at the possibility of such an evil as to act like the alarmists of old is what I am by no means sure of." The alarmists of old were those who had disapproved the coalition with North: that coalition had put Pitt in power for seventeen years, and the memory of it was by no means dead: Fox's contempt for the alarmists was a little misplaced.

English politicians will apparently never learn that the English people expect them to fight each other, hammer and tongs. Year after year, hatchets are buried, unions are cemented, old sores are healed, pipes of peace are smoked: year after year the same complacent oratory anoints these reconciliations: and year after year the reconciled parties are equally taken aback by the boos and hisses of the electorate. Long before Disraeli laid it down that England does not love coalitions, the events of 1783 had made it plain to any man of common observation that consistency in likes and dislikes weighs quite as heavily with the public as consistency in policies.

The new alarmists were mostly those who had refused to join in the secession of 1797. Fox had been angry with them for spoiling his gesture. From Philip Francis he had separated with "no return, no acknowledgment, not a single word at parting." He had been unjust to Tierney, a valuable subordinate, who later led the party in the Commons. Tierney carried his reprobation of the Grenvilles so far as to take office under Addington. Sheridan, without going quite so far, made it clear that he was not going to be disgraced by Fox's new connection. By taking this line he incurred a most ungenerous accusation of betraying Fox. Since 1797 he had taken an independent line, sometimes voting with and sometimes against ministers. His opposition had been almost single-handed and at times extremely effective: even Fox in his letters was unable to deny him a little grudging admiration from time to time. Sheridan had become a power in Parliament, principally because of his refusal to compromise. He was boldly consistent. He rated his opponents in order of their support of the war: that is to say, he hated Addington much, Pitt more, and the Grenvilles most. Fox at first complains that "Sheridan will not vote with me for fear of being found in Pitt's company," conduct which he describes as "intolerable." If Sheridan was scrupulous about Pitt, he was likely to stick at the Grenvilles altogether, and he did. Fox was infuriated: Sheridan was "past praying for," he was "mad with vanity and folly." And all because he had learnt a lesson from the coalition with North, which Fox could never learn.

Sheridan loved acting alone. He could not defer the whole time to Fox's judgment, which had proved invariably wrong. Like Burke in 1790, he was at the end of his patience. He had no use for retreats into private life, and preferred more lively company to that of Fox, after Fox had settled down. In a word, he was a bad Foxite: and as such all good Foxites were bound to regard him as a traitor and a renegade. Such was Creevey's view.

Creevey was the perfect Foxite. This jolly, drunken, prattling little man found his idol in Fox and his temple in Brooks's. He was the embodiment of the Foxite type, whose notion of politics, it was said, consisted in preferring a fat man who loved women to a thin man who was insensible to their charms. When Fox was committing political suicide, the worst Creevey could bring himself to say was that he was "damned imprudent." A month later all is well again: "Old Charley was himself and of course was exquisitely delightful. Unfettered by any hopes or fears—by any systems or connections, he turned his huge understanding loose amongst these skirmishers, and it soon settled, with its usual and beautiful perspicuity, all the points that came within the decision of reasoning, judgment, experience and knowledge of mankind. In addition to the correctness of his views and delineations, he was all fire and simplicity and sweet temper." Not naturally a modest man, Creevey bowed the knee to Fox: "I am more certain from every day's experience that the leader of the party to which I belong is as superior in talents, in enlightened views, in public and private virtues, to all other party leaders as one human being can be to another. He must therefore give many, many votes that I may think are wrong, before I vote against him or not with him. I scarcely know an earthly blessing I would purchase at the expense of those sensations I feel towards the incomparable Charley."

This was the sort of man who joined the cry against Sheridan when he dared to differ from Fox. Creevey can find no words bad enough for Windham the Bloodhound: "No friend of Fox can ever forget or forgive the bitter malignity with which Windham pursued and hunted down the great and amiable creature." But he is quite sorry for Windham the ally of Fox: "Fox and Windham," he sighs, "those proscribed victims of fortune." Tierney invited Creevey to dinner to discuss Fox's leadership: but Creevey gave them the toast "Devotion to Fox"—"and so we all got to loggerheads directly, and jawed and drank till twelve or one o'clock, and I suppose I was devilish abusive, for they are all as shy as be damned of me ever since." As for Sheridan, "for the last three months he has been damning Fox in the midst of his enemies, and in his drunken and unguarded moments has not spared him even in the circles of his most devoted admirers." Thus Fox's abuse gave the cue for general ostracism. Sheridan's tragic decline did not begin till Fox was dead: but it was Fox who dealt him the deadliest blow.

3. *Pitt Returns to Power, 1804*

The Doctor's administration became weaker every day: his pills and medicines and prescriptions, as all his measures were described, were treated less and less respectfully by the House. Pitt simply waited until the absurdity of his being in a minority, while Addington ruled, should become unbearable. In April, 1804, after propounding various silly plans for coalition with Pitt, Addington finally retired, and Pitt reigned in his stead.

Pitt had large views about the basis of his new government. This war, after all, was not like the last. Napoleon was sweeping across Europe: it was no war of opinion. He wanted a comprehensive cabinet. In his previous cabinet he had suffered too much from the war-mania of the Grenvilles. He had now two alternatives: to form a government without the Grenvilles, or to form a government in which the Grenvilles were balanced by Fox. The former would be precarious. The latter was almost the least he could do, since Fox as well as Grenville had helped him to beat Addington. He needed all the support he could get. Besides, his health was failing. He felt his weakness, both in cabinet and in Parliament: England was in the midst of a war of self-preservation: he decided on an all-embracing government. Fox and Grey on the one side were to balance Windham, Grenville, Spencer, and Fitzwilliam on the other: Pitt and Dundas would form the core.

He had reckoned without the King. "The whole tenor of Mr. Fox's conduct," the King wrote, "since he quitted his seat at the Board of Treasury, when under age, and more particularly at the Whig club and other factious meetings, rendered his expulsion from the Privy Council indispensable, and obliges the King to express his astonishment that Mr. Pitt should one moment harbour the thought of bringing such a man before his royal notice." He would be willing to give Mr. Fox a foreign embassy, he said: but rather than have him again as Secretary of State he would prefer a civil war. The objection was entirely personal. To Grey the King had no objection. But to the man who had led his son (so he thought) into wicked ways, and tried to climb into power on his son's shoulders, he was unrelenting. Pitt knew he was on dangerous ground. Twice in the last four years George the Third's mind had given way. He had had to be humoured on the Catholic question:

now he had to be humoured over Fox. Pitt's proposals were submitted in a mutilated form. Fox raised no objection to his personal exclusion, and urged both Grey and the Grenvilles to go in with Pitt. That Grey should refuse was natural enough: but the world was astonished to find that Grenville was in the plot. Grenville's action in refusing to join Pitt's cabinet without Fox has been represented as a noble sacrifice to friendship. It was nothing of the sort. It was a stab in the back to the man to whom he owed all the importance he had. He took this step, not out of allegiance to Fox, with whom he had no single principle in common, but out of malignant rancour against Pitt, whom he could never forgive for having supported the Peace of Amiens. Fox had no desire to oppose the government, as peace was out of the question. The initiative of opposition came from the Grenvilles, who by refusing to act on Fox's suggestion, tricked him into the false position of opposing a government that deserved to be supported, with the assistance of a politician who deserved to be impeached.

When Pitt realised that he was dealing with a cabal, all his spirit was aroused. "I will teach that proud man," he said of Grenville, "that I can do without him, though I think my health such that it may cost me my life." Fox, for his part, was furious with Pitt, thinking that he had given way to the King too easily. "A mean, low-minded dog" was the sort of thing he would say about Pitt in moments of bitterness. In this way Pitt was opposed by the man he had wanted as his Foreign Secretary, and Fox found himself in opposition to the man with whom he had urged his friends to join, and all through the intrigues of Grenville.

The situation of parties was strangely familiar. As in 1784, Pitt had to scrape together a lutestring administration, consisting of William and Pitt, as it was said: but once again he had the country with him. Once again, Fox had joined hands with the extreme right wing of the opposite party, to form an opposition held together by no public principle at all, execrated by the public, and deeply disapproved by his closest friends. "The Grenvillites and Windhamites," says Creevey, "have to a man stuck fast to Fox and refuse to treat with Pitt. The Prince, too, loads Fox with caresses." It was all delightfully convivial: the penitent old Whigs were charming. Stowe was a delightful place for a week-end, and Carlton House was great fun: but it was bad politics. He was acting once again on personal grounds, in contravention of public interest. He disliked Pitt, as he had disliked Shelburne: he liked Grenville, as he had liked North.

Pitt, like Shelburne, he had come to regard as a minister dependent entirely on the Crown. His own conspiracies he excused on the grounds that any methods were legitimate against the power of the Crown. "Without coalitions," he declared, "*nothing* can be done against the Crown." This excuse was disproved by the whole of his previous experience. In Fox's first cabinet it had been Shelburne who proposed the reform of Parliament and was outvoted. It had been Pitt who renewed the question during the coalition government, when North killed it. Pitt had governed for a little short of twenty years: so far was he from depending on the Crown, that George the Third regarded him with terror, and complained to all and sundry of his minister's tyranny. The first time the King frustrated him in anything, Pitt haughtily resigned, having between 1783 and 1801 reduced the power of the Crown to a phantom, retained his popularity throughout, and introduced enough liberal measures to satisfy a generation. During this entire period, Fox's one contribution towards popular government had been to form a project of a ramshackle administration, which, if it ever came into power, was going to depend, for every single vote it got in either House, upon how much bribery and patronage the Prince Regent could strew in its path:—a path which at the best could not lead beyond the next general election. Finally, how much resistance to the crown could be expected of a Fox-Grenville coalition? No more, of course, than from a Fox-North coalition. The King could drive a coach and four through the resistance of such an army of opposites. All the objects for which Fox persuaded himself that he wanted power had to be sacrificed every time to the allies without whom he persuaded himself that he would never attain power. His letters do not, like those of other party leaders, discuss the prospects in this or that constituency: they discuss whether Lord Spencer is likely to come in, or whether Lord Sandwich is worth getting hold of, or how pleasant it would be if Lord Fitzwilliam could be fitted into an arrangement. It was all a family affair. Never a glance beyond the walls of Parliament: none of Pitt's eagle concentration on the course of public opinion: at the most a reluctant admission that some particularly glaring breach of principle may cause an outcry, a false alarm, another of those popular scares.

The most valuable of all clues to Fox's career is contained in a letter to Lord Lauderdale, in which he convicts himself out of his own mouth. "I do not deny the truth of the objection you state to this junction, but it applies to all junctions of the kind, and would, if attended to, make all resistance to the Crown more impossible even than as it is. No strong confederacy since the Restoration, perhaps not before, ever did exist without the accession of obnoxious persons: Shaftesbury, Buckingham, etc., in Charles II's time; Danby and many others at the time of the Revolution; after the Revolution many more, and even Sunderland himself. In our times, first the Grenvilles with Lord Rockingham, and afterwards Lord North with us. I know this last instance is always quoted against us because we were ultimately unsuccessful, but, after all that can be said, it will be difficult to show when the power of the Whigs ever made so strong a struggle against the Crown, the Crown being thoroughly in earnest and exerting all its resources." There speaks the unteachable Stuart. He is trying to prove that a certain course of action will be right and successful in the nineteenth century: he points to all that was wrong and disastrous in the seventeenth. The "confederacies" that resisted Charles and James were formed of men whose power depended on their wealth or personal influence: their lack of success and of cohesion is one of the marvels of history. All that had happened since then, the growth of a powerful public opinion, organised by men like Place and Cartwright, voiced by men like Cobbett: this, which was the backbone of Pitt's position, to the cultivation of which Pitt gave half his mind, was altogether lost on Fox. He never realised that Pitt got his power from below: he never attempted to get his own power from below. To him, Pitt was a mere appendage of the Court: and he himself was a turbulent aristocrat, forming "confederacies" with other turbulent nobles to terrorise the Court. He saw politics through the eyes of a Monmouth born out of time. How else could he pretend to represent the coalition with North as the culmination of the power of the Whigs, if the Whigs to him meant anything beyond a few families? The Crown, he says, was "in earnest and exerting all its resources." To achieve what? A dissolution, an election, an appeal to the people against this monstrous confederacy of latter-day Shaftesburys and Sunderlands. The Crown won: and what was the result? The election, by an unprecedented vote, of an independent Whig, who in the course of the next seventeen years ruled like a Mayor of the Palace, so certain was he of his popular backing. At the end of that time Fox had learnt so little of the nature of post-revolution politics that he could write that "the only glimmering of hope which I see is from the Court, when that shall fall into other hands." Fox's conduct during the Regency crisis of 1788 is the exact counterpart of Shaftesbury's conduct over the Exclusion Bill of 1679. The one saw his ruin, the other saw his only glimmering of hope, when the Court should fall into other hands. Shaftesbury was taken unawares by the strength and efficacy of the popular resistance when he tried to exclude the Duke of York from the succession: Fox created a public reaction in favour of the King when he tried to anticipate the succession of the Prince of Wales.

If Fox sincerely believed in both his propositions, that without coalitions nothing could be done against the Crown, and that without the Prince of Wales nothing could be done against Pitt, he may well have despaired of public life, and wished himself a subject of Bonaparte. For it was unlikely that the Prince, much as he disliked Pitt, would turn him out, merely in order to give Fox the chance of "doing something against the Crown." Fox was arguing in a circle, that without royal influence he would never be able to destroy royal influence. Only a Stuart could achieve such logic as that. Only James the Second, when he attempted to unite Catholics and Dissenters against the established church, had rivalled the ineptitude of Fox in attempting to unite himself, the Prince and Grenville against Pitt, the King, and the people. The great bulwarks against royal influence were the two-party system and the solidarity of cabinets; Fox twice disrupted the party system and twice formed a heterogeneous government.

Both the seventeenth century Whig and the eighteenth century Whig were so engrossed in their struggles with the Crown that they forgot about the people. The Whig historians make just the same mistake. Macaulay is never happier than when he is pouring ridicule upon the civilisation of our ancestors, in order to point the glories of the nineteenth century. Page after page is devoted to demonstrating how ill they were educated, how seldom they washed, how slow they travelled, how miserably small their trade statistics were. All this proves nothing. It is the superficial oddities in a past generation that catch the eye and give glamour to the narrative: the underlying resemblance passes unnoticed. Macaulay casts his powerful limelight upon the virtues of eminent Whigs and the vices of eminent Tories: the people of England never appear upon his historical stage at all: at the most, they are allowed to hover in the wings and murmur "Rhubarb! Rhubarb!" at the more crucial moments of the drama. History such as this is a caricature of what really happened. Because Macaulay spelt correctly, travelled in trains, enjoyed his hip-bath, and made four thousand a year, it does not follow that all those who did not enjoy these advantages were children of darkness. Least of all does the facile view of history as a progressive evolution succeed in explaining why the eighteenth century produced so much more real ability than the nineteenth. It is unlikely that when the Houses of Parliament were full of brilliant men, and resounded with an eloquence of which the secret has been lost, the whole of the outside world was wrapped in intellectual night. In reality, there was a powerful, independent, and well-informed public opinion, then as now. With every election, in spite of purchase and bribery and intimidation, the pendulum swung free: the robust opinions of the taverns had its effect on the opinion of the corporations, and the corporations kept a strict watch on their Parliament-man. The machinery for the expression of opinions was imperfect: but the materials for the formation of opinions were not yet polluted at the source. It was a crude sort of control, but it was independent, and it was sometimes astonishingly efficient.

Shaftesbury came up against this public opinion in 1679; James the Second was ousted by it; William the Third was in continual friction with it; Walpole deferred to it in 1733 and 1739; Pitt himself was nearly beaten by it in the Otchakoff crisis. Fox was up against it from 1782 until the end of his life. But all the time Fox imagined that he was up against the Crown. He was fighting the old battle of the Whig oligarchy, against whom the people had always been ready to ally themselves with the King. Pitt saw that the alliance between the Crown and people was bound to be the winning side, and to that extent Pitt became a Tory. Once in power, he dominated the King as much as any of the old Whigs: but he saved both King and people from a return of the Whig oligarchy. Pitt's accusation against Fox was in its way as unjust as Fox's accusation against Pitt. Pitt was not a courtier: nor was Fox a mere republican. They were both of them at heart reformers. What kept them apart, what kept Pitt on top and Fox below, was the difference in their methods. Fox allied himself with any fellow-aristocrats he could find: Pitt struck his roots in the esteem of the people. It was a matter of temperament.

4. Pitt's Last Government, 1804-1806

Pitt, as has been seen, was afraid that the strain of governing alone would kill him. So excessively feeble was his cabinet, in which Melville (formerly Dundas) was the only important subordinate, that he had recourse to Addington, and actually took him in again. Not that the assistance of his brains was needed, but the Doctor had a personal following in the Commons of some fifty country gentlemen who trusted in his comfortable stupidity; and Pitt needed every vote he could get. So that the House of Commons was once again clearly divided into two parties. On one side were those who had supported both the peace and the renewal of the war. On the other side were those who had opposed the peace, allied with those who had opposed the war. The former had a majority of about a hundred and fifty.

Addington's accession put Fox's nose very much out of joint. "He (Pitt) certainly gained more in numbers by his junction with the Doctor than I thought he would, but his loss in reputation from that and other causes is incalculable." Pitt, in fact, was to lose in reputation by joining a man with whom he had only a personal quarrel, while Fox joined a man from whom he differed on every public issue. "The next two questions of importance," Fox continues, "will, if he has any feeling, hurt him beyond measure: 1st, the tenth Report of the Naval Commissioners against Lord Melville, 2nd, the Catholic question."

Lord Melville has hitherto appeared by the name of Henry Dundas. Dundas was a Scottish lawyer, who had come into politics during the American war, of which he was at first a strenuous supporter. His feeling cooled rapidly, and he contrived with great skill to attach himself to Shelburne without seeming to betray North, until, when North joined Fox, he could abuse his old leader to his heart's content. He was a mainstay of Pitt's cabinet in one capacity after another, and the only colleague to whom Pitt gave his confidence. In Scotland particularly he ruled supreme, using his patronage as President of the Indian Board of Control, that very patronage Fox had tried to seize, in such a way as to make Scotland a solid electoral bloc. Amongst other things, he had been Treasurer of the Navy for sixteen years, in which office he had allowed one of his clerks to borrow from the public monies in his hands. It was not done on a large scale, and the public lost nothing from it, but it was a contravention at least of the spirit of an act drafted by Melville himself to regulate the use of naval funds. All this was revealed in the famous Tenth Report in 1805, and caused the greatest jubilation among the Whigs. If Melville could be convicted of misappropriation, Pitt would lose his First Lord of the Admiralty, his most capable colleague, and his only intimate friend. They moved a stringent censure on him. Fox supported the motion with a vehemence which many thought a little out of place in Lord Holland's son. "I should be ashamed of myself," he declared, "if I belonged to the same class of society with Lord Melville"—strong words, coming from the son of "the public defaulter of unaccounted millions," about a man who had connived at the loan of the interest on a few thousands. The opposition had the support of Addington, who hated Melville with the hatred of a stupid man for a very clever man who openly derides him. The Grenvilles, who had sat in cabinet with Melville for years, hounded him down with malignant jealousy. The numbers for and against the censure were even. The Speaker gave his casting vote with the opposition. Pitt crumpled up in tears: he felt as Fox would have felt if Fitzpatrick had been caught cheating at cards: he did not live to see his friend honourably acquitted. The personal loss was terrible: the public loss no less. He lost his best man: he lost with him Addington, who resigned on the grounds that he had sheltered Melville, and Addington's fifty votes.

The second question which Fox predicted would hurt Pitt beyond measure, "if he has any feeling," was the Catholic question. In 1801, Pitt had resigned because the King refused to allow Irish Catholics to sit in the United Parliament, a concession to which Pitt felt himself morally bound. It was a most honourable step. Pitt had to give way for fear of a fresh outbreak of the King's insanity: yet he had to show that he was sincere in his intention to make the concession: so he resigned, promising the King never to raise the question again. Three years later, the Irish question was eclipsed by the renewal of the war and the risk of invasion: Pitt was called back to power by universal demand: the Catholic question was not so much as mentioned. Fox now conceived that this was an excellent stick with which to beat him. Pitt could be accused of betraying the Irish nation. The pledge never to raise the question again could be interpreted as a pledge never to take office again: in which case there would be two politicians who saw their only hope in the Prince of Wales. Little did Fox imagine that he would soon make the very same concession himself.

Catholic Emancipation had been a handicap to many parties: in this instance it was used as a debating advantage. But Parliament knew that Pitt was fully as much in earnest on it as Fox. Fox, moreover, gave himself away. Addington was the principal opponent of emancipation. He soon left Pitt's cabinet in a huff: and Fox was making eager advances to him within a few weeks of attacking Pitt in the disguise of a champion of religious toleration. Neither his approaches to the enemy of emancipation, nor his own promise not to demand emancipation, were yet divulged to a wondering world: but, even so, the House could distinguish by this time between Fox the religious liberator and Fox the artful dodger: and the motion was crushingly defeated.

When he lost Addington, Pitt went down to Weymouth, where the King was staying, to implore permission to make another offer to both Fox and Grenville. But George the Third was immovable: he declared that Fox acted from personal dislike to himself: and indeed, if Fox's letters were opened in the post (as Fox suspected), the King did not speak without book. Pitt returned disappointed to carry on alone, opposed by the very men he wanted as colleagues, the very men who accused him of not pressing their claims on the King, though the want of their assistance was, he felt sure, going to cost him his life.

Pitt had survived two blows at himself: two blows at his country killed him. In November came the news of the fall of Ulm, a setback only partially redeemed by Trafalgar a few days later; and Trafalgar itself was a doubtful set-off to the loss of Nelson. The ways in which Pitt and Fox responded to the news were painfully divergent. "England," said Pitt, "has saved herself by her exertions, and will as I trust save Europe by her example." "It is a great event," said Fox, "and by its solid as well as brilliant advantages, far more than compensates for the temporary succour which it will certainly afford to Pitt in his distress. I am very sorry for poor Nelson: for though his conduct at Naples was atrocious, I believe he was at bottom a good man, and it is hard he should not enjoy (and no man would have enjoyed it more) the popularity and glory of this last business." The succour was very temporary: Pitt's distress was completed by the news of Austerlitz. In January, 1806, he went home to die. "Sunt lacrimæ rerum," said Fox, "et mentem mortalia tangunt": all opposition was suspended at once. On the 23rd, his death was known. "I am very sorry, very, very sorry," said Fox. "This is not a time to lose talents like his." When Grenville, that proud man, heard the news, he burst into "an agony of tears."

CHAPTER TWENTY-FOUR

1. *Fox and Pitt, 1806*

Pitt died leaving no successor. Canning was too young, Portland was too obscure: Melville was on his trial. The right wing of Pitt's party inclined towards Grenville, the left towards Addington. So Fox achieved his object in joining with them, and found himself with a Parliamentary majority once more after twenty-two years. The King sent for Grenville, who said that he could not form a government without consulting Fox. "I understand it to be so," said the King, "and I meant it to be so." Grenville became Prime Minister, with Fox as his Foreign Secretary, and the real head of the government.

To have remained in public life at all after the events of 1784; to have kept a following; to have arranged yet another coalition: each of these was an extraordinary achievement for a man in Fox's position. But to have returned to power in the long run; to have overcome the King's resentment; to have lived down the coalition, the Regency scandal, and his adulation of Napoleon: this gives the measure of Fox's ability. He had no outside popularity worth mentioning; among politicians he was generally regarded as impossible; except for Pitt's early death, his luck was dreadful: yet he was in office again. It was ability, sheer ability, that made him indispensable at a time when everything else militated against him, and even his own inclination was for retirement. When Pitt went, there was no other figure in the the landscape but Fox. When Fox went too, all was mediocrity. All that bad luck and bad management can do to ruin a career, they had done for Fox. He was the prince of bunglers, the "proscribed victim of fortune": but he was still a giant, and, when Pitt died, the only giant.

He came into office in 1806, as in 1783, with the sole objective of giving "a good stout blow to the influence of the Crown." It was this high ideal that he had utilised to justify each in turn of his attacks upon the constitution and the party system, and not least to justify his latest coalition with Grenville. Of this coalition, as of so many of his political moves, it was necessary to confess that "nothing but success could justify it." Much may be granted to it, but not success. Fox's previous coalition had held office for nine months: this coalition held office for fourteen months. Fox's previous coalition had put the Tories in for twenty-two years: this one put them in for twenty-three.

The first thing to be done was to bury Pitt, and to pay his debts, which were exorbitant. Fox was willing enough to pay the debts, but on the proposal of a public funeral he raised objections which deserve examination. The motion put forward by Pitt's supporters demanded a monument "to the memory of that excellent states-man." Fox opposed this motion. "I cannot," he said, "so far forget my public duty, as to subscribe to the condemnation of those principles, by agreeing to the motion before the House." On the face of it, this was rather a fine attitude to adopt. He had more to lose than to gain by seeming to be ungenerous. Scrupulous attention to truth is not a character of lapidary inscriptions. A noble speech in the grand manner about his dead rival might have gone far to obliterate the memory of the methods Fox had adopted against him when he was alive. By taking the opposite course, he was making a heavy draft upon his reputation for magnanimity. But the question goes deeper than expediency. Everyone knew that Fox was the soul of generosity: everyone knew that he hated Pitt. The question was, who was Fox that he should claim to pass judgment on Pitt's statesmanship?

There were few points of contact between Fox's mind and Pitt's. Pitt was primarily a financier: and Fox, while admitting the excellence of his finance, underrated its importance as a branch of government. Fox, on the other hand, was supreme as a critic of foreign policy, although his direction of foreign policy, wherever he was in power, was crippled by his lack of credit in his own country. He knew enough to realise that Pitt was a bad diplomatist and a vile war-minister: but it was not on these grounds that he impugned his statesmanship. It was as a contravener of Whig principles that Fox attacked Pitt: it was because he "unfortunately lent his brilliant talents and his commanding eloquence to the support of the system of government which has pervaded the whole of the present reign"—in other words, to increasing the royal influence. This charge was altogether unfounded. Pitt had done nothing of the sort. He had, it is true, enjoyed the confidence of the King, but that was no crime against Whig principles. His power was from the people, whose confidence in him was absolute from his twenty-fourth year till his death. A Tory might argue that his domination over the King had been excessive. No man since Walpole had ruled his sovereign with a higher hand. If Pitt had once lost the popular confidence, George the Third would have grasped at the opportunity of divesting himself of his tyrannical minister. The only check on Pitt's power was his fear of a return of the King's madness: from the dread of provoking the King to madness, he had resigned on the first occasion in seventeen years on which he encountered any resistance in the closet. To accuse Pitt of depending on royal influence was as rational as to accuse Fox of depending on Sheridan. And the accusation did not come with a very good grace from the man who had distributed among his friends positions in the government which was to depend on the arbitrary will of an unpopular Regent.

Fox might have attacked Pitt's claim to statesmanship on a dozen grounds: this, which he selected, was the least substantial of all. There was a case against Pitt for having gone to war, or at any rate for not having resigned when war became inevitable. There was a case against his repressive legislation. There was a very strong case against his conduct of the war, against his crazy strategy and his abominable choice of generals. All this might have been urged against his memory. Pitt had done the State some service, and Fox knew it: but his disservices, in undertaking the direction of a war for which he was wholly unfit, were a very great, if not a preponderant, subtraction from his services. Under Pitt, in 1797, England's fortunes sank lower than for a century before or since. A large part of the blame was his. Few can have seen that very monument, for which Fox refused to vote, without asking whether its eulogy was earned.

Beside his father, Pitt shrivels into a small man. Beside Fox, he appears cold and uninspiring. Both his father and his rival were men of genius; he was not. It was said of him that his mind seemed to be worked by the motion of his tongue, like a clock by its pendulum: an unenviable contrast to Fox, whose volubility could never keep pace with the onrush of his thoughts. Pitt did generous things in a calculating manner: he did disagreeable things with an air of relish. He had almost every human merit in abundance. His intellect was vast and perfectly developed: his public virtues were above praise: he inherited that rare faculty, which Johnson acutely ascribed to his father, the "faculty of putting the state in motion": he had a large share of social qualities, wit and generosity. Time has been unkind to him. He was a bigger man than he is usually accounted: but he was not as big a man as Fox. Pitt was of the same consistency throughout:he was all of a piece. In his private affairs, in party affairs, in affairs of state, he was the same man: cold, hard, brilliant, disinterested, and solitary. Fox was the very reverse. He was never normal: whenever he did not rise above the accepted standards of conduct, he fell below them. In affairs of state, he was at one moment a masterly critic of diplomacy, at another a contemptible critic of finance. In private life he was the unchallenged master of the art of pleasing: in the conduct of a party, his clumsiness was only equalled by his lack of principle. He was always either much superior or much inferior to Pitt. When he was punishing Pitt in the Otchakoff debates, he shone with all the genius of insight and judgment. When Pitt was punishing him in the Regency debates, he appeared like a naughty schoolboy, whose stupidity is more tiresome even than his offence. He had no middle course: Pitt had no extremes.

If he had attacked Pitt from the high ground, Fox's words would have carried weight. He might have accused him of a lack of liberalism, and he would have been right. But he chose the low ground—he accused him of a lack of Whiggism, and there he was wrong. Pitt was an illiberal man, but a good Whig. Fox was the apostle of liberalism, but an incorrigible sinner against Whig constitutional principles.

> "Drop upon Fox's grave a tear:
> 'Twill trickle to his rival's bier,"

says Scott, in his elegy on them both. It is painful that Fox should have dropped nothing on his rival's bier but an aspersion, but at all events it was the least warrantable aspersion he could have found. The two of them are inseparably linked in history. Characters live on after policies are forgotten, and in character the contrast is overwhelming in Fox's favour. Fox is the easy winner in the affections of posterity. He could well have afforded to leave Pitt's merits to speak for themselves.

Four years earlier, he had refused to support a proposal for a memorial for Burke, on the grounds that Burke's pamphlet on the *Conduct on the Minority* had wounded him more deeply than he could pretend to have forgiven. Who could have foreseen in 1781, when Pitt and Sheridan and Burke were following his lead in the most splendid of Parliamentary campaigns, that Fox would live to repudiate all three of his great contemporaries? It was through no lack of generosity, for few men were more ready to sacrifice public to private considerations. But the iron had entered into his soul. Long years of opposition under a free constitution had made him receptive to Jacobinism, and the issue between French and English principles went too deep for any ties of friendship, gratitude, or common generosity.

2. Fox's Last Government, 1806

In constituting this ministry, as in constituing the joint ministry with North, Fox was under the painful necessity of deciding how far to sacrifice his principles for the sake of his personnel. Like the captain of a ramshackle ship, he had to assess the relative value of the cargo and the crew. On this occasion, he needed all the hands he could muster. He had to exercise a drastic elimination of the cargo. The Broad-Bottomed Administration, as it was nicknamed, left harbour with a fine complement of men: but it had no ballast at all. Every Whig principle was thrown overboard, in order that the boat might be completely manned. The crew was an admirable, if a mixed, assemblage: the King provided a favourable breeze: but what the boat carried nobody could say, nor where it was heading, for even the compass had been jettisoned.

Grenville as Prime Minister was at least without the opportunities for mischief-making of which he had availed himself in 1800. Even in order to make sure of Grenville, Fox had to perpetrate a disgraceful job. Grenville had been auditor of the Treasury at £4000 a year for the last twelve years. He was reluctant to abandon a large salary, for which no work whatever was done: yet it was illegal for him to be First Lord of the Treasury and Auditor simultaneously. A public man cannot audit his own accounts, even in theory. But Fox was too good-natured to suggest that Grenville should surrender this fat sinecure: instead, he passed a bill to allow the same man to hold both offices, not in order to enable Grenville to be Prime Minister, but to enable him to retain a sinecure of which he had no real need, and for which the Prime Minister's salary more than compensated him.

This was a pretty start for a ministry which was to give a stout blow to the influence of the Crown. An even larger concession had to be made to secure the support of Addington. Addington's following in the Commons was valuable, but it was dearly bought, as Pitt had found, at the price of his presence in the cabinet. "The Doctor," said Canning, "is like the measles—everybody has him once." Fox decided to have him, but, sure enough, after a few months he had to go. His inclusion was the death-blow to the hopes of the Irish Catholics. No cabinet with Addington in it would ever grant emancipation. So that also was thrown overboard, although it was the very policy that Fox had taunted Pitt with abandoning, less than a year before. Fox excused himself in the very same way as Pitt excused himself: to raise the question now, he explained, would endanger the King's sanity. But the Catholics could remember the time when he had not been so solicitous for the King's sanity.

Erskine made an indifferent Lord Chancellor, having so little knowledge of Equity that his decisions were known as the Apocrypha: but this fault was redeemed by the impartiality he showed in presiding over the impeachment of Lord Melville. This disgraceful prosecution was undertaken in no judicial spirit. The Whig underlings regarded it, in Creevey's words, as "famous sport." The Whig peers voted in platoons for verdicts unsupported by a scrap of evidence. The real offender, the clerk who had misapplied the money, was given a full indemnity in the hopes that his evidence would incriminate the chosen person. Much depended on the Lord Chancellor, whose reputation was that of a wayward and partisan advocate. But Erskine rose to the occasion, and Melville was acquitted on every charge. It is fair to say that Fox took little interest in the proceedings.

An innovation in flagrant contravention of Whig principles was the inclusion of the Lord Chief Justice in the cabinet. This was a direct menace at once to the independence of the judicial bench, and to the collective responsibility of the cabinet. It was undesirable that the same man should hear, as a judge, a prosecution that he had advised, as a minister, to be instituted: it was even more undesirable that the other members of the cabinet should be held responsible for a miscarriage of justice in the King's Bench. Fox, however, could not understand what the outcry was about: he airily remarked that he had never had an easier case to defend than this: he denied the collective responsibility of the cabinet altogether and ridiculed the separation of the judicial from the legislative functions. By this pronouncement he added the coping-stone to his edifice of imaginary constitutional theory. He had in turn mistaken the functions of the Crown, the Lords, and the Commons: now he mistook the functions of the judiciary. It was solely a matter of convenience. He wanted the Chief Justice in the cabinet: the justification he invented in his usual way.

For the rest of the personnel, Windham became Secretary for War and Colonies, a post where he was able to continue the bad work of his previous administrations, and even to excel all his former extravagances by preparing a scheme for the capture of Chile by a force of 4000 men. Sheridan was so far forgiven as to be re-instated as Treasurer of the Navy. For the Chancellor of the Exchequer, Fox selected Lansdowne's son, Lord Henry Petty, who was only twenty-four years old. Fox thought the world of this young man. It was a good appointment, and a posthumous amend to the old statesman, who had died the previous year, whom Fox had hated so wantonly, and ruined himself by hating.

One achievement of Fox's last administration atoned for many of his broken promises. The abolition of the slave trade had been an annual question in Parliament for many years. Wilberforce led the movement: Pitt and Fox lent it their finest oratory: but the vested interests were too strong for them all. At last, in 1806, Fox carried a resolution condemning the trade. This was the prelude to a rather ineffectual bill, which passed the following year. These first measures were very ill-considered, and combined the greatest damage to trade with the least benefit to the Africans. It was long before the trade, and longer still before the institution of slavery was suppressed. But Fox's motion marked the turn of the tide. It was a personal triumph for him: it was also a fine conclusion to his Parliamentary career, for his speech against the slave trade in June, 1806, was the last he ever made.

3. Overtures for Peace, 1806

Even at the time of taking office, Fox had misgivings about his health, and there had been suggestions that he should take a peerage and hand over the Foreign Office to his young nephew Holland. But he felt that he must first let his coalition justify its existence, before he could hand over the reins with a clear conscience. "Don't think me selfish, young one," he wrote, "the slave trade and peace are two such glorious things, I can't give them up, even to you. If I can manage *them*, I will then retire." He had done what he could towards the suppression of the slave trade: now was the time to prove this theory that Napoleon was at bottom a frustrated pacifist.

He had many handicaps. His colleagues in the cabinet were still for war at any price, and for war in as many corners of the globe as possible. The actual business of providing the sinews of war left little leisure to explore the possibilities of peace: within a month of taking over, Fox is described as "quite warlike" in his outlook. To crown all, a new enemy suddenly entered the fray against us: the King of Prussia invaded and appropriated Hanover. Prussia was Fox's old diplomatic mainstay: Hanover was the pet aversion of the Whigs. But there was nothing for it but to take up the challenge. Fox moved an address to assure His Majesty that the House participated in His Majesty's paternal feelings in the loss of Hanover; and supported the declaration of war in a speech which Windham described as a brilliant warwhoop.

These disappointments were inevitable. Fox was perfectly in earnest in his dealings with Napoleon. He was fortunate in having Talleyrand for his opposite number. Being himself incapable of pretence, and not thinking that pretence was a part of diplomacy, he felt at ease with a man on whom pretence would be thrown away. They knew each other, and they both admired each other's country. Talleyrand knew exactly how uncomfortably Fox was situated with his colleagues, and Fox must have realised that Talleyrand was at this very time applying the brake to Napoleon's forward policy more energetically than anyone else had dared. Fox and Talleyrand were thrown into intercourse by a lucky accident.

A French lunatic secured admission to the Foreign Office, and divulged to Fox a plan for the murder of Napoleon. He was arrested: and Fox wrote to Talleyrand, asking him to warn the Emperor of the danger, though the courtesy of the letter was rather marred by a pedantic description of Napoleon as "Chef des Francais." Talleyrand replied with exquisite tact: "Je me rejouis du nouveau caractère que, par cette démarche, la guerre a déjà pris." Fox wisely saw an opening in this, and followed it up with a suggestion of negotiations. Talleyrand was all agreement: "L'Empereur désire la paix avec l'Angleterre. Il est homme. Père de ses sujets, il souhaite leur procurer les douceurs de la paix." This was the initiation of along interchange of letters, in which both parties displayed the most admirable commonsense, without receding from the obstinacy of the Grenville school of diplomacy. Finally, in June, a discussion took place. England was at first represented by Lord Yarmouth, the famous prototype of Disraeli's Lord Monmouth, who in Fox's opinion bungled the affair by producing his full powers too soon. Yarmouth was certainly an unsatisfactory emissary, and seems to have been chosen for the task as casually as Tom Grenville twenty years before. He was not merely hoodwinked, but actually cuckolded, by the French representative: he was finally superseded when it transpired that he was using his position to gamble in the funds. Talleyrand put the blame upon his successor, Lord Lauderdale. Talleyrand did not like Lauderdale, who had been one of Fox's faithful forty in 1793, when he himself was in London, being insulted by society in general, and by Lord Grenville in particular. Much had happened since then: but Talleyrand's transition from a follower of Danton into a follower of Napoleon was not half so devious as the evolution by which Lauderdale became the representative of a Grenville government. The irony of the Fox-Grenville coalition was not lost on Talleyrand: "ils nous envoient un ambassadeur jacobin," he grumbled. But by the time the negotiations had failed, the Foreign Office was in other hands than Fox's.

4. Illness and Death, 1806

He was ten years older than Pitt had been, and his fifty-seven years had been for the most part no less active. His corpulent frame had always been difficult to exercise, and now a swelling in the legs at last convinced him that he was suffering from dropsy. In June, his official activities became almost insupportable: in July, he was confined to his bed, in acute pain. Trotter was sent for, and lovingly administered large doses of Virgil and Ariosto at the bedside. Some days he was well enough for an afternoon drive as far as Holland House, but as August came on he was imprisoned in his little house in Stable Yard. There the great and the famous brought their sympathy. The Prince came almost every day. His followers, and even some of his enemies, remained in London from a curiously profound emotion. There was a painful parting interview with Sheridan, who now stood on the brink of his own tragedy. But as August wore on, Fox began to be less able to receive his visitors; and with every day, his longing to see his country home increased. It was only a matter of twenty miles or so: but the doctors forbade it, at least until he had been tapped for dropsy. This nauseating operation was performed, and gave him some relief. At the end of August he was able to travel half the journey, as far as Chiswick, that lovely Palladian villa of the Duke of Devonshire's, which still stands unconcerned among the untidy western outgrowths of London.

At Chiswick he had to stop in order to be tapped again. For a few days he lingered there, sometimes strong enough to be wheeled round the gardens or the galleries, discoursing on vegetables or paintings; more generally in bed, listening while his wife read him out Crabbe's *Parish Register*, which the poet had sent him in manuscript for his approval, or while his nephew read to him from Johnson's *Lives of the Poets*. Trotter meanwhile was kept busy with a vast correspondence. The nation was suddenly moved. England realised that the greatest Englishman of his generation was dying: a man whom everyone had wronged, yet whom everyone at heart admired. Dissenters who had denounced him as a loose liver, Tories who had denounced him as a Jacobin, democrats who had denounced him as a traitor to the people: all who had fastened on his particular faults recognised, when he was dying, that they were the faults of greatness. England without

266

Fox would be a more peaceful polity; but it would have lost the colour and the glow of his warm heart and his impetuous mind. Probably other politicians had secretly entertained those disloyal and unpatriotic thoughts, those violent impulses of pique and rage and despair, which Fox alone had never troubled to conceal. It was impossible to bear malice against a man who had never hidden anything, either of his public or his private life, or pretended to be anything but what he was. He had challenged the disapproval of the world; he had given his enemies every possible advantage, his critics every possible foothold; and still by the sheer weight of a great intellect and a noble character he had overcome them all. He increased men's faith in human nature. He had never attempted to deceive his fellow-men: he had so consistently deceived himself. The common people, whose confidence he had forfeited long ago, knew in their hearts that the worst of leaders was still the best of friends. They were moved, as Wordsworth said,

> "For he must die who is their stay,
> Their glory disappear."*

Though, as the loyal Whitbread confessed, he had "overset the public opinion with regard to statesmen," he had won their hearts without their votes. He had been rash when other men were prudent, mild when other men were harsh; in an age of armaments and imperialism, he had kept the humanities alive. His success is no measure of his importance. "If I have not acted much," he said, "you will allow that I have spoken much, and I have felt more." It was what he had felt in all his years of political impotence that endeared him even to those who differed from him the most.

A little time after his second operation, he was strong enough for a Sunday drive with Elizabeth. "He kept my hand in his all the time we were out, made me kiss him several times, and admired the Thames that we saw in the road back from Kew Bridge, and made me repeat from *Cooper's Hill:*

> " 'Thames, the most loved of all the Ocean's sons
> By his old sire, to his embraces runs;
> Hasting to pay his tribute to the sea,
> Like mortal life to meet eternity.' "

* Wordsworth. *Lines composed at Grasmere during a walk one Evening after a stormy day, the Author having just read in a Newspaper that the Dissolution of Mr. Fox was hourly expected.*

That excursion was the longest he could undertake. St. Anne's Hill faded into the background as he lost strength at Chiswick.

Fitzpatrick was there, the young man whose indifference to money had excelled his own, now a General; Lord Holland, born for the destruction of the Jews, the pious recipient of all those educative letters; Henry Petty, to whom he had made up some of the wrongs he had done to Shelburne; Caroline Fox, his niece and Shelburne's; a Miss Willoughby, one of his natural daughters; and his host, Devonshire, whose Georgiana had died only that spring.

He and Elizabeth had made a compact that, whichever should die first, the other should show no sign of grief. But she failed him. "When he felt that I was almost in hysterics he looked up and said, 'Oh fie, Liz, is this your promise?' . . . But, my God, who could do it?" For several days this agony went on. Fox was calm enough: and his faculties were clear. He had strength enough to discuss foreign politics to Holland in French, or to express himself in Italian—"O sostegno della mia vita"—to his wife. But a cold sweat hung upon him; his liver was afterwards found to be terribly diseased; and his legs swelled, the water sometimes gushing from the puncture. About sunset on the 13th of September he said: "I die happy, but I pity you." Then, as if that were a little sententious, he looked up at his wife, and said: "It don't signify, my dearest, dearest Liz."

He is buried in Westminster Abbey.

Index